Advanced Language Lessons

Sheldon and Company

SHELDON'S

ADVANCED

LANGUAGE LESSONS

GRAMMAR AND COMPOSITION

SHELDON AND COMPANY

NEW YORK AND CHICAGO

TYPOGRAPHY BY J. S. CUSHING & CO., BOSTON, MASS., U.S.A.

PREFACE.

———◦○◦———

To experienced teachers it has long been evident that pupils trained in old-style grammar too often lack the power of expression. Indeed, it has been charged, that though their heads are full of theory, and though they have hundreds of rules at the end of their tongues, they are unable to write a single clear, strong, smooth English sentence.

Sheldon's Language Lessons will be welcomed by all who believe that technical grammar should be developed side by side with practical composition. In the second book of this comprehensive series, rules and principles are accompanied by illustrative extracts from good authors, and followed by attractive problems in construction.

In connection with sentence building, punctuation is introduced; and the rules are correlated with the laws of English expression.

By easy lessons in synonyms and figures, and occasional reference to the fundamental principles of effective discourse, students are gradually prepared for a systematic view of rhetoric.

A method of English work exceedingly valuable in high schools has been simplified, and adapted to the needs of lower grades. Numerous well-defined plans for experiments in narration and description are presented, together with models and suggestions designed to encourage habits of thoughtful observation, and to stimulate a taste for good literature. Every lesson has borne the test of the classroom, and has proved repeatedly the educating power of what has been called "laboratory work in English."

The Appendix contains an introductory outline of versification, a complete system of diagrams applied to typical sentences, and a brief sketch of the English language, with ample material for elementary work in the analysis of words.

Selections from the works of Lowell, Saxe, Longfellow, Holmes, and Hawthorne, are offered for study by permission of, and by arrangement with, Messrs. Houghton, Mifflin, & Co. Extracts from other copyrighted works are used through the favor of the Century Company and of the publishers of "The Critic."

ADVANCED LANGUAGE LESSONS.

GRAMMAR AND COMPOSITION.

LESSON I.

THE SENTENCE.

Think of some fact, and make a statement.

EXAMPLES. — Wild flowers are beautiful.

Stars shine at night.

Think of something you wish to know, and ask a question.

EXAMPLES. — Have you studied your lessons?

Why do clouds float in the air?

Think of something you wish done, and give an order or command.

EXAMPLES. — Let me see your drawing.

Ask the teacher to explain the example.

Suppose yourself to be very much interested, surprised, or excited, and express your thought by making an exclamation.

EXAMPLES. — What beautiful flowers you have !

How glad I am to see you !

The bell is ringing !   We are late !

A thought expressed in words is called a SENTENCE.

In how many different ways have you expressed thought?

A thought expressed in the form of a statement is called a DECLARATIVE SENTENCE.

A thought expressed in the form of a question is called an INTERROGATIVE SENTENCE.

A thought expressed in the form of a command is called an IMPERATIVE SENTENCE.

A thought expressed in the form of an exclamation is called an EXCLAMATORY SENTENCE.

LESSON II.

KINDS OF SENTENCE. — PUNCTUATION.

Study the following sentences, and be prepared to write them from dictation : —

1. See that black cloud!
2. It has hidden the sun.
3. How dark it seems!
4. It will rain very soon.
5. Do you like to hear the thunder?
6. How grand it sounds!
7. Come into the library.
8. Is it not a pleasant room?
9. This is my favorite chair.
10. I always study by this window.
11. Shall I show you my favorite books?
12. How are books written?
13. We express our thoughts in words.
14. A book expresses somebody's thoughts.
15. I wish I could write a book!

Which of the above are declarative sentences? Why?
Which of the above are interrogative sentences? Why?
Which of the above are imperative sentences? Why?
Which of the above are exclamatory sentences? Why?
With what kind of letter does each sentence begin?

A declarative sentence is one used to state or declare something.

An interrogative sentence is one used to ask a question.

An imperative sentence is one used to express a command.

An exclamatory sentence is one used to express an emotion.

In the preceding examples, a period (.) is placed at the close of what kind of sentences? At the close of what kind of sentences is an interrogation point (?) placed? An exclamation mark (!) is placed at the close of what kind?

The first word of every sentence should begin with a capital letter.

A declarative and an imperative sentence should end with a period.

An interrogative sentence should end with an interrogation point.

An exclamatory sentence should end with an exclamation mark.

LESSON III.

THE PARAGRAPH.

WILLIAM PENN'S TREATY WITH THE RED MAN.

Two hundred years ago William Penn called the Indian chiefs to a great council on the banks of the Delaware. Unarmed, and in the plain dress of the Quaker, he and his companions met the Red Men under an elm tree.

Standing before them, he said, "My friends, we have met on the broad pathway of faith and good will. We are all of one flesh and blood. Being brethren, no advantage shall be taken on either side.   When disputes arise, we will settle them in council.   Between us there shall be nothing but friendship."

The chiefs replied, " While the rivers run, and the sun and moon shall shine, we will live at peace with William Penn and his children."

The treaty made under the old elm tree was never broken by the Indians.   They were always friendly with Penn and his people.   The Quaker coat and hat proved a better defense than the sword or rifle.

What does the first group of sentences tell about?   When, where, and how did William Penn meet the Red Men?

What is the subject of the second group of sentences?   What did Penn say as he stood before the Indian chiefs?

What is the subject of the third division of the story?   In what words did the chiefs promise to live at peace with William Penn and his people?

What is the subject of the fourth division of the story?   What advantages resulted to Penn and his people from the treaty made under the old elm tree?

How many principal divisions are there in the story of " William Penn's Treaty with the Red Man "?

Do all the sentences in each division relate to the same subject of thought?

Each of these divisions is called a PARAGRAPH.

A paragraph is one of the parts into which a prose composition is divided.   It may consist of a single sentence, or of a series of sentences relating to the same subject of thought.

Write from memory, in four paragraphs, the story of "William Penn's Treaty with the Red Man."

LESSON IV.

WORDS USED AS NAMES.

1. *Write the names of five objects you saw on your way to school this morning.*

2. *Write the names of five objects in this room.*

3. *Write the first or given names of five friends, beginning each with a capital letter.*

4. *Write five names which stand for things that can be thought about, but never seen.*

A word used as a name is called a NOUN.

LESSON V.

WORDS USED TO ASSERT.

1. Birds sing.
2. Birds fly.
3. Birds build nests.
4. The birds have flown.

In the first sentence, what word is used to assert something about birds?

What word is used in the second sentence to assert something about birds?

What is said about birds in the third sentence? How many words are there in the sentence? Which of the words are names? Is the second word used as a name? Is it used to tell or assert something of birds?

Words like *sing, fly, build,* used to assert, are called VERBS.

In the fourth sentence, what two words together assert something about birds?

A verb may be made up of one or more words.

Complete the following sentences by supplying verbs : —

1. Trees ——.
2. Stars ——.
3. The wind ——.
4. The lightning ——.
5. The thunder ——.
6. The sun ——.
7. I —— a rainbow.
8. Fishes ——.
9. Bees —— honey.
10. The clock ——.
11. The bell ——.
12. Boys —— ball.
13. Girls —— violets.
14. People —— ——.
15. Snow —— the ground.
16. The ice ——.
17. Spring —— ——.
18. Foxes —— grapes.
19. I —— —— a story.
20. Who —— —— a song?

LESSON VI.

WORDS USED WITH NOUNS.

1. Cool water is a refreshing drink.
2. Have you the answer to the fifth example?
3. You were early this morning.
4. Bring me the red apples from the large basket.

What kind of water is spoken of in the first sentence? Which word tells what kind of water? What kind of drink is mentioned? Which word tells the kind of drink?

What example is spoken of in the second sentence? Which word tells the example we mean? Which word limits the noun *answer?*

In the third sentence, which word tells a particular morning?

What kind of apples are spoken of in the fourth sentence?

Which word qualifies the noun *apples ?* Which words qualify the noun *basket ?*

Words like *cool, refreshing, fifth, this, the, red,* and *large,* used to limit or qualify the meaning of a noun or a pronoun, are called ADJECTIVES.

Point out the adjectives in the following sentences : —

1. A black crow sat in a tall tree.
2. She held in her beak a small piece of cheese.
3. A sly fox came under the tree.
4. He wanted some cheese for his breakfast.
5. He praised the crow's shiny black coat.
6. He praised her graceful form.
7. He wished to hear her beautiful voice.
8. The foolish crow tried to sing.
9. The coveted cheese fell to the ground.
10. The mischievous fox seized it, and ran.
11. The silly crow never finished her song.
12. Beware of insincere praise.
13. The wise Æsop wrote many fables.
14. He closed each fable with some good advice.
15. This bit of good advice is called the " moral."

LESSON VII.

EXERCISES.

1. *Study the sentences in the preceding lesson and be prepared to write them from dictation.*
2. *Make a list of ten nouns found in the sentences.*
3. *Make a list of ten verbs found in the sentences.*
4. *Write five sentences, each of which shall contain a noun, a verb, and an adjective.*

LESSON VIII.

WORDS USED TO TELL HOW, WHEN, WHERE.

1. The brook runs noisily over the pebbles.
2. It will soon reach the river.
3. The river flows onward.

How does the brook run?   Which word tells how it runs?
When will the brook reach the river?   Which word tells when?
Where does the river flow?   Which word tells the direction?
Words like *noisily, soon,* and *onward,* used to modify the
meaning of a verb, are called ADVERBS.

*Copy the following, filling the blanks with suitable
adverbs : —*

1. The children slept ——.
2. They were —— dreaming.
3. The moon shone ——.
4. —— the smooth snow glistened!
5. The north wind was blowing ——.
6. Jack Frost was working ——.
7. —— the clock struck twelve.
8. Sleigh bells jingled ——.
9. Santa Claus rode ——.
10. —— did he come in?
11. I do —— know.   Do you?
12. He —— filled the stockings.
13. —— he drove ——.
14. Next morning all rose ——.
15. Oh! —— the children shouted.

LESSON IX.

MODIFIERS OF ADVERBS AND ADJECTIVES.

1. It is a very pleasant day.
2. The carriage is almost here.
3. Do not drive too fast.
4. We will ride only two hours.

What adjective describes the day? What word modifies the adjective?

What adverb tells where the carriage is? What word modifies the adverb?

What two adverbs modify the verb *drive?* What word modifies one of the adverbs?

What adjective modifies the noun *hours?* What word modifies the adjective?

Words like *very, almost, too,* and *only,* used to modify the meaning of an adjective or an adverb, are called ADVERBS.

Point out the adverbs in the following sentences : —

1. The mountain is almost visible through the mists.
2. I have heard several very good stories lately.
3. Have you a fairly good memory?
4. A friend gave me some very excellent advice.
5. Do not keep too many irons in the fire.
6. Through wind and wave, right onward steer!
7. The branches sighed overhead in scarcely audible whispers.
8. Does the magnetic needle always point directly northward?

LESSON X.

COMPOSITION.

AN ANXIOUS MOTHER.

Audubon once came upon a wild duck with her brood. The mother raised her feathers, and hissed ; the ducklings skulked and hid in every direction. His well-trained dog, however, hunted them all out, and brought them to the bag without injury. All this time the old duck fluttered before the dog to draw away his attention. When the little ones were all in the bag, she came and stood before the sportsman, as if deeply grieved. What could he do less than give her back her babies? The mother, he says, seemed to smile her gratitude, and he felt a great joy in her happiness.

What did Audubon once see? When the duck raised her feathers, and hissed, what did the ducklings do? When the dog found the little birds, and brought them to his master's bag, what did the mother duck do? Did the sportsman feel sorry for her? What did he do? What does the great observer of birds tell us about the gratitude of the mother? Did he enjoy her happiness?

1. *Write in your own words the story told by Audubon. Describe as if you had been present : —*

    1. The appearance of the little family.
    2. The well-trained dog catching the ducklings.
    3. The anxiety of the mother duck.
    4. The kindness of the great naturalist.
    5. The lesson taught by the incident.

2. *Give an account of some similar incident you have witnessed, or, if you prefer, write a story from the following notes :* —

Dr. Livingstone once met a brood of little ostriches led by a male who pretended to be lame, that he might attract attention from his tender charge.

Try to imagine, and then describe, the capture of the small ostriches, the appeal of the anxious father, the result.

LESSON XI.

THE DECLARATIVE SENTENCE. — SUBJECT AND PREDICATE.

1. Dogs bark.
2. The birds flew away.
3. The children skate gracefully.
4. The shadows of the clouds rest on the mountain.

What animals bark? About what is something said in the first sentence?

What is the second sentence about?

What is the third sentence about?

Of what is something said in the fourth sentence?

Dogs do what? What did the birds do? The children do what? The shadows of the clouds do what?

The subject of a sentence is the part which mentions that about which something is said.

The predicate of a sentence is that part which states what is said about the subject.

Either the subject or the predicate may be expressed in a single word, or may be made up of several words.

1. *Complete the following sentences by supplying predicates : —*

    1. Wild violets —— ——.
    2. A rolling stone —— —— ——.
    3. The ten o'clock train —— ——.
    4. The best oranges —— —— ——.
    5. Sixty minutes —— —— ——.
    6. The flag of our country —— ——.
    7. The needle of the compass —— ——.
    8. The moss-covered bucket —— —— —— ——.

2. *Complete the following sentences by supplying subjects : —*

    1. —— —— —— should be finished with a period.
    2. —— can learn to talk.
    3. —— build paper nests.
    4. —— walk on the ceiling.
    5. —— —— has five petals.
    6. —— spoil the garden.
    7. —— —— have round leaves.
    8. —— —— —— grows in China.
    9. —— —— flies about in the night.
    10. —— —— made music all the evening.

LESSON XII.

THE INTERROGATIVE SENTENCE. — SUBJECT AND PREDICATE.

    1. Have you studied your lesson?
    2. What did Harry say?
    3. How came these books here?

The subjects and predicates of an interrogative sentence will be readily seen if the sentence be first changed to the declarative form. Thus the above sentences may be rewritten : —

     1. You have studied your lesson.
     2. Harry did say ——.
     3. These books came here ——.

It is then evident that *you, Harry,* and *these books,* are respectively the subjects, and *have studied your lesson, did say* ——, and *came here* ——, are the predicates of the sentences.

Rewrite the following sentences in the declarative form, and tell the subject and predicate of each: —

     1. Was Audubon a great naturalist?
     2. Had he a very kind heart?
     3. Could his dog have caught the mother duck?
     4. Would you have given back the ducklings?
     5. Are some animals very intelligent?
     6. Is your dog very brave?

Mention the subject and predicate of each of the following sentences: —

     1. Can you keep a secret?
     2. Must I tell you the whole story?
     3. Will you come with me?
     4. Ought we to go home now?
     5. Will next year be leap year?
     6. Has the thrush a beautiful song?
     7. Is the lion a king among beasts?
     8. Have you seen the falls of Niagara?
     9. Have we a national park?
    10. Should every line of poetry begin with a capital?

LESSON XIII.

THE IMPERATIVE SENTENCE. — SUBJECT AND PREDICATE.

   1. Listen.
   2. Read carefully.
   3. Copy the marked paragraphs.

The subject of an imperative sentence is the pronoun *thou* or *you*, representing the person or persons commanded. Usually the subject is not expressed, but understood.

The predicate is the word or words expressing the command or request.

Write imperative sentences, using the following as predicates or parts of predicates : —

sing	touch	go
remember	whisper	listen
come	try	ask
think	tell	knock

LESSON XIV.

THE EXCLAMATORY SENTENCE. — SUBJECT AND PREDICATE.

   1. This is cruel!
   2. How could you do it!
   3. Oh, leave me!

The first sentence is declarative in form. Its subject is *this;* and its predicate, *is cruel.*

The second sentence is interrogative in form. Its subject is *you;* and its predicate, *could do it how.*

The third sentence is imperative in form. Its subject is *thou* or *you* understood; and its predicate, *leave me.*

Exclamatory sentences are either declarative, interrogative, or imperative in form, and their subjects and predicates are determined accordingly.

Tell the form of each of the following exclamatory sentences, and point out its subject and predicate : —

1. It cannot be done!
2. What shall we do!
3. Come here quickly!
4. Soldier, rest!
5. The Eternal City shall be free!
6. This is my own, my native land!
7. Thou, too, sail on, O Ship of State!
8. I was once a barefoot boy!
9. How pleasant is Saturday night!
10. Woodman, forbear thy stroke!

LESSON XV.

COMPOSITION.

A MORTIFYING MISTAKE.

I studied my tables over and over, and backward and
    forward too ;
But I couldn't remember six times nine, and I didn't
    know what to do,
Till sister told me to play with my doll, and not to bother
    my head.
"If you call her 'Fifty-four' for a while, you'll learn it
    by heart," she said.

So I took my favorite, Mary Ann (though I thought 'twas
    a dreadful shame
To give such a perfectly lovely child such a perfectly
    horrid name),
And I called her my dear little " Fifty-four " a hundred
    times, till I knew
The answer of six times nine as well as the answer of
    two times two.

Next day Elizabeth Wigglesworth, who always acts so
    proud,
Said, " Six times nine is fifty-two ; " and I nearly laughed
    aloud !
But I wished I hadn't when teacher said, " Now, Dorothy,
    tell, if you can,"
For I thought of my doll, and — sakes alive ! — I answered
    — " *Mary Ann !* "   ANNA M. PRATT.

This poem from " St. Nicholas " will show you how to make
an interesting story out of an every-day experience.

*Recall some occurrence in the schoolroom, and give the
leading incidents as clearly as you can.   Choose, if you like,
one of the following subjects : —*

A Mouse's Short Visit.	**An Absurd Mistake.**
A Lesson in Obedience.	**An Undeserved Reproof.**

HINTS.

1. Select a title for your story.   2. Keep the title in
your mind, and think carefully before you begin to write.
3. Write down the principal points you mean to mention.
4. From these notes complete your story, making as many
paragraphs as there are topics in your outline.

LESSON XVI.

SIMPLE AND MODIFIED SUBJECT.

1. The great wheel stopped.
2. The dusty old mill was still.
3. William's first letter came yesterday.

What one word in the subject of the first sentence tells what stopped? What part of speech is it? What do the other words do? Which is the principal word? Which words are modifiers of the principal word?

What is the subject of the second sentence? What word in the subject is a noun? What three adjectives modify it?

What is the subject of the third sentence? What is the principal word in the subject? Do the first two words modify the noun *letter?*

The principal word in a subject is called the SIMPLE SUBJECT.

The simple subject, together with the word or words which limit it, is called the MODIFIED SUBJECT.

Find out the simple subject and the modified subject in each of the following sentences : —

1. The tallest trees grow in Australia.
2. The largest trees grow in California.
3. The trailing arbutus is the Mayflower of Plymouth.
4. Many precious stones come from Africa.
5. Five little squirrels live in a hollow tree.
6. Their busy parents gather nuts for winter.
7. The most delicate ferns grow in shady places.
8. A good name is a great treasure.
9. The sunset clouds are beautiful.

Complete the following sentences by supplying suitable modifiers for the simple subjects : —

1. —— —— clouds floated in the sky.
2. —— —— music filled the air.
3. —— —— clock ticked steadily.
4. —— —— poppies grow among the wheat.
5. —— —— roses covered the porch.
6. —— —— knife has three blades.
7. —— —— bird catches the worm.
8. —— —— cloud hid the sun.
9. —— —— flowers grow in the woods.
10. —— —— —— evenings are pleasant.
11. —— —— hills look blue. ,
12. —— —— umbrella came from London.

LESSON XVII.

SIMPLE AND MODIFIED PREDICATE.

1. The summer rain falls softly.
2. The wind blows furiously.

What is the predicate of the first sentence? What word modifies the verb in the first sentence? Do the two words together tell more about the subject than the verb alone?

What is the predicate of the second sentence? By what word is it modified? Do these two words together make a more complete assertion about the subject *wind* than the verb alone does?

The verb in the predicate is called the SIMPLE PREDICATE, or the PREDICATE.

The simple predicate of the first sentence is *falls;* of the second, *blows.*

The simple predicate, together with its modifiers, is called the MODIFIED PREDICATE.

The modified predicate in the first sentence is *falls softly;* in the second, *blows furiously.*

Mention the simple predicate and the modified predicate in each of the following sentences :—

1. The century plant never blossoms twice.
2. The tired horses trotted steadily homeward.
3. Kitty was here just now.
4. Now the full moon rises slowly.
5. Presently a sweet voice sang softly.
6. Never speak unkindly.
7. The stormy waves thundered louder.
8. The lightning flashed vividly.
9. Gradually the storm died away.
10. The singing lark soared continually higher.

Complete the following sentences by supplying suitable modifiers for the simple predicates :—

1. The cold north winds blow ——.
2. The thrush sings ——.
3. The cat approached —— ——.
4. May we go ——?
5. The tide rises —— ——.
6. —— the door bell rang ——.
7. Will you —— come —— ——?
8. The young robins —— ate ——.
9. —— we have come —— ——.
10. Plants grow —— ——.
11. Oak trees —— live ——.
12. The train rushes —— ——.

LESSON XVIII.

REVIEW.

1. Words used to modify nouns are called what? Give an illustration.

2. Words used to modify verbs are called what? Give an illustration.

3. Words used to modify adjectives and adverbs are called what? Give illustrations.

4. Point out the adjectives and adverbs in the selection entitled "An Anxious Mother," Lesson X.

5. Into what two parts may every sentence be divided? Give illustrations.

6. What is the simple subject of a sentence? The modified subject? Illustrate.

7. What is the simple predicate of a sentence? The modified predicate? Illustrate.

8. Write five sentences, drawing a line under the simple subject and the simple predicate of each.

LESSON XIX.

OBJECTIVE COMPLEMENTS OF VERBS.

1. The lambs play.
2. The girls found a nest.
3. Trees grow.
4. The boy hit the ball.

What is the predicate of the first sentence? Why? What do the lambs do? Does *play* make a complete assertion about *lambs?*

What do trees do? Does the predicate *grow* make a complete assertion about *trees?*

What is the predicate of the second sentence? Does the verb alone make a complete assertion? Could the girls find and not find something? What word completes the assertion made by the verb *found?*

Does the verb *hit* make a complete assertion about the subject *boy?* What word completes the assertion?

Nouns that complete the assertion made by the verb, like *nest* and *ball* above, are therefore called COMPLEMENTS.

A noun that completes the assertion made by the verb, and names that on which the action terminates, is called the OBJECT OF THE VERB, or the OBJECTIVE COMPLEMENT.

Mention the simple predicate in each sentence below, and tell its objective complement : —

1. We climbed the steep stony path.
2. We could see the river below.
3. A cloud obscured the sun.
4. Its shadow covered the fields.
5. The haymakers saw the cloud.
6. They gathered the hay quickly.
7. The wind rustled the poplar leaves.
8. The birds sought their leafy shelter.
9. How the thirsty plants welcomed the shower!
10. See the bright rainbow!
11. Hear the sparrow's happy song!
12. A wise son maketh a glad father.
13. A soft answer turneth away wrath.
14. Have you enjoyed the vacation?
15. How doth the little busy bee
    Improve each shining hour!

LESSON XX.

COMPOSITION.

Write an account of the last picnic you attended. Tell in a simple and straightforward way what you did and what you saw.

HINTS.

On what day of the week was the excursion? What can you say of the weather?

What preparations had you made? Who went with you?

Did you make the journey in a car, a carriage, or a boat? What did you see on the way?

What did you most enjoy during the day? Describe the scenes and amusements.

Tell what happened on the way home, and give your opinion of the picnic.

You may, if you prefer, write a composition on one of the following subjects: —

A NUTTING PARTY.

Describe the weather, the party, the place. Tell what kind of nuts you gathered, what animals you saw, where you ate luncheon. Tell about your journey home. Describe the collection of things you gathered.

A HUNT FOR WILD FLOWERS.

Tell where you went, what you found, what you looked for longest. Name the friends who went with you. Tell about their mishaps and successes. Describe the most beautiful spot you found. Tell what you took home.

LESSON XXI.

PREDICATE NOUNS.

1. That man is a physician.
2. The girl became an artist.
3. The child will be a builder.

Read the subject and predicate of the first sentence. Does the verb make a complete assertion about the subject? What noun is necessary to complete the assertion? What is the complement in the first sentence?

What noun is the complement in the second sentence? Why?

What noun is the complement in the third sentence? Why?

Notice that while the nouns *physician, artist,* and *builder,* are complements, they do not name anything on which the action terminates. *Physician* refers to the same individual as the subject *man,* and explains it. *Artist* refers to the same person as *girl,* and explains that noun. *Builder* refers to and explains the noun *child.*

A noun used like *physician, artist,* or *builder,* — to complete the assertion of the verb, and refer to or explain the subject, — is called a PREDICATE NOUN.

Mention the predicates in the following sentences, and tell the predicate noun belonging to each : —

1. Hans Christian Andersen was a Dane.
2. Copenhagen was his home.
3. He was the children's favorite story-teller.
4. A popular story is his " Ugly Duckling."
5. The " duckling " was really a cygnet.
6. The cygnet became a beautiful swan.

7. Can you be a hero?
8. Abraham Lincoln was a great man.
9. He became President.
10. Cornelia was a Roman mother.
11. Two Roman boys were her sons.
12. A chrysalis becomes a butterfly.
13. A thing of beauty is a joy forever.

LESSON XXII.

PREDICATE ADJECTIVES.

1. The old pine is straight.
2. The green fields are beautiful.
3. Children should be obedient.

What is the predicate of the first sentence? Does it assert an action of the tree, or a quality? What does the adjective *straight* do?

What is the predicate of the second sentence? Is the subject represented as doing anything? What is asserted of fields? What word completes the assertion? What part of speech is it?

What is the predicate of the third sentence? Does it make a complete assertion? What word completes the assertion? What part of speech is it? What word does it modify?

Adjectives used like *straight, beautiful,* and *obedient,* — to complete the predicate, and modify the subject, — are called PREDICATE ADJECTIVES.

Because a predicate adjective completes the assertion of the verb, it is called a COMPLEMENT.

Predicate adjectives and predicate nouns are called ATTRIBUTIVE COMPLEMENTS.

Mention the predicates in the following sentences ; point out the attributive complement in each case, telling whether it is a predicate adjective or a predicate noun : —

1. November days often seem chilly.
2. How cheerful the open fire looks !
3. How pleasant the long evenings are !
4. Mountain scenery is sublime.
5. On high mountains the weather is always cold.
6. Brave boys should be kind.
7. Is not sleep wonderful ?
8. The live oak is an evergreen.
9. Oak wood is strong.
10. In the autumn, oak leaves become brown.
11. Among the ancient Britons, the oak was a sacred tree.

LESSON XXIII.

THE COMPLETE PREDICATE.

1. Dorothy reads many stories.
2. These peaches are ripe.
3. My pony is a gentle creature.

What is the predicate of the first sentence ? Of the second ? Of the third ?

What is the complement of the predicate in the first sentence ? What kind of complement is it ? Why ?

What is the complement of the predicate in the second sentence ? What kind of complement is it ? Why ?

What is the complement of the predicate in the third sentence ? What kind of complement is it ? Why ?

A simple predicate, together with an objective or attributive complement, is called a COMPLETE PREDICATE.

Complete the following sentences by supplying the simple predicates with suitable complements. Tell in each instance whether the complement supplied is objective or attributive.

1. Pride must have —— ——.
2. A small leak may sink —— —— ——.
3. Some days must be ——.
4. The hour has seemed ——.
5. Always keep —— ——.
6. William Penn was —— ——.
7. He founded ——.
8. The Indians were —— ——.
9. King Crœsus was —— ——.
10. Remember —— —— ——.
11. The moon is —— ——.
12. Oh, give me —— —— —— —— ——.
13. The Lord is —— ——.
14. —— are the peacemakers.

LESSON XXIV.

COMPOSITION.

A TENDER-HEARTED SOLDIER.

A Southern newspaper tells the story of a soldier who saw a little kitten on the battlefield. Shot and shell were falling around him; but he sprang from his horse, and saved the kitten. It afterward became the pet of the company, and often took its nap on the top of a cannon.

The bravest are the kindest. The coward is always cruel to those weaker than himself. He kills flies, and steps on caterpillars, and pulls off butterflies' wings. He thinks it fun to torment kittens, and whip horses. Sometimes he trips up small boys, and teases his sisters. He never touches anything big enough to hit back. He does not know that

> "The bravest are the tenderest;
> The loving are the daring."

Study carefully the story of "A Tender-hearted Soldier," and then write a similar account of "A Tender-hearted Boy." Without using unnecessary words, tell : —

    1. Where the lad found a kitten.
    2. What he did with it.
    3. How it improved in appearance.
    4. What he taught his new pet.
    5. How he defended it from a dog.

You may, if you prefer, write a composition on one of the following subjects : —

    The Rescue of an Unhappy Dog.
    The Sufferings of a Colony of Ants.
    The Victims of a Bad Boy.
    A Gentle Little Girl and her Dumb Friends.
    A Brave Boy and his Pets.

LESSON XXV.

WORDS USED INSTEAD OF NOUNS.

    1. I met a friend and asked him to go with you and me.

    2. He asked his mother to lend us her boat.

    3. She said that we might use it.

What does the word *I* stand for? In place of what noun is *him* used? What word denotes the person spoken to?

In place of what noun is *he* used? *His?* What words represent the person speaking and another? In place of what noun is *her* used? *She?* What does *we* represent? *It?*

Words like *I, you, we, us,* which are used to denote the person speaking or the person spoken to, are called PRONOUNS.

Words like *he, she, his, her,* and *it,* used instead of nouns, are also called PRONOUNS.

A pronoun is a word used instead of a noun.

The noun in place of which the pronoun is used is called its ANTECEDENT.

Mention the pronouns in the following sentences : —

1. Trees drop their leaves in autumn.

2. I could hear the strange notes of wild geese as they followed their leader.

3. The sunshine touched the waves, and they glittered like gold.

4. We cannot honor our country with too deep a reverence.

5. Dame Barbara snatched the silken scarf.
   She leaned far out on the window sill,
   And shook it forth with a royal will.
   "Shoot, if you must, this old gray head,
   But spare your country's flag," she said. — WHITTIER.

6. Lives of great men all remind us
   We can make our lives sublime. — LONGFELLOW.

7. The rivers rush into the sea,
   By castle and town they go ;
   The winds behind them merrily
   Their noisy trumpets blow. — LONGFELLOW.

8. The babbling brook doth leap when I come by,
Because my feet find measure with its call ;
The birds know when the friend they love is nigh,
For I am known to them, both great and small.

JONES VERY.

9. Remember now thy Creator in the days of thy youth. — BIBLE.

Copy the following sentences, filling the blanks with suitable pronouns : —

1. —— father said —— would write —— a letter.

2. —— know —— will keep —— promise.

3. Have —— ever seen puss carry —— kittens in —— mouth ?

4. —— might think —— would hurt ——, but —— do not cry.

5. —— can fly —— kites to-day, but —— must mend —— first.

6. —— teacher explained to —— how a partridge tries to protect —— chickens when a person comes near ——.

7. See that tall pine : —— has a crow's nest on one of —— highest branches.

8. Let —— take —— knife. —— will sharpen ——.

9. The boys are going fishing. May —— go with ——?

10. —— neighbors will move into —— new house next week.

11. Ask Henry if —— watch is right.

12. The tree sends —— roots deep into the earth.

13. Alice thinks that —— has written —— exercise without a mistake.

3

LESSON XXVI.

REVIEW.

1. Write three sentences in which the verbs have objective complements.

2. Write three sentences in which the verbs are followed by predicate nouns.

3. Write three sentences in which the verbs are followed by predicate adjectives.

4. Distinguish between a modified predicate and a complete predicate.

5. Point out the objective complements and the attributive complements in the selection entitled "A Tender-hearted Soldier," Lesson XXIV.

6. A word used instead of a noun is called what? Point out the personal pronouns in the selection entitled "William Penn's Treaty with the Red Man," Lesson III.

LESSON XXVII.

WORDS USED TO SHOW RELATION.

1. The house *near* the lake is deserted.
2. Our teacher is kind *to* us.
3. We rested *under* a great elm.

Read the phrase in the first sentence. What word does it modify? What kind of word is *lake?*

Read the phrase in the second sentence. What does it modify? What kind of word is *us?*

Read the phrase in the third sentence. What word does it modify? What kind of word is *elm?*

Words used like *near, to, under,* — to introduce a phrase, and show the relation of a noun or pronoun following to some other word, — are called PREPOSITIONS.

That a preposition shows the relation of the noun or pronoun following it to some other word will be shown by rewriting each of the following sentences several times, using a different preposition each time.

Thus, in the sentence,

The worm crawled —— the leaf,

the prepositions *to, under, over, on, around, near,* etc., may be successively used in the blank.

Give for each of the following sentences two or more prepositions that may be successively used in the blank. Be careful that only appropriate prepositions are used.

1. We came home —— the shower.
2. Will you read —— me?
3. This letter is —— Sarah.
4. I found this book —— your chair.
5. The birds flew —— us.
6. We walked —— building.
7. The bird flew —— tree.

A preposition is a word used in a phrase to show the relation of a noun or pronoun that follows it to the word which the phrase limits.

Mention the prepositions in the sentences in Lesson XXVIII., and tell between what words each one shows relation.

LESSON XXVIII.

PHRASES.

1. The children *in the grove* are happy.
2. They are playing *among the trees.*
3. Would you like to be *with them?*

What children are happy? Which words tell what children are happy? Do these three words taken together modify *children?*

They are playing where? Which words tell where they are playing? Do these three words taken together modify the verb *are playing?*

Where would you like to be? Which words tell the place? Do these two words taken together modify the verb *be?*

Two or more words taken together and used (like *in the grove, among the trees, with them*) to limit or modify, as an adjective or adverb is used, are called a PHRASE.

Point out the phrases in the following sentences, and tell what word each one modifies, and whether it is used like an adjective or like an adverb : —

1. The water of the ocean is salt.
2. Rivers pour fresh water into the ocean.
3. Glaciers flow slowly downward toward the sea.
4. White strawberries grow in Chile.
5. Humboldt discovered potatoes in Mexico.
6. New York is the largest city in the United States.
7. Brooklyn is a city of homes.
8. Did some one knock at the door?
9. A word of three syllables is a trisyllable.
10. The cold winter is a season of rest for many plants.

11. In winter the reindeer lives chiefly upon lichens.

12. There is a steamboat on the lake.

13. In New Hampshire, the Old Man of the Mountains looks down on Profile Lake.

14. The wise men from the East followed the Star of Bethlehem.

15. At night the light from Vesuvius is seen in the city of Naples.

LESSON XXIX.

WORDS USED TO CONNECT.

1. Men *and* women gathered in the village.
2. They came in wagons *or* on horseback.
3. Many remained *until* night came on.
4. Some went home happy, *but* all were tired.

What does the word *and* connect in the first sentence? *Or* in the second? *Until* in the third? *But* in the fourth?

Words used like *and, until, or, but,* — to connect words, phrases, clauses, or sentences, — are called CONJUNCTIONS.

A series of words like *until night came on,* when used to explain or limit a word in the principal sentence, is called a CLAUSE.

Sentences like *some went home happy,* and *all were tired,* when connected by a conjunction to form one sentence, are called CLAUSES or MEMBERS OF THE SENTENCE.

A conjunction is a word used to connect words, phrases, clauses, or sentences.

Mention the conjunctions in the following sentences, and tell what each connects : —

1. Time and tide wait for no man.
2. Have you been well since I saw you?

3. Is this stone a diamond, or a crystal of quartz?

4. We looked for the cardinal flower, but we did not find it.

5. Shall you spend the vacation at home, or in Boston?

6. To-morrow will be pleasant, for the sunset is bright.

7. The brook will be dry unless we have rain soon.

8. I hope that it will not rain before we go home.

9. I have read the entire letter, though the handwriting is not plain.

10. Spiders catch flies, and wasps catch spiders.

11. If you will help me, we can do it.

12. Poplar leaves rustle easily, because their stems are flattened sidewise.

13. Blessed are the meek, for they shall inherit the earth.

14. The well looked up with its eye of blue,
And asked the sky for rain and dew.

Copy the following sentences, supplying suitable conjunc-tions in place of the blanks: —

1. Water —— oil will not mix.

2. The ice cracked —— it did not give way.

3. We will go on Monday —— on Tuesday.

4. You cannot learn —— you do not study.

5. —— you study the lesson, it will seem easy.

6. Wait —— I come.

7. We made a fire —— it was so cold.

8. I was not looking for a four-leaved clover —— I have found it.

9. How many years have passed —— this country was discovered?

10. Have you a gold watch, —— a silver one?

LESSON XXX.

COMPOSITION.

A CHANCE ACQUAINTANCE.

He was a very pretty little creature, with a beautiful bang hiding a pair of soft, gentle brown eyes. His manners were perfect. He never spoke a loud word, and was so quiet at the table, that if you had not seen him come into the dining-room you would never have known he was there. His toilet was as perfect as his manners, from his necktie to the last curl in his bushy tail. Yes, of course it was the dog Tobey. No one received more attention, and no one could have been less affected. When you patted him on the head, his jolly tail responded in the merriest fashion. He had one trick that would delight you. If you dropped a spool, no matter where it went, Tobey would not stop until he found it, and returned it to you. And if you rolled his own special ball through the railing of the piazza, where it would hide in the shrubbery and tall grass, Tobey would go nearly wild with delight, and hunt until he found it, and returned it to you, when he would dance and caper until you threw it again. Indeed, more than once I saw Tobey continue the game long after he was tired out, because some thoughtless child would throw the ball with no thought of the tiny little fellow who worked so hard to bring it back. But, no matter how tired Tobey was, he always was cheerful while the game lasted, though he panted when he went back to his rug.

MARGARET HASTINGS.

Study carefully the account of Tobey, and then write a similar composition about some dog you have met.

1. Where did you first see the dog?
2. Tell of its appearance.
3. Describe its intelligence.
4. Give some incidents showing its disposition.
5. Add your opinion of the animal.

If you prefer to do so, you may write on one of the following subjects:—

> **An Intelligent Dog.**
>
> **One of my Kittens.**
>
> **My Mother's Canary.**
>
> **The Elephant in the Park.**
>
> **The Gentlest Horse I ever Saw.**

LESSON XXXI.

INTERJECTIONS.

1. Aha! now I have caught you.
2. What! can't you go?
3. Oh, how beautiful it is!

What is the subject of each of the above sentences? What is the predicate of each? What words have no grammatical connection with other words in the sentences?

Words used like *aha, what, oh,* to express surprise or emotion, are called INTERJECTIONS.

An interjection is a word used to express surprise or emotion.

Mention the words that are used as interjections in the following sentences : —

1. Hark! I hear the bell.
2. Hurry! We shall be late.
3. Halloo! Here we are.
4. Wait! They are not ready yet.
5. Hush! Do not waken the baby.
6. Come, come, do not cry over spilled milk!
7. Well, well, begin again!
8. Hurrah! We have won the game.
9. Why, how quickly you have done it!
10. Indeed! I am very much surprised.
11. No, indeed! I cannot think of it.
12. O Mary! That was my last chance.
13. Ah! Is it you?
14. Oh, how glad I am to see you!

Write twelve sentences, using one of the following words as an interjection in each : —

O	why	help
oh	hush	come
ah	there	stop
alas	halloo	see
hurrah	look	hark
well	aha	wait

An exclamation point (!) is usually placed immediately after the interjection. When the interjection forms a part of an exclamatory sentence, the point may be placed at the end of the sentence.

LESSON XXXII.

A, AN, AND *THE.*

1. A man gave me the orange.
2. The man gave me an orange.
3. The man gave me a peach.

Words that limit or qualify nouns are adjectives : therefore *a, an,* and *the* in the sentences above, are ADJECTIVES. These three little words are, however, usually called ARTICLES.

In the first sentence above, does *a man* mean some particular man, or any man?

In the second sentence, does *the man* mean any man, or a particular man? How does the expression *the orange* differ from *an orange?*

Because the article *the* is used to point out a particular man or particular orange, it is called the DEFINITE ARTICLE.

Because the articles *a* and *an* are used when speaking or writing without regard to particular objects, they are called INDEFINITE ARTICLES.

The definite article *the* is used when either one or more than one object is spoken of; as, the man, the men.

The indefinite articles *a* and *an* may be used only when a single object is spoken of; as, a pear, an oyster.

A is used before words beginning with a consonant sound ; as, a peach, a ripe apple. *An* is used before a word beginning with a vowel sound ; as, an elephant, an elegant dress.

The is used before words beginning with either a vowel or a consonant sound ; as, the pear, the oyster, the elephant, the elegant dress.

Complete the following sentences by supplying articles. Give a reason for the one you use in each blank.

1. Oaks often live more than —— hundred years.
2. I once planted —— acorn.
3. Now —— tree which grew from it is —— foot high.
4. Let us go to —— post office.
5. I may receive —— letter.
6. I once read —— story of —— elephant.
7. —— man tried to teach —— elephant to perform tricks.
8. —— elephant was found practicing —— tricks alone on —— moonlight evening.

LESSON XXXIII.

COMMA. — SERIES OF WORDS.

1. Pines, birches, spruces, and hemlocks grow around my house.

2. Great, wide, beautiful, wonderful world, you are beautifully dressed.

3. The happy children run, jump, dance, and shout.

What part of speech is the word *pines?* *Birches?* *Spruces?* *Hemlocks?*

In the second sentence, what part of speech is *great?* *Wide?* *Beautiful?* *Wonderful?*

In the third sentence, what part of speech is *run?* *Jump?* *Dance?* *Shout?*

A mark like the one used between the words in the sentences at the head of the lesson is called a COMMA.

Place a comma after each word in a series of words alike in grammatical construction.

Combine the following sets of sentences into single sentences, and insert commas according to the above rule:—

EXAMPLE. — I have roses in my garden.
I have lilies in my garden.
I have pansies in my garden.
I have pinks in my garden.
I have roses, lilies, pansies, and pinks in my garden.

1. Tobey was a bright dog.
Tobey was a little dog.
Tobey was a shaggy dog.
Tobey was a brown dog.

2. He was polite.
He was handsome.
He was quiet.
He was jolly.

3. We bring coffee from the West Indies.
We bring sugar from the West Indies.
We bring spices from the West Indies.
We bring dyestuffs from the West Indies.

4. Intemperance leads to poverty.
Intemperance leads to crime.
Intemperance leads to degradation.

5. Abraham Lincoln was a great man.
Abraham Lincoln was a good man.
Abraham Lincoln was a noble man.

6. A heavy mist came in from the sea.
A cold mist came in from the sea.
A dense mist came in from the sea.
A penetrating mist came in from the sea.

LESSON XXXIV.

STUDY OF SELECTION.

GENERAL JUNOT.

In 1793, when Bonaparte was besieging Toulon, which was then in the possession of the English, he was one day directing the construction of a battery. The enemy perceived the work, and opened a warm fire. Bonaparte was anxious to send off a dispatch, and asked for a sergeant who could write. One immediately stepped out of the ranks, and wrote a letter to his dictation. It was scarcely finished when a cannon ball fell between them, and covered the paper with dust. The sergeant, looking towards the English lines, said, "Gentlemen, I am much obliged to you. I did not think you were so polite. I was just wanting some sand for my letter."

The expression and the coolness of the sergeant struck Napoleon, and he did not forget the incident. The sergeant was soon promoted, and finally became a general. He was the brave Junot, whose name is so often found in the annals of French campaigns.

By what other name do you know Bonaparte? On what occasion did he wish to send a dispatch? How did he find a man to prepare the letter? What happened while the young sergeant was writing? What did he remark? Have you ever seen sand used instead of blotting paper?

What reward did Junot receive for his coolness? How long ago did all this happen? Do you know the names of Napoleon's marshals? Do you know what battles Napoleon won? Have you ever heard of Waterloo?

Write in your own words a description of the coolness of General Junot in the face of danger.

Equivalent expressions : —

1. Besieging, investing, attacking. 2. Directing, superintending, looking after. 3. Opened a warm fire, began to fire upon. 4. Anxious, desirous of. 5. Finished, ended, completed. 6. Covered, besprinkled. 7. Expression, remark, saying. 8. Struck, impressed. 9. Promoted, advanced. 10. Brave, valiant, courageous. 11. Annals, records, history.

LESSON XXXV.

ABBREVIATIONS.

1. Doctor James Knight Johnson resides in South Manchester, Thetford County, Missouri.

2. Dr. James K. Johnson resides in S. Manchester, Thetford Co., Mo.

Compare these two ways of writing the same thing. In the second example, how is the title *Doctor* shortened? How is the name *Knight* shortened? How is the word *South* shortened? The word *County?* What is the shortened form of the name *Missouri?* What mark is placed after each of these short forms?

Shortened forms like *Dr.* for *Doctor*, *S.* for *South*, *Co.* for *County*, are called ABBREVIATIONS.

Every abbreviation should be followed by a period.

Learn the following abbreviations : —

amt.	amount	Aug.	August
ans.	answer	chap.	chapter
Apr.	April	C.O.D.	Collect on delivery

Cr.	Creditor	lb.	pound
cts.	cents	Nov.	November
Dec.	December	Oct.	October
do.	ditto. The same	oz.	ounce
doz.	dozen	p.	page
Dr.	Debtor or Doctor	pt.	pint
Esq.	Esquire	qt.	quart
ex.	example	Rev.	Reverend
Feb.	February	Sept.	September
ft.	foot or feet	Sr. or Sen.	Senior
Gen.	General	Supt.	Superintendent
Hon.	Honorable	U.S.A.	United States of
Jan.	January		America
Jr. or Jun.	Junior	yd.	yard

Write ten sentences, using correctly at least twenty of the above abbreviations.

LESSON XXXVI.

CONTRACTIONS.

1. Why don't you go to the beach?
2. It's a fine day: I'll go with you.
3. We'll watch the waves come in.

In shortening *do not* to *don't,* what letter is left out? Where is the apostrophe placed? What two words are shortened to make the word *it's?* What letter is omitted? Where is the apostrophe placed? What is the short form of *I will?* How many letters are omitted? Where is the apostrophe placed? What is the short form of *we will?* How many letters are omitted? Where is the apostrophe placed?

A shortened form of words, in which the apostrophe shows the place of omitted letter or letters, is called a CONTRACTION.

Contractions may be used in conversation, whether oral or written. They are sometimes used in poetry in order to secure the desired number of syllables in a line.

Commit to memory, and use in sentences, the following contractions : —

I'm *for* I am	can't *for* cannot
you're *for* you are	weren't *for* were not
we're *for* we are	haven't *for* have not
they're *for* they are	they've *for* they have
there's *for* there is	I'd *for* I would
'tis or it's *for* it is	she's *for* she is *or* she has
isn't *for* is not	he's *for* he is *or* he has
doesn't *for* does not	let's *for* let us
didn't *for* did not	o'er *for* over
hasn't *for* has not	o'clock *for* of the clock
thro' *for* through	ne'er *for* never

LESSON XXXVII.

QUOTATIONS.

1. "Annie, here is a letter for you," said Harry.

2. As soon as Annie saw the writing, she exclaimed, "Oh! it is from auntie, I know!"

3. "Well, when you have read it," said Harry, "please give me the stamp."

Are there any words in the first sentence which Harry did not say? Read his exact words. When we give the exact words used by another, we make a DIRECT QUOTATION.

What direct quotation is made in the second sentence?

Read Harry's last remark just as he made it.

In the first sentence, notice the double commas above the beginning and end of the quotation. These are called QUOTATION MARKS. Is the second quotation also inclosed in quotation marks? In the third sentence, which words were not spoken by Harry? Do these words divide the quotation into two parts? Is each part inclosed in quotation marks?

Does the first quotation begin with a capital? The second? The third?

A direct quotation should be inclosed by quotation marks (" ").

Begin with a capital the first word of a direct quotation.

Copy the following fable, carefully noticing the capitals and all marks of punctuation : —

THE CRICKET AND THE ANT.

A cricket came one cold day in winter to her neighbor, the ant, and said, " My dear neighbor, let me have a little food, for I am very hungry and have nothing to eat."

" Did you lay up no food for the winter ? " asked the ant.

"Indeed, I had no time to store up food," was the answer.

" No time, Madam Cricket ! What did you have to do in summer ? "

" I was singing all the time," replied the cricket.

" Very good," said the ant. " If you sung in summer, you may dance in winter."

After studying Lesson XXXVIII., rewrite the fable of " The Cricket and the Ant," changing the quotations from the direct form to the indirect.

LESSON XXXVIII.

INDIRECT QUOTATIONS.

1. A wise man once said that he could not afford to waste his time in making money.

2. A wise man once said, " I cannot afford to waste my time in making money."

Do these two sentences tell the same thing? How do they differ? Are the exact words of the speaker given in the first sentence? Are they changed in the second?

Are any quotation marks used in the first sentence? In the second?

When we tell in our own words what another has said, we make an INDIRECT QUOTATION.

An indirect quotation should not be inclosed in quotation marks, and it need not begin with a capital.

Rewrite the following fable, changing the indirect quotations so that they shall be direct : —

THE OX AND THE FLY.

An ox was grazing in the field when a fly alighted on one of his horns. Presently the fly asked him if her weight did not inconvenience him.

The ox did not notice her until she spoke again, saying that she would willingly fly away if he thought her too heavy.

Then the ox replied that she might make herself quite easy, for he had not known when she alighted, and probably should not know when she thought best to fly away.

LESSON XXXIX.

COMPOSITION.

A LITTLE KNIGHT OF THE NINETEENTH CENTURY.

We met him on the elevated road. He was about twelve years old. His hat, a shabby felt, was pulled down as far as possible on his head ; his trousers were ragged and faded ; his jacket was much too large. There was nothing remarkable about this boy until you looked sharply into his face ; then you saw an expression that made you think he was a boy who would not be moved to do a thing until he had thought it over. Beside him, on the next seat, tied carefully, was a very large bundle of papers. He looked up, saw us standing, and at once removed his papers to the floor, saying, "Here's a seat." We thanked him, and then he discovered that one of us was standing. Immediately he jumped up, and insisted on giving up his own seat. He was so cordial that it would have been discourteous to refuse. His face was cheerful, and you could not feel that he suffered, in spite of the poor, thin clothes. He picked up his bundle of papers — which he told us contained six hundred — long before the train stopped at City Hall, and, in reply to the question why he took up his burden so soon, he answered, giving it another hitch higher up on his shoulder to balance it more evenly, "I want to get used to it."

Read thoughtfully the description of a newsboy. Recall some similar incident, and write a composition on " An Unknown Hero."

LESSON XL.

RULES FOR THE USE OF CAPITALS.

1. Begin the first word of every sentence with a capital.

Stately elms grew on the lawn.
The gentle rain refreshes the thirsty flowers.

2. Begin the first word of every line of poetry with a capital.

No mortal builder's most rare device
Could match this winter palace of ice. — LOWELL.

3. Begin with a capital the first word of a quotation, precept, or question, if introduced in a direct form.

DIRECT. — The father of modern philosophy said, "Knowledge is power."

INDIRECT. — The father of modern philosophy said that knowledge is power.

4. Begin every proper noun with a capital.

Paris is the capital of France.
Having collected his army, Hannibal began his march.

5. Begin with capitals words derived from proper nouns.

The English language is spoken in many European countries.
Thomas Moore was an Irish poet.

6. Begin with capitals all appellations of God and of Jesus Christ.

The Lord is my shepherd.
The hope of my spirit turns trembling to Thee. — MOORE.

7. Begin with capitals titles of honor and respect.

His Excellency the Governor of Massachusetts was present, and made a speech.

8. Write with capitals the pronoun I and the interjection O.

If I were not Alexander, I would be Diogenes.
Guide me, O thou great Jehovah !

9. Begin with a capital the names of the days of the week and the months of the year.

School will open the first Tuesday in September.
The last Thursday in November is usually a day of public thanksgiving.

10. Begin with a capital the important words in the subject of a composition.

You have written compositions on " An Anxious Mother," " A Mortifying Mistake," " A Tender-hearted Soldier."

Justify the use of the capitals in the following. Write the sentences from dictation.

1. Have you read Irving's " Sketch-Book " ?
2. A Mohammedan mosque is a place of worship.
3. A lecture will be given by President Adams.
4. The author of " Home, Sweet Home," was an American named John Howard Payne, who was born in June, 1792.
5. The vessel was flying before the wind.
6. The bleak winds of March
   Made her tremble and shiver.
7. Remember the maxim, " Know thyself."
8. Dr. S. Weir Mitchell is the author of " In War Times," a story which originally appeared in "The Atlantic Monthly."

9. In the New Testament is found the question, "O death, where is thy sting?"

10. "Little Lord Fauntleroy" is a charming story for children.

11. The poetry of Milton differs from that of Dante as the hieroglyphics of Egypt differ from the picture writing of Mexico.

12. To me the meanest flower that blows can give
Thoughts that do often lie too deep for tears.

LESSON XLI.

REVIEW.

1. Words used to show relation are called what? Illustrate.

2. What is a phrase? Illustrate.

3. Mention what a phrase may do. Illustrate.

4. Point out the phrases in the selection "General Junot," Lesson XXXIV., and tell what each modifies.

5. Illustrate the different uses of conjunctions.

6. Point out the conjunctions in the selection entitled "A Chance Acquaintance," Lesson XXX.

7. Write three sentences in which interjections are used.

8. Mention the three adjectives that are called articles. How do *a* and *an* differ from *the*?

9. What mark is used to separate a series of nouns, adjectives, verbs, or adverbs?

10. Write five sentences, each containing an abbreviation.

11. Write five sentences, each containing a contraction.

12. Write five sentences in which quotation marks are used.

13. Give, with illustrations, ten rules for the use of capitals.

LESSON XLII.

COMPOSITION.

A LETTER.

My dear Sir:

Let me present to you a new friend of mine, well recommended from beyond the waters, and of a pleasant quality in himself: Mr. Henry Barnard, from Connecticut, New England. When he visits Glasgow, will you explain to him a little what he has to see; give him furtherance and welcome such as a stranger needs and merits?

I have never yet seen your worthy brother, but mean surely to do it. I shall hear of you, perhaps see you, in Annandale, where we hope ere long to be.

With true good wishes,

Ever faithfully,

Thomas Carlyle.

To D. Hope, Esq.

Study carefully Thomas Carlyle's letter of introduction, then write a similar letter, introducing one of your friends to a relative in another city.

LESSON XLIII.

THE PARTS OF SPEECH.

A sentence is a thought expressed in words. We use sentences when speaking. The words of which sentences are composed are therefore called PARTS OF SPEECH. They are classified as NOUNS, PRONOUNS, ADJECTIVES, VERBS, ADVERBS, PREPOSITIONS, CONJUNCTIONS, and INTERJECTIONS.

They may be defined as follows : —

A noun is a word used as a name.

A pronoun is a word used instead of a noun.

An adjective is a word used to limit or qualify the meaning of a noun or pronoun.

A verb is a word used to assert something about some person or thing.

An adverb is a word used to modify the meaning of a verb, an adjective, or another adverb.

A preposition is a word used in a phrase to show the relation of the noun or pronoun following it, to the word which the phrase limits.

A conjunction is a word used to connect words, phrases, clauses, or sentences.

An interjection is a word used to express surprise or emotion.

Read the following extract, and tell the part of speech of each Italicized word.

THE STUDY OF WORDS.

The *study* of *words* has *always* been regarded as one of the *most valuable* of *intellectual* disciplines, independently of *its* great *importance* as a guide *to* the right *practical use* of *words.*

The habit of thorough *investigation into* the *meaning* of words, and of exact discrimination in the use of *them,* *is indispensable* to precision and accuracy *of thought;* and *it* is surprising how soon the process *becomes spontaneous* and *almost mechanical* and *unconscious,* so that one often finds himself making nice yet *sound distinctions between particular* words which *he is not* aware that he has ever made the *subject* of critical *analysis.* —G. P. MARSH.

LESSON XLIV.

COMMON AND PROPER NOUNS.

1. A *city* is the capital of a *state.*
2. *Columbus* is the capital of *Ohio.*
3. *Florence* is a good *girl.*
4. *Huron* is a large *lake.*

Can you tell from the first sentence alone, what city and what state are meant? Can you tell from the second sentence, what city and state are meant? How do the nouns *city* and *state* differ from *Columbus* and *Ohio?* Which nouns begin with capitals?

Is *Florence* the name of a particular individual? Is *girl* the name of a particular individual only, or may each of many individuals be called a girl?

In the fourth sentence, which noun is a particular name? Which noun may be applied to many other things of the same sort? Which nouns begin with capitals?

Nouns like *city, state, girl, lake,* which are the names of classes of persons or objects, are called COMMON NOUNS.

Nouns like *Columbus, Ohio, Florence, Huron*, which are the names of particular individuals, places, or objects, are called PROPER NOUNS.

Some proper nouns are made up of two or more words, as *Jersey City, Ralph Waldo Emerson, Emancipation Proclamation, Declaration of Independence.*

A common noun is the name common to all of a class of individuals or objects.

A proper noun is the name of a particular individual or object.

The first letter of a proper noun should always be a capital.

Write ten sentences, each containing a common noun.
Write ten sentences, each containing a proper noun.

Mention the nouns in the following sentences. State of each whether it is common, or proper, and why.

1. The old town of Salem in Massachusetts was once a famous seaport, and ships sailed out of its harbor to the ends of the world.

2. Up from the meadows rich with corn,
   Clear in the cool September morn,
   The clustered spires of Frederick stand,
   Green-walled by the hills of Maryland. — WHITTIER.

3. Whoever has made a voyage up the Hudson must remember the Catskill Mountains.

4. What rice is to the Hindu, what wheat is to the European, the banana is to the natives of the tropical islands.

5. The whole German race honor the robin ; and the Scotch and the French consider the wren sacred.

6. And now the glad, leafy midsummer, full of blossoms and the song of nightingales, is come.

7. As Longstone looks now, so it looked many years ago, when Grace Darling was living there with her father and mother.

8. The soul of Jonathan was knit with the soul of David.

9. No man can gather cherries in Kent at the season of Christmas!

10. Welcome, O wind of the East! from the caves of the misty Atlantic.

11. An acre in Middlesex is better than a principality in Utopia. — MACAULAY.

12. No truer American ever existed than Thoreau.

EMERSON.

13. A barge across Loch Katrine flew,
High stood the henchman on the prow. — SCOTT.

14. The catbird is found in certain seasons all over North America, from Florida to Canada, and from the Atlantic coast to the Pacific Ocean.

15. High up in the tower of the old moss-covered church, against which the winds and storms of many years have beaten, hangs the village bell.

LESSON XLV.

COLLECTIVE, ABSTRACT, AND VERBAL NOUNS.

1. A *flock* of birds flew over our heads.

2. There were ten men on the *committee*.

3. A *family* of five moved into the house.

Is *flock* the name of a single individual, or of several taken together? Does *committee* mean one man, or a number taken together? Of what is *family* the name?

Nouns like *flock, committee, family,* etc., which are the names of a collection of objects, are called COLLECTIVE NOUNS.

1. *Politeness* is *kindness* kindly expressed.
2. *Beauty* is its own excuse for being.
3. *Pride* goeth before destruction.

Is *politeness* the name of a person, or a quality of a person?
Is *kindness* the name of a quality?
Is *beauty* the name of a thing, or of an attribute of a thing?
Is *pride* the name of a quality?

Nouns like *politeness, kindness, beauty, pride,* etc., which are names of qualities or attributes of objects, are called ABSTRACT NOUNS.

1. *Skating* and *coasting* are winter sports.
2. Boys enjoy *walking* and *rowing.*

Is *skating* the name of an action? Of what is *coasting* the name? *Walking? Rowing?*

Nouns like *skating, coasting, walking, rowing,* etc., which are used as names of actions, are called VERBAL NOUNS.

A collective noun is the name of a collection of objects.

An abstract noun is the name of a quality or attribute considered apart from its object.

A verbal noun is the name of an action.

State whether the nouns in the following sentences are proper, common, collective, abstract, verbal, and why.

1. Man is a thinking being.
2. A little weeping would ease my heart.

3. Attention is the stuff that memory is made of, and memory is accumulated genius.

4. Walking is a healthful exercise.

5. The other weapon with which he conquered all obstacles in science was patience. — EMERSON.

6.   Wounds are not healed
By the unbending of the bow that made them.

LONGFELLOW.

7. They say of Giotto, that he introduced goodness into the art of painting. — BANCROFT.

8. That they surpass the European species in sweetness, tenderness, and melody, I have no doubt; and that our mocking bird in his native haunts in the South surpasses any bird in the world in fluency, variety, and execution, is highly probable. — BURROUGHS.

9. There have been holy men who hid themselves
Deep in the woody wilderness, and gave
Their lives to thought and prayer. — BRYANT.

10. All the hearts of men were softened
By the pathos of his music;
For he sang of peace and freedom,
Sang of beauty, love, and longing;
Sang of death, and life undying. — LONGFELLOW.

11. Hang around your walls pictures which shall tell stories of mercy, hope, courage, faith, and charity. — MITCHELL.

12. The boast of heraldry, the pomp of power,
And all that beauty, all that wealth e'er gave,
Await alike the inevitable hour:
The paths of glory lead but to the grave. — GRAY.

Write ten sentences each containing a collective noun. Write ten sentences each containing an abstract noun. Write ten sentences each containing a verbal noun.

LESSON XLVI.

THE CHOICE OF WORDS.

1. Edison *invented* the electric doll.
2. Newton *discovered* the law of gravitation.

Did Edison construct the first electric doll? Had the law of gravitation always existed? In what respect do the verbs in the foregoing sentences agree in meaning? In what respect do they differ?

Complete the following sentences by supplying the proper words : —

1. Columbus —— America.
2. Howe —— the sewing machine.
3. Who —— the planet Neptune?
4. Who —— the telephone?
5. Whitney —— the cotton gin.
6. The Phœnicians —— Britain.
7. Stephenson —— the locomotive engine.
8. What navigators have tried to —— the North Pole?
9. De Soto —— the Mississippi River.
10. Who —— the trolley?
11. Galileo —— Jupiter's satellites with the telescope which he is said to have ——.
12. The barometer was —— by Torricelli.

LESSON XLVII.

THE PARAGRAPH.

CARRIER PIGEONS.

The use of pigeons for carrying messages was practiced by the Romans two thousand years ago. Navigators from Egypt were accustomed to take on board their ships carriers, which they released from time to time, to bear messages to their families. William, Prince of Orange, employed pigeons to carry letters to the besieged city of Leyden in 1574; and so delighted was he with their faithfulness, that he ordered them to be fed on strawberries, and to be embalmed after death. During the siege of Paris in 1871, pigeons were employed to carry messages to and from the city. These postboys were out of the reach of the German soldiers.

The carrier pigeon is by nature strongly attached to its home. In training it is taken, perhaps, a mile from home in a basket, and let loose. Then the distance is increased daily, until the bird can be moved to any distance, when, on being released, it will take a direct course for home. Once trained, the bird, with the letter tied to its wings or to its feet, is set free, rises high in the air, makes one or two circular flights, and then darts off in the proper direction, like an arrow.

Into how many parts is the selection divided? What does the first paragraph tell? What does the second paragraph describe? How wide is the margin at the left of the page? How wide is the space at the beginning of the first line of each paragraph?

Write from memory what you have learned about carrier pigeons. In your composition mention : —

1. Pigeons as messengers among the ancients; how the Prince of Orange rewarded carrier pigeons for carrying letters to Leyden; pigeons as postboys during the siege of Paris.

2. The training of carrier pigeons; why they can be trained to return home; how the distance is increased; where the letter is tied; what the bird does when it is set free.

LESSON XLVIII.

GENDER AND PERSON OF NOUNS.

1. John, boy, brother, heir, manservant.
2. Mary, girl, sister, heiress, maidservant.
3. Knife, cup, pen, farm, inkstand.
4. Child, teacher, parent, neighbor, cousin.

Of what sex are the objects denoted by the nouns in the first line?

Of what sex are the objects denoted by the nouns in the second line?

Do the nouns in the third line, *knife, cup,* etc., denote objects of either sex, or without sex?

Do the nouns in the fourth line, *child, teacher,* etc., denote objects of one sex, or of either?

Nouns like *John, boy, brother, heir, manservant,* etc., which denote objects of the male sex, are called MASCULINE NOUNS, or NOUNS OF THE MASCULINE GENDER.

Nouns like *Mary, girl, sister, heiress, maidservant,* etc., which denote objects of the female sex, are called FEMININE NOUNS, or NOUNS OF THE FEMININE GENDER.

Nouns like *knife, cup, pen, farm, inkstand*, etc., which denote objects without sex, are called NEUTER NOUNS, or NOUNS OF THE NEUTER GENDER.

Nouns like *child, teacher, parent, neighbor, cousin*, etc., which may be applied to either sex, are by some grammarians said to be of the COMMON GENDER. The gender of such nouns is usually indicated by the context, and they are said to be masculine or feminine, as the context determines.

A noun is of the FIRST PERSON when it is the name of the person or persons speaking, and is in apposition with a pronoun of the first person; as, I, *John*, will go.

A noun is of the SECOND PERSON when it is the name of the person addressed; as, Thou, *God*, seest me.

All other nouns are of the THIRD PERSON.

Nouns do not change their *form* to denote the different persons.

Make a list of the masculine nouns in the following sentences. Of the feminine. Of the neuter. Are all of these nouns of the third person? Why?

1. Mary has a bed of mignonette in her father's garden.

2. The sweetest word that ear hath heard
   Is the blessed name of " Mother."

3. Chisel in hand stood a sculptor boy,
   With his marble block before him.

4. A cloth weaver whose name was Columbus once lived in the city of Genoa.

5. At one end of the island stands the lighthouse, with the little cottage attached, where live the keeper and his family.

LESSON XLIX.

HOW TO TELL THE GENDER OF NOUNS.

The gender of nouns is distinguished in three ways : —

1. *By different words ; as,* —

MASCULINE.	FEMININE.	MASCULINE.	FEMININE.
brother	sister	nephew	niece
earl	countess	sir	madam
father	mother	son	daughter
king	queen	uncle	aunt
man	woman	wizard	witch

Most given or Christian names are of this class, and show of which gender they are : James, Patrick ; Sarah, Kate.

2. *By different endings ; as,* —

MASCULINE.	FEMININE.	MASCULINE.	FEMININE.
count	countess	duke	duchess
heir	heiress	executor	executrix
actor	actress	hero	heroine
tiger	tigress	Julius	Julia
emperor	empress	Paul	Pauline

3. *By prefixing a distinguishing word ; as,* —

manservant, maidservant ; male child, female child.

Be prepared to write the feminine of the following nouns by adding ess :—

Quaker	Jew	prior
baron	poet	heir
giant	priest	count
tailor	patron	lion

Be prepared to write the feminine of the following nouns by changing the ending er, or, *or* rer *into* ress: —

founder	actor	enchanter
arbiter	proprietor	sorcerer
adventurer	traitor	benefactor
ambassador	idolater	protector

LESSON L.

STUDY OF SELECTION.

ICHABOD CRANE AND HIS BORROWED HORSE.

The animal was a broken-down plow-horse that had outlived almost everything but his viciousness. He was gaunt and shagged, with a ewe neck, and a head like a hammer. His rusty mane and tail were tangled and knotted with burs. One eye had lost its pupil, and was glaring and spectral; but the other had the gleam of a genuine devil in it. Still he must have had fire and mettle in his day, if we may judge from the name he bore of Gunpowder. He had, in fact, been a favorite steed of his master's, the choleric Van Ripper, who was a furious rider, and had infused, very probably, some of his own spirit into the animal; for, old and broken-down as he looked, there was more of the lurking devil in him than in any young filly in the country.

Ichabod was a suitable figure for such a steed. He rode with short stirrup, which brought his knees nearly up to the pommel of the saddle. His sharp elbows stuck out like grasshoppers'; he carried his whip perpendicularly in his hand like a scepter; and, as his horse jogged on, the motion of his arms was not unlike the flapping of a pair of wings. A small wool hat rested on the top of his nose, for so his scanty strip of forehead might be called; and the skirts of his black coat fluttered out almost to the horse's tail. Such was the appearance of Ichabod and his steed as they shambled out of the gate of Hans Van Ripper, and it was altogether such an apparition as is seldom to be met with in broad daylight. — IRVING.

1. *Study very carefully the sketch from Washington Irving's " Legend of Sleepy Hollow."*

Was the horse young? Was it a saddle-horse? Was it smooth and beautiful? Notice the words that describe the head, the neck, the mane, the tail, the eyes. What is said of the disposition of the animal? Do you think the name " Gunpowder " suggests a fiery temper? Who owned the broken-down plow-horse?

How did Ichabod look on horseback? What is said of his knees? Of his elbows? How did he carry his whip? How did his arms move as the horse jogged along? Notice his hat, his forehead, the skirt of his coat. What do you understand by the word *shambled?*

2. *Try to imagine, and then describe, Ichabod Crane and his borrowed horse as they rode away from the gate of Hans Van Ripper.*

3. *Read Irving's sketch again. Now read aloud your own composition. Which description sounds better? Which is more laughable? What points have you omitted?*

4. *Try to imagine the accident that happened to Ichabod Crane, and complete in your own way the story of his misfortunes.*

5. *Compare again your work with the original, and improve your composition by adding interesting incidents.*

LESSON LI.

NUMBER OF NOUNS.

1. The girl reads.
2. The girls read.
3. The man works.
4. The men work.

Mention the noun in the first sentence. Does it denote one, or more than one? Mention the noun in the second sentence. Does it denote one, or more than one?

How many does the noun in the third sentence denote? The noun in the fourth?

Nouns like *girl* and *man*, which denote but one, are in the SINGULAR NUMBER.

Nouns like *girls* and *men*, which denote more than one, are in the PLURAL NUMBER.

Point out the nouns in the following sentences. Tell the kind and number, and give reasons.

1. The mind should have its palace halls
   Hung with rich gifts and pictures rare.

J. W. MILLER.

2. Of all the old festivals, however, that of Christmas awakens the strongest and most heartfelt associations.

IRVING.

3. New England, at least, is not based on any Roman ruins. We have not to lay the foundations of our houses on the ashes of a former civilization. — THOREAU.

4. Order is a lovely nymph, the child of beauty and wisdom ; her attendants are comfort, neatness, and activity ; her abode is the valley of happiness. — JOHNSON.

5. How pleasantly the rising moon,
   Between the shadows of the mows,
   Looked on them through the great elm boughs !

WHITTIER.

6. As for marigolds, poppies, hollyhocks, and valorous sunflowers, we shall never have a garden without them, both for their own sake and for the sake of old-fashioned folks who used to love them. — BEECHER.

7. When heats as of a tropic clime
   Burned all our inland valleys through,
   Three friends, the guests of summer time,
   Pitched their white tent where sea winds blew.

WHITTIER.

8. The crows flapped over by twos and threes,
   In the pool drowsed the cattle up to their knees,
   The little birds sang as if it were
   The one day of summer in all the year,
   And the very leaves seemed to sing on the trees.

LOWELL.

LESSON LII.

HOW TO FORM THE PLURAL OF NOUNS.

SINGULAR.	PLURAL.	SINGULAR.	PLURAL.
boy	boys	glass	glasses
lesson	lessons	watch	watches
house	houses	bush	bushes
town	towns	fox	foxes

What letter is added to the nouns *boy, lesson, house, town,* to form the plural?

The plural of nouns is usually formed by annexing *s* to the singular.

With what letter does the noun *glass* end? With what two letters does the noun *watch* end? The noun *bush?* With what letter does the noun *fox* end? How is the plural of each of these nouns formed?

The plural of nouns ending in *s*, *ch*, *sh*, or *x*, is formed by annexing *es* to the singular.

1. *Write sentences, using the plural of each of the following nouns :* —

bench	chair	moss	match
box	circus	pen	blush
light	suffix	brush	patch

2. *Copy the following, and notice how each plural is formed :* —

SINGULAR.	PLURAL.	SINGULAR.	PLURAL.
alley	alleys	jelly	jellies
essay	essays	duty	duties
journey	journeys	ruby	rubies

When the singular ends in *y* preceded by a vowel (*a*, *e*, *i*, *o*, or *u*), the plural is formed by annexing *s;* but when the final *y* is preceded by a consonant, the plural is formed by changing *y* into *i*, and annexing *es.*

3. *Write sentences, using the plurals of the following nouns :* —

enemy	jury	poppy
colony	ferry	city
fury	dairy	copy

4. *Form the plurals of the following nouns : —*

By annexing *s*.		By changing *f* or *fe* into *ves*.	
gulf	fife	life	wife
proof	safe	loaf	beef
grief	strife	knife	half
dwarf	roof	self	thief

Most nouns ending in *f* or *fe* form their plural by annexing *s*. A few form their plural by changing *f* or *fe* into *v*, and annexing *es*.

5. *Write sentences, using the plurals of : —*

Annex *s*.		Annex *es*.	
quarto	proviso	calico	tomato
palmetto	canto	grotto	cargo
memento	tyro	torpedo	negro
folio	piano	buffalo	potato
halo	solo	tornado	veto

When the singular ends in *o* preceded by a vowel, the plural is formed by annexing *s*. The plural of most nouns ending in *o* preceded by a consonant is formed by annexing *es*.

Learn the following plurals : —

Man, men ; woman, women ; goose, geese ; foot, feet ; mouse, mice ; tooth, teeth ; child, children ; ox, oxen ; louse, lice ; memorandum, memorandums or memoranda ; son-in-law, sons-in-law ; man-servant, men-servants ; 5, 5's ; alumna, alumnæ ; alumnus, alumni ; index, indexes or indices.

LESSON LIII.

CHOICE OF WORDS.

1. My uncle sent me a *number* of foreign postage stamps, and my cousin sent me a *quantity* of maple sugar.

2. There is *less* carelessness on the cable road, and therefore *fewer* accidents.

Do you think the stamps could be counted? Could the maple sugar be weighed?.

In speaking of things that may be counted, use *number.* In speaking of substances that may be measured or weighed, use *quantity.*

Which word means smaller in number, — *less,* or *fewer?* Which refers to something that cannot be counted?

In referring to numbers, use *fewer.* In speaking of quantity, use *less.*

Construct six sentences, using the words quantity *and* number *with nice discrimination.*

Write three sentences containing the word less, *and three containing the word* fewer.

LESSON LIV.

COMPOSITION.

FIVE PEAS IN ONE POD.

Once there were five peas growing in one pod. The peas were green, the pod was green, the vine was green, the leaves were green; and they thought all the world was green. The warm sun shone on the vine, the summer rain watered it. The shell grew larger, and the peas grew bigger and bigger.

"Are we to lie here cooped up forever?" asked one.

"I am tired of it," said another.

"I fear we shall become hard," said a third.

"I want to see what there is outside," said a fourth; while the fifth, a very little pea, cried because he could not get out.

At length the vine turned yellow, the pod turned yellow, and the peas turned yellow.

"All the world is turning yellow," said the peas, with one voice.

Then there came an earthquake. The pod burst open with a crack, and all five peas rolled out into the yellow sunshine. A little boy clutched them, and said they were fine peas for his pea shooter. He put the biggest one into his gun, and shot it out.

"Catch me if you can!" said the big pea.

"I shall fly straight into the sun," said the next one.

"I shall travel farthest," said the third pea.

"Let me alone," said the fourth.

"What is to be will be," said the little pea, as he shot up, and lodged in an empty flowerpot in the window of a room where lay a poor sick girl.

Pretty soon the little pea sprouted, and began to grow into a beautiful vine.

"Dear mother, I think I shall get well," said the little girl one day; "for my pea is growing famously."

"God grant it!" said the mother; and she took a stick and tied a string to it, so that the green vine might have something to cling to.

After many days there stood a beautiful pink pea blossom smiling in the warm sunshine. The little girl kissed it, and said, " Now I am sure I am going to get well."

HANS ANDERSEN.

Study carefully the story of the " Five Peas in One Pod." Observe the arrangement of the paragraphs, and the use of quotation marks.

Write in your own words one of the following tales : —

Cinderella.	Whittington and his Cat.
Ali Baba.	Little Red Riding Hood.
John Gilpin.	The Golden Fleece.

LESSON LV.

NOUNS IN THE NOMINATIVE CASE.

1. The summer rain falls softly.
2. Shakespeare was a great poet.

What is the simple subject of the first sentence? Why? What part of speech is it? What is the simple predicate of the first sentence? What part of speech is it?

A noun used like *rain*, as a simple subject, is called the SUBJECT OF THE VERB.

Point out a predicate noun in the second sentence. Does it refer to the same person as the subject?

A predicate noun like *poet*, referring to the same person or thing as the subject, is said to be in the NOMINATIVE CASE.

By the *case* of a noun, we mean its relation to other words in the sentence. The case of the subject of a verb is called the SUBJECT NOMINATIVE ; the case of a predicate noun is called the PREDICATE NOMINATIVE.

In the following sentences, point out each noun that is a subject nominative or a predicate nominative, and give the reason in each instance : —

1. The summer breeze sighs gently.
2. Stanley is a great explorer.
3. Ruth and Lucy are studious girls.
4. The linden is a beautiful tree.
5. The captain and the mate are brave sailors.
6. It was a night of lovely June,
   High rode in cloudless blue the moon. — SCOTT.
7. John Gilpin was a citizen
   Of credit and renown,
   A trainband captain eke was he,
   Of famous London town. — COWPER.
8. The twilight is sad and cloudy,
   The wind blows wild and free,
   And like the wings of sea birds
   Flash the whitecaps of the sea. — LONGFELLOW.

LESSON LVI.

NOUNS IN THE OBJECTIVE CASE.

1. The dead leaves covered the ground.
2. The rabbits jumped across our path.

What is the subject of the verb *covered?* What did the leaves cover? Is *ground* a predicate noun? Why not? Does it name the object of the action expressed by the verb *covered ?*

A noun like *ground*, used in the predicate to name that on which the action expressed by the verb terminates, is called the OBJECT OF THE VERB.

What is the simple predicate of the second sentence? By what is it modified? What part of speech is *across?* What part of speech is *path?*

A noun used like *path*, with a preposition, to form a limiting phrase, is said to be the OBJECT OF THE PREPOSITION.

A noun which is used as the object of a verb or of a preposition is in the OBJECTIVE CASE.

Name the case of each noun in the following sentences, giving the reason in every instance : —

1. The frost has killed the flowers.
2. The Normans conquered England.
3. The waves break on the shore.
4. The bird built its nest in a climbing rosebush near the house.
5. The gray-haired boatman rowed us across the little inlet to the sea.
6. Did you see the ships sail into the harbor?
7. The triumph of modern art in writing is manifested in the structure of the paragraph. — EARLE.
8. I climbed up to the old mill on top of the hill, and then went down through the green meadows by the side of the river.
9. Far up the blue sky a fair rainbow unrolled
    Its soft-tinted pinions of purple and gold. — WELBY.
10. I stood on the bridge at midnight,
     As the clocks were striking the hour,
     And the moon rose o'er the city,
     Behind the dark church tower. — LONGFELLOW.
11. The sun broke forth again in the east, and gilded the mountain tops. — BARBAULD.

LESSON LVII.

COMPOSITION FROM OUTLINE.

Write a composition from the following outline : —

HOW WE CAMPED OUT.

1. The plans for the outing.
2. The persons invited to join our party.
3. Our preparations for a week in the woods.
4. The place we chose for our tent.
5. The food and the cooking.
6. Disadvantages of life in camp.
7. What occupations we enjoyed.
8. What we collected and brought home.

If you have never camped out, you will perhaps prefer to write on one of the following subjects : —

A Saturday Afternoon.	Thanksgiving Day.
A Visit to the Museum.	A Fishing Excursion.
A Shopping Expedition.	Having my Picture Taken.

LESSON LVIII.

NOUNS IN THE POSSESSIVE CASE.

1. Arthur's bicycle is very light.
2. We escaped the storm's fury.
3. He has children's books for sale.

What is the simple subject of the first sentence? What word tells you who owns the bicycle? What does the word *Arthur's* denote? What is added to the word *Arthur*, when used to denote ownership or possession?

A noun used like *Arthur's*, to denote ownership or possession, is said to be in the POSSESSIVE CASE.

What does the noun *storm's* denote in the second sentence? What is annexed to the noun *storm*, when used to denote source or origin?

A noun used like *storm's*, to denote source or origin, is said to be in the POSSESSIVE CASE.

What books are for sale? What does the noun *children's* denote? What is added to the noun to denote that the books are suitable for children?

A noun used like *children's*, to denote fitness, is said to be in the POSSESSIVE CASE.

The possessive case is always found in connection with another noun, expressed or understood, whose meaning it limits by connecting with it the idea of origin, fitness, or possession.

Tell the case of each noun in the following sentences, and give the reason. If in the possessive case, state whether origin, fitness, or possession is indicated.

1. The ship's sails are white.
2. The clock's hands are always moving.
3. Frank's call sounded loud and clear.
4. My mother's voice is soft and sweet,
   Like music on my ear.
5. Each man's chimney is his golden milestone.

LONGFELLOW.

6. Happy hearts are watching out
   The old year's latest night.
7. The blue sky is the temple's arch. — WHITTIER.
8. A soldier's death thou hast boldly died,
   A soldier's grave won by it. — L. E. LANDON.

LESSON LIX.

FORMATION OF THE POSSESSIVE CASE.

POSSESSIVE SINGULAR.	POSSESSIVE PLURAL.
A woman's dresses.	The women's dresses.
A fairy's wings.	The fairies' wings.
A lass's laughter.	The lasses' laughter.

What is added to the nouns *woman, fairy,* and *lass,* to form the possessive singular?

The possessive singular of nouns is formed by annexing an *apostrophe* and *s* to the nominative.

What is the possessive plural of *woman ?* Does the nominative plural end in *s ?* How is the possessive plural formed ? What is the possessive plural of *fairy ?* Of *lass ?* With what letter does the nominative plural of these nouns end? How is the possessive plural formed?

When the nominative plural does not end in *s*, the possessive plural is formed by annexing an *apostrophe* and *s ;* but, when the nominative plural ends in *s*, the possessive plural is formed by annexing simply the *apostrophe*.

Write both the possessive singular and the possessive plural of each of the following nouns : —

ox	parent	fox	angel	butterfly	teacher
scholar	farmer	wasp	friend	company	Indian

State the difference in meaning between these pairs of expressions, and tell what makes the difference : —

1. The pupil's efforts.
   The pupils' efforts.

2. The rainbow's tints.
   The rainbows' tints.

3. The band's music.
   The bands' music.
4. The tree's fruit.
   The trees' fruit.
5. The servant's wages.
   The servants' wages.
6. The patriot's devotion.
   The patriots' devotion.
7. A fly's wings.
   Flies' wings.
8. The teacher's patience.
   The teachers' patience.
9. The man's duty.
   The men's duty.
10. Woman's work.
    Women's work.

• A noun of more than one syllable, ending in an *s* or a *z* sound, sometimes (like a plural) omits the *s* following the apostrophe, in order to avoid the repetition of hissing sounds. Thus, *princess, princess'; conscience, conscience'*.

LESSON LX.

POSSESSIVE NOUNS EQUIVALENT TO PHRASES.

1. A man's voice.
2. A lion's roar.
3. The tree's leaves.
4. The voice of a man.
5. The roar of a lion.
6. The leaves of the tree.

Are *a man's voice* and *the voice of a man* equivalent expressions? What is the difference in their form? In what case is *man's?* What does it show? What do you call the expression, *of a man?* What does the phrase limit?

A lion's roar is equivalent to what? How is the change made?

By what is the noun *leaves* modified or limited in the third expression? By what is the noun *leaves* modified or limited in the sixth expression?

A noun in the possessive case is frequently equivalent to a phrase, — the preposition *of* followed by the same noun.

6

Rewrite the following expressions, using an equivalent phrase in place of each possessive noun: —

The sun's rays.   America's history.
The story's end.   The navigator's compass.
A bird's wing.   The ship's crew.
The parrot's beak.   A mother's love.
A lily's perfume.   The mountain's height.
The acorn's cup.   The ocean's waves.
A flower's petals.   A father's care.
The river's bed.   The doctor's skill.
A man's reputation.   The forest's shade.
The book's cover.   A city's population.

Rewrite the following, using an equivalent possessive noun in place of each Italicized phrase: —

The streets *of the city.*
The sweetness *of music.*
The depth *of the river.*
The walls *of the castle.*
The nest *of the swallow.*
Dreams *of boyhood.*
The wand *of a fairy.*
The hands *of a watch.*
The cell *of the prisoner.*
The verdict *of the jury.*
The conscience *of a man.*
The colors *of the rainbow.*
The voice *of the singer.*
The beauty *of the landscape.*
The friends *of his childhood.*
The blue eyes *of the child.*

LESSON LXI.

CHOICE OF WORDS.

Study carefully the words in the following pairs. Use each word correctly in two sentences.

PEACEABLE. Quiet in reference to outside disturbance.
PEACEFUL. Quiet in reference to inside disturbance.

EXAMPLES. — He is peaceable who makes no tumult.
He is peaceful who lives in calm enjoyment.

STOP. To cease to go forward.
STAY. To continue in a place.

THINK. To employ the intellect.
GUESS. To hit upon by accident.

LIKE. To be pleased with in a moderate degree.
LOVE. To delight in with preëminence.

EMPTY. Containing nothing.
VACANT. Unoccupied.

LESSON LXII.

COMPOSITION.

HOW CRUSOE MADE POTTERY.

It would make you pity me, or rather laugh at me, to know how many awkward ways I took to make earthen vessels; what odd, misshapen, ugly things I made; how many of them fell in, and how many fell out, the clay not being stiff enough to bear its own weight; how some cracked by the great heat of the sun; and how others crumbled into dust the moment I touched them.

In short, after having labored hard for two months to find the right kind of clay, — to dig it, to bring it home, and to shape it, — I had only two great ugly earthen things not worthy to be called jars.

Now, it happened one day that I made a hotter fire than usual for cooking my meat; and when I went to put it out, after I had done with it, I found in the ashes a broken piece of one of my earthenware vessels, burnt as hard as a stone and as red as a tile.

I was agreeably surprised to see it, and said to myself that certainly these vessels might be made to burn whole if they would burn broken.

I had no notion of a kiln such as potters use, nor of glazing the pots with lead, although I had some lead; but I placed three large pipkins and two jars in a pile, one upon another, and heaped my firewood all round them, with a great mass of embers underneath.

The fire I plied with fresh fuel round the outside and on the top till I saw the jars inside were red-hot through and through, and I observed that they did not crack at all. When I saw that they were clear red, I let them stand in that heat for five or six hours.

At last I found that one of the jars, though it did not crack, had begun to melt, or run. The sand which was mixed with the clay had melted by the violence of the heat, and would have run into glass if I had gone on.

So I slacked my fire gradually till the earthenware began to lose its red color; and watching all night, — lest the fire should die out too fast, — I had in the morning three very good pipkins and two jars, as hard burnt as could be desired, and one of them perfectly glazed with the melted sand.

After studying carefully the simple narrative style of the extract from " Robinson Crusoe," write an account of one of your own experiences. Perhaps you will choose one of the following subjects : —

How we Made Maple Sugar.   A Good Way to Catch Rats.

Our Snow Fort.   How to Make a Kite.

An Experiment in Building.   My First Attempt at Cooking.

LESSON LXIII.

NOUNS IN APPOSITION.

1. Longfellow the poet lived in Cambridge.

2. Longfellow lived in Cambridge, a city near Boston.

What word in the first sentence is used to explain the noun *Longfellow?* If there were several men by the name of Longfellow, which word would help to explain the one we mean?

What word in the second sentence means the same as *Cambridge*, and explains it?

Nouns used like *poet* and *city*, to explain or limit the meaning of other nouns, and referring to the same persons or things, are said to be IN APPOSITION WITH those nouns.

With what noun is *poet* in apposition? With what noun is *city* in apposition?

The *case* of a noun in apposition is the same as the case of the noun which it explains.

In what case is *Longfellow?* Why? In what case is *poet?* Why? In what case is *Cambridge?* Why?

When two or more possessives are in apposition, only one takes the sign ; as, —

Longfellow the poet's home was in Cambridge.

Here *Longfellow* is in the possessive case because it denotes the ownership of the house. The noun *poet's* is in the possessive case because it is in apposition with *Longfellow*. But only the noun *poet's* takes the sign.

A noun in apposition, if accompanied by modifiers, should be set off by commas. If the appositive has no modifiers, no commas are needed ; as, —

The Emperor William reviewed the German troops.
William, the Emperor of Germany, reviewed the troops.

Tell the case of each noun in the following sentences, and give the reason. Give the reason for each punctuation mark.

1. Swift, the author of "Gulliver's Travels," had a brilliant intellect and a selfish heart.

2. Those green-coated musicians the frogs make holiday in the neighboring marshes.

3. The lark, that airy little musician, is known as an early riser.

4. Miss Alcott, the author of "Little Women," lived in Concord.

5. Sir Walter Scott, the novelist and poet, had a very strong affection for animals.

6. It was the great hall of William Rufus; the hall which had resounded with acclamations at the inauguration of thirty kings; the hall which had witnessed the just sentence of Bacon and the just absolution of Somers.

MACAULAY.

LESSON LXIV.

STUDY OF SELECTION.

HABITS OF FLOWERS.

Nearly all flowers turn towards the light, as if they loved it. This habit can be seen by watching plants that are standing near a window. The flowers will all be bent towards the light, if the pots are allowed always to stand in the same position. But by turning them round a little every day, while the blossoms are opening, the plants can be made to show flowers on all sides.

Some flowers shut themselves up at night, as if they were going to sleep, and open again in the morning.

A lazy bee was once imprisoned in a tulip. Perhaps he had done a hard day's work in gathering honey, and at last had become sleepy. At any rate, he staid too long in the flower, and so was shut in for the night.

The daisy is one of the flowers that close at night. When it shuts itself up, it forms a little green ball, not unlike a pea, and can hardly be known from the green grass amidst which it lies. But look next morning, and the ball is open, showing, as the poet says, "a golden tuft within a silver crown." It is a very beautiful sight indeed to see the grass spangled with daisies shining in the bright sun. It is said that this flower was at first called *day's eye*, because it opens its eye at the dawn of day, and that afterward the name became *daisy*.

The golden flowers of the dandelion are shut up every night; and they are folded so closely together in their green coverings, that they look like buds which have never been opened.   In places where the sun is very hot, the dandelion shuts itself up, even during the day : in this way it is sheltered in its green covering from the sun, and kept from fading.

Some flowers hang down their heads at night, as if nodding in their sleep ; but in the morning they lift them up again to welcome the light.   Other flowers have a particular time to open.   The evening primrose, for example, is so called, because it does not open till evening.   Through spring, summer, and autumn, we have a constant succession of flowers, each having its own season, and opening at its appointed time every year.

In what direction do flowers always turn?   How can you make a plant show flowers on all sides?

Do flowers close at night?

What happened one afternoon to a bee that lingered too long in a tulip?

How does the daisy look at night?   What does the poet say of the daisy?   Why is the flower called daisy?

When does the dandelion close its golden flowers?

Do flowers sometimes droop at night?   Do certain flowers open at a particular hour of the day?   At an appointed time of the year?

1. *Write from memory what you have learned of the habits of flowers.*

2. *Find out by observation, and then describe, the habits of the dandelion blossom, the clover leaf, the morning-glory.*

3. *Write a composition on " The Habits of Strange Plants."   You will find in botanical text-books and encyclopædias interesting accounts of the Venus's flytrap, the pitcher plant, the sensitive plant, the night-blooming cereus.*

LESSON LXV.

HOW TO PARSE NOUNS.

To parse a noun, state : —

1. *Class* — whether it is common, proper, collective, abstract, or verbal, and why.
2. *Gender* — whether it is masculine, feminine, or neuter, and why.
3. *Number* — whether it is singular or plural, and why.
4. *Case* — whether it is in the nominative, objective, or possessive, and why.

The person of nouns may be omitted in parsing, since a noun used as a subject is always in the third person.

MODEL FOR ORAL EXERCISE.

A bound volume has a charm in my eyes similar to what scraps of manuscript possess for the good Mussulman. — HAWTHORNE.

VOLUME is a common noun because it is the name of a class of things ; it is of the neuter gender because it is the name of something without sex ; it is of the singular number because it denotes but one ; it is in the nominative case because it is the subject of the verb *has.*

CHARM is an abstract noun because it is the name of a quality ; it is of the neuter gender because it is a name without sex ; it is of the singular number because it denotes but one ; it is in the objective case because it is the object of the verb *has.*

EYES is a common noun because it is a name common to a class of things ; it is of the neuter gender because it is the name of objects without sex ; it is of the plural number because it denotes more than one ; it is in the objective case because it is the object of the preposition *in.*

SCRAPS is a common noun because it is a name of a class of objects ; it is of the neuter gender because it is the name of objects without sex ; it is of the plural number because it denotes more than one ; it is in the nominative case because it is the subject of the verb *possess.*

MANUSCRIPT is a common noun because it is the name of a class of objects ; it is of the neuter gender because it is the name of an object without sex ; it is of the singular number because it denotes but one ; it is in the objective case because it is the object of the preposition *of.*

MUSSULMAN is a proper noun because it is the name of one of a particular people ; it is of the masculine gender because it is the name of a male person ; it is of the singular number because it denotes but one ; it is in the objective case because it is the object of the preposition *for.*

After the reasons for the several classifications are well understood, a briefer form may be used ; as, —

VOLUME is a noun, common, neuter, singular, nominative, subject of the verb *has.*

MODEL FOR WRITTEN EXERCISE.

NOUNS.	CLASS.	GENDER.	NUMBER.	CASE.
volume	common	neuter	singular	nominative
charm	abstract	neuter	singular	objective
scraps	common	neuter	plural	nominative
Mussulman	proper	masculine	singular	objective

Parse according to the model the nouns in Lesson LXIV.

LESSON LXVI.

PERSONAL PRONOUNS.

1. I stood on the bridge at midnight.

2. Listen, my children, and you shall hear
   Of the midnight ride of Paul Revere.

3. Let him not boast who puts his armor on
   As he who puts it off, the battle done.

4.   Words of welcome and gladness
   Fell from her beautiful lips, and blessed the
   cup as she gave it.

What part of speech is *I* in the first sentence? *You,* in the second sentence? *He, his, him,* in the third? *It,* in the fourth?

Pronouns used to denote the person or persons speaking are said to be of the first person; as, *I, my, me, we, our, us.*

Pronouns used to denote the person or persons spoken to are said to be of the second person; as, *thou, thy, thine, you, your.*

Pronouns used to denote persons or things spoken of are said to be of the third person; as, *he, she, it, his, her, its, they, their, them.*

Pronouns that have a different form for each person and number are called PERSONAL PRONOUNS.

Point out the personal pronouns in the following sentences : —

1. We judge ourselves by what we feel capable of doing, while others judge us by what we have already done. — LONGFELLOW.

2. I vowed that I would dedicate my powers
To thee and thine : have I not kept the vow?

3. Spider, your web is so light that a dewdrop is enough to break it.

4.   And she glides
Into his darker musings with a mild
And healing sympathy, that steals away
Their sharpness ere he is aware. — BRYANT.

5.   And we like, too, old Winter's greeting :
His touch is cold, but his heart is warm ;
So, though he may bring to us wind and storm,
We look with a smile on his well-known form,
        And ours is a gladsome greeting.

6. Give every man thine ear, but few thy voice :
Take each man's censure, but reserve thy judgment.

7. Our hearts, our hopes, are all with thee,
Our hearts, our hopes, our prayers, our tears,
Our faith triumphant o'er our fears,
Are all with thee, — are all with thee!

LONGFELLOW.

LESSON LXVII.

PERSONAL PRONOUNS.

NUMBER, GENDER, AND CASE.

Pronouns, like nouns, are of the singular or plural number ; of the masculine, feminine, or neuter gender ; and in the nominative, possessive, or objective case.

The following table gives the different personal pronouns with their modifications : —

DECLENSION OF PERSONAL PRONOUNS.

The First Person.

SINGULAR.		PLURAL.	
Nom.	I	*Nom.*	we
Poss.	my	*Poss.*	our
Obj.	me	*Obj.*	us

The Second Person.

ANCIENT FORM.		COMMON FORM.	

	SINGULAR.	PLURAL.		SINGULAR.	PLURAL.
Nom.	thou	ye	*Nom.*	you	you
Poss.	thy	your	*Poss.*	your	your
Obj.	thee	you	*Obj.*	you	you

The Third Person.

	SINGULAR.			PLURAL.	
	Masculine.	*Feminine.*	*Neuter.*		*All genders.*
Nom.	he	she	it	*Nom.*	they
Poss.	his	her	its	*Poss.*	their
Obj.	him	her	it	*Obj.*	them

The pronouns *thou, thy, thee,* and *ye,* are not now used, except in poetry or in prayer. They will be found, however, in old writings, particularly in the Bible.

Mine and *thine* are sometimes used for *my* and *thy* before words beginning with a vowel sound; as, —

Mine eyes have seen the glory of the coming of the Lord.

If thine enemy hunger, feed him.

The English language lacks a pronoun of singular number, common gender; for example, *Who has lost his or her book?* In such cases, the masculine form is usually preferred.

Point out the personal pronouns in the following sen-
tences. Give the person, number, gender, and case of each,
with reasons.

1. Ah! what would the world be to us
    If the children were no more?

2. And I'd feed the hungry, and clothe the poor,
    And all should bless me who left our door.

    WHITTIER.

3. If we say, The darkness shall cover us — in the
darkness, as in the light, our obligations are yet with us.

    WEBSTER.

4. Sister and brother wound their arms around each
other, and the golden light came streaming in, and fell upon
them. — DICKENS.

5.   The land
    Is never lost that has a son to right her.

6. Oh, hear your father, noble youth! hear him.

    SCHILLER.

7. He grew to be revered and admired by his towns-
men, who had at first known him only as an oddity.

    EMERSON.

8. I know not how long it was before, to his unspeak-
able joy, he beheld the huge shape of the giant, like a cloud
on the far-off edge of the sea. — HAWTHORNE.

9. Ye sons of freedom, wake to glory!

10. Wit makes its own welcome, and levels all distinctions. — EMERSON.

11. How poor they are that have not patience!

    SHAKESPEARE.

12. The mind of the scholar, if you would have it large and liberal, should come in contact with other minds.

13.   Whene'er a noble deed is wrought,
        Whene'er is spoken a noble thought,
            Our hearts, in glad surprise,
            To higher levels rise. — LONGFELLOW.

14.   'Tis willing hand! 'tis cheerful heart!
            The two best friends I know.
        Around the hearth come joy and mirth,
            Where'er their faces glow. — MACKAY.

LESSON LXVIII.

CHOICE OF WORDS.

1. The minister *hastened* up the aisle.
2. The boy *hurried* toward the schoolhouse.

Do you think of any difference between the motion of the minister and that of the boy? Which was quiet, but rapid? Which was both rapid and irregular?

Hasten and *hurry* both imply a quick movement; *hurry* always adds the idea of excitement or irregularity.

Construct four original sentences illustrating the correct use of : —

       hasten   hurry

Construct sentences to show the proper use of the following words : —

enough	healthy	pride
sufficient	wholesome	vanity

LESSON LXIX.

COMPOSITION.

A LETTER.

ELMWOOD, CAMBRIDGE, MASS.,
Jan. 2, 1890.

DEAR FRIENDS:

Here I am again in the house where I was born longer ago than you can remember, though I wish you more New Year's Days than I have ever had. 'Tis a pleasant old house, just about twice as old as I am, four miles from Boston, in what was once the country, and is now a populous suburb.

My library occupies two rooms opening into each other by arches at the side of the ample chimneys. The trees I look out on are the earliest things I remember.

Now for out of doors. What do you suppose the thermometer is about on this second day of January? I was going to say he was standing on his head: at any rate, he has forgotten what he is about, and is marking sixty-three degrees Fahrenheit on the north side of the house and in the shade!

I forgot one thing. There are plenty of mice in the wall, and, now that I can't go to the play with you, I assist at their little tragedies and comedies behind the wainscot in the night hours, and build up plots in my fancy. 'Tis a French company, for I hear them distinctly say, "*Wee, wee.*"

Good by, and take care of yourselves till I come with the daffodils. I wish you both many a happy New Year and a share for me in some of them. Poets seem to live long nowadays, and I, too, live in Arcadia after my own fashion.

Affectionately yours,

JAMES RUSSELL LOWELL.

TO THE MISSES LAWRENCE,
  LONDON, ENGLAND.

Study carefully the arrangement of the letter and the style.

Write a letter to one of your relatives who has never seen your home. Describe : —

1. The location of the house.
2. Your room and its contents.
3. The view from your windows.
4. Your occupations.

LESSON LXX.

COMPOUND PERSONAL PRONOUNS.

1. I enjoyed myself. We enjoyed ourselves.
2. You enjoyed yourself. You enjoyed yourselves.
3. He enjoyed himself. They enjoyed themselves.

Pronouns like *myself, yourself, himself, ourselves, themselves,* etc., which are formed by annexing *self* or *selves* to one of the personal pronouns, are called COMPOUND PERSONAL PRONOUNS.

What other compound personal pronouns may be formed besides those given above?

Mention the compound personal pronouns of the masculine gender. Mention those of the feminine gender. Mention those that are neuter. Which are used for either gender?

Which of the compound personal pronouns are of the first person? Which are of the second? Which are of the third?

Which compound personal pronouns are of the singular number? Which are plural? What word is used to form the singulars? What to form the plurals?

In what case are all the compound personal pronouns in the sentences at the beginning of this lesson?

The compound personal pronouns are usually in the objective case.

Sometimes, when used to emphasize a noun or pronoun, they are by apposition in the nominative case; thus, —

> I myself will do it.
> The general himself ordered it.
> You yourselves have defeated it.

Tell the gender, person, number, and case of each compound personal pronoun in the following sentences : —

1. If you would have it well done, — I am only repeating your maxim, —
   You must do it yourself, you must not leave it to others.

2. Let us, then, be what we are, and speak what we think, and in all things
   Keep ourselves loyal to truth.

3. My father is old, and has nobody but myself to love him. Hard as you think his heart is, it would break to lose me.

4. He who destroys a good book kills reason itself.

   MILTON.

5. Each man makes his own stature, builds himself.

   YOUNG.

LESSON LXXI.

ABSOLUTE POSSESSIVE PRONOUNS.

This house is my house.
This house is mine.

This house is thy house.
This house is thine.

This house is her house.
This house is hers.

This house is our house.
This house is ours.

This house is your house.
This house is yours.

This house is their house.
This house is theirs.

What is the difference between the first and second sentences? Do they mean the same? The word *mine* in the second sentence takes the place of what words in the first? The words *thine, hers, ours, yours,* and *theirs,* take the place respectively of what words?

When the noun qualified by the possessive pronouns *my, thy, her, our, your,* or *their,* is omitted, these pronouns are changed to *mine, thine, hers, ours, yours,* and *theirs.*

The pronouns *mine, thine, hers, ours, yours,* and *theirs,* are called ABSOLUTE POSSESSIVE PRONOUNS because they are used independently of a noun. Be careful not to use an apostrophe in writing these absolute possessives.

Rewrite the following sentences, substituting an appropriate absolute possessive pronoun for the Italicized words : —

1. This bouquet is *your bouquet.*
2. That bouquet is *my bouquet.*
3. The apples in the basket are *their apples.*
4. All the largest apples are *my apples.*
5. What a happy life *your life* must be !
6. A sad fate is *my fate.*
7. Is the tent in the woods *your tent?*
8. *His class* is the most diligent class in the school.
9. The fastest horses are *their horses.*

My, thy, our, your, and *their* are always in the possessive case ; but *hers, ours, yours,* and *theirs* are never in the possessive case. They are used in the nominative or the objective case.

Suppose we ask the question, *Whose book was lost?*

These answers might be given : —

Mine was lost.   Hers was lost.   Ours was lost.   Yours was lost. Theirs was lost.

In each of these answers, the absolute possessive is in what case ? Why ?

Suppose we ask the question, *Who lost his book ?*

These answers might be given : —

I lost mine.   She lost hers.   We lost ours.   You lost yours. They lost theirs.

In each of these answers, the absolute possessive would be in what case ?   Why ?

Write a similar set of answers to each of the following questions, and state whether the pronouns are in the nominative or the objective case : —

1. Whose house was burned?
2. Whose trees were struck by lightning?
3. Whose boats are the best in the harbor?
4. Whose fault was it that the watch was lost?
5. Is the brown-and-white setter your dog?
6. Whose roses were blighted by the storm?
7. Are the books in the library your books?
8. Whose carriage was used?
9. In whose garden did the gardener plant the vines?

Point out the possessive pronouns and the absolute possessives in the following sentences. Give the person, number, gender, and case of each.

1. I have learned to seek my happiness by limiting my desires. — JOHN STUART MILL.
2. We have met the enemy, and they are ours. — PERRY.
3. "A dainty pair," the prudent matron said,
   "But thine they are not." — BRYANT.
4. The deadliest foe of all our race,
   And hateful unto me and mine!
5. Yours has the suffering been,
   The memory shall be ours.
6. But knowing well captivity,
   Sweet bird! I could not wish for thine. — BYRON.
7. No time is this for hands long over-worn
   To task their strength. — WHITTIER.
8. Come, good people, all and each,
   Come and listen to our speech!
   In your presence here I stand,
   With a trumpet in my hand. — LONGFELLOW.

LESSON LXXII.

STUDY OF SELECTION.

THE BLUE JAYS.

I once had the chance of doing a kindness to a household of blue jays, which they received with very friendly condescension. I had had my eye for some time upon a nest, and was puzzled by a constant fluttering of what seemed full-grown wings in it whenever I drew nigh. At last I climbed the tree, in spite of angry protests from the old birds against my intrusion. The mystery had a very simple solution. In building the nest, a long piece of packthread had been somewhat loosely woven in. Three of the young birds had contrived to entangle themselves in it, and had become full grown without being able to launch themselves upon the air. One was unharmed; another had so tightly twisted the cord about its shank that one foot was curled up and seemed paralyzed; the third, in its struggles to escape, had sawn through the flesh of the thigh and so much harmed itself, that I thought it humane to put an end to its misery. When I took out my knife to cut their hempen bonds, the heads of the family seemed to divine my friendly intent. Suddenly ceasing their cries and threats, they perched quietly within reach of my hand, and watched me in my work of manumission. This, owing to the fluttering terror of the prisoners, was an affair of some delicacy; but ere long I was rewarded by seeing one of them fly away to a neighboring tree, while the cripple, making a parachute of his wings, came lightly to the ground, and hopped off as well as he could with one leg, obsequiously waited on by his elders.   A week later I had the satisfaction of meeting him in the pine walk, in good spirits, and already so far recovered as to be able to balance himself with the lame foot.   I have no doubt that in his old age he accounted for his lameness by some handsome story of a wound received at the famous Battle of the Pines, where one tribe, overcome by numbers, was driven from its ancient camping ground. — LOWELL.

Study carefully Lowell's account of the imprisoned blue jays.

Tell the story in your own words.   You may, if you wish, use the following equivalent expressions :—

Intrusion = unwelcome entry.

Launch themselves on the air = fly.

Humane = kind, merciful.

Manumission = setting free.

Making a parachute of = spreading.

Overcome = conquered.

Satisfaction = pleasure.

Accounted for = excused.

Camping ground = stronghold.

Describe in a similar way an accident you have seen.

Before you begin to write, increase your knowledge of the subject :—

1. By observation.
2. By experiment.
3. By reading and study.
4. By conversation.

The following subjects will probably remind you of a familiar incident :—

A Mouse that we Caught in a Trap.

Some Ants that Moved a Straw.

Two Birds that Built a Nest in our Apple Tree.

A Canary Bird that Left its Home.

LESSON LXXIII.

PUNCTUATION. — THE COMMA.

A comma (,) is placed after each word in a series of words alike in grammatical construction; thus, —

The wisest, brightest, meanest, of mankind.

Infancy, childhood, youth, manhood, age, are different stages in human life.

1. If the last word of the series is preceded by a conjunction, a comma is not placed after it; thus, —

Ease, indulgence, luxury, and sloth make man a poor, sordid, selfish, and wretched being.

2. If the words in a series are severally connected by conjunctions, a comma is not used; thus, —

The air and earth and water teem with delighted existence.
The mind is that which knows and feels and thinks.

3. If only one word follows the series, a comma is not placed after the last word of the series; thus, —

He was a resolute, self-possessed, decided man.
David was a wise, good, pious king.
They taught, urged, threatened, lectured him.

4. If the series is composed of pairs of words, a comma is placed after each pair; thus, —

Draw from life the utmost it will yield for honor and usefulness, culture and enjoyment, health and affection.

Explain the use of the comma in the following sentences. Write the sentences from dictation.

1. Let all the ends thou aim'st at be thy country's, Thy God's, and truth's. — SHAKESPEARE.

2. To idle, silly, flattering words,
   I pray you ne'er give heed.

3. Faith, hope, and charity are three cardinal virtues.

4. We should be kind, sympathetic, and helpful to all.

5. Strength, health, love, wisdom, peace, hope, are the elementary atoms of happiness.

6. God gives us the soul; but genius, talent, and ability we must get through education.

7. Griefs, joys, fears, hopes, suspicions, and counsels may all be imparted to a true friend.

8. How deeply and warmly and spotlessly Earth's nakedness is clothed!

9. The wit, the sage, the orator, the hero, the whole family of genius, furnished forth their treasures, and gave them nobly to the nation's exigence.

10. The one serviceable, safe, certain, remunerative, attainable quality in every study and every pursuit is the quality of attention. — DICKENS.

11. Walled towns, stored arsenals, guns, and ammunition are of no avail, unless the people be courageous.

12. In old Rome the public roads beginning at the Forum proceeded north, south, east, west, to the center of every province of the empire.

13. It is a story of labors, of trials, of patient forbearance, of long-suffering.

14. No one can find peace but in the growth of an enlightened, firm, disinterested, holy mind.

15. The back of the chair was curiously carved in open-work, so as to represent flowers and fruit and foliage.

16. Cause and effect, means and ends, seed and fruit, cannot be severed. — EMERSON.

17. How nobly those inverted commas, those italics, those capitals, bring out the writer's wit, and relieve the eye! They are as good as jokes, though you mayn't quite perceive the point. — THACKERAY.

18. The rich and the poor, the wise and the ignorant, the strong and the weak, are all brothers.

19. Were all these changing beauties of form and color to disappear, how unsightly and dull and dreary would be this world of ours!

20. Poverty and sickness, oppression and misery, were the lot of the French peasantry in the eighteenth century.

21. Shining and tall and fair and straight
As the pillar that stood by the Beautiful Gate.

LOWELL.

LESSON LXXIV.

PRONOUN AND ANTECEDENT.

1. The man lost *his* pocketbook and all the money *he* had with *him*.

2. The woman lost *her* pocketbook and all the money *she* had with *her*.

3. The men lost *their* pocketbooks and all the money *they* had with *them*.

In place of what noun is the pronoun *his* used? The pronoun *he?* The pronoun *him?*

In place of what noun is the pronoun *her* used? The pronoun *she?*

In place of what noun is the pronoun *their* used? The pronoun *they?* The pronoun *them?*

The noun for which a pronoun stands is called its ANTECEDENT.

What is the antecedent of *his?* Of *he?* Of *him?* What is the gender of *man?* What is the person? The number? The pronouns *he, his,* and *him,* are in what person, number, and gender?

In the second sentence, what are the person, number, and gender of *woman?* Of *she* and *her?*

What are the person, number, and gender of *men* in the third sentence? Of *they, their,* and *them?*

A pronoun must agree with its antecedent in person, number, and gender.

Point out the antecedent of each personal pronoun in the following sentences, and give the person, number, and gender of both the antecedent and the pronoun: —

  1. A light broke in upon my brain, —
        It was the carol of a bird ;
     It ceased, and then it came again,
        The sweetest song ear ever heard. — BYRON.
  2. My country, 'tis of thee,
     Sweet land of liberty,
          Of thee I sing. — S. F. SMITH.
  3. When a man has not a good reason for doing a thing, he has one good reason for letting it alone. — SCOTT.
  4. God's ways seem dark, but soon or late
        They touch the shining hills of day. — WHITTIER.
  5. I have ships that went to sea
        More than fifty years ago ;
     None have yet come home to me,
        But are sailing to and fro. — COFFIN.

6. Comrades, leave me here a little, while as yet 'tis
　　　early morn :
　　Leave me here, and when you want me, sound upon
　　　the bugle horn. — TENNYSON.

7. There is always room for a man of force, and he
makes room for many. — EMERSON.

8. With spiders I had friendship made,
　　And watched them in their sullen trade,
　　Had seen the mice by moonlight play,
　　And why should I feel less than they ? — BYRON.

9. Sweet streamlet ! What a bright life must have
been yours ! What flowers must have fringed your gliding
way, what rosy clouds you have reflected, what lilies you
have nourished, what stars have risen to tell you their
secret ere they have set ! — CONWAY.

LESSON LXXV.

TWO OR MORE ANTECEDENTS.

1. Ethel and Elaine had their pictures taken.
2. Ethel or Elaine had her picture taken.

What are the antecedents of *their?* In what number is each
antecedent? By what are the antecedents connected? Does the
connective make us consider both girls together? Have the two,
thus, a singular, or a plural significance? Is the pronoun *their*
singular, or plural?

**When a pronoun has two or more singular antecedents con-
nected by *and*, it must agree with them in the plural number.**

How many antecedents has *her* in the second sentence? In
what number is each? By what are the antecedents connected?

Does this connective make us consider the girls together, or separately? Does the sentence mean that one, or both, had their pictures taken? In what number is *her?*

When a pronoun has two or more singular antecedents connected by *or* or *nor*, it must agree with each in the singular number.

But when one of the antecedents is plural, the pronoun must be plural also.

When a pronoun has for an antecedent a collective noun in the singular which stands for many as one whole, the pronoun must agree with it in the singular.

The board holds its regular meetings on the first Tuesday of each month.

Mention the antecedents of the pronouns in the following sentences, and tell in what number each is. Tell in what number each pronoun is, and why.

1. James and Edward lost their way.
2. James or Edward lost his way.
3. The maple and the chestnut shed their leaves in the fall.
4. Either the elm or the maple throws its shadow across my window.
5. Neither George nor Harry is willing to go.
6. Either James or Henry will come and bring his games with him.
7. Such was the appearance of Ichabod and his steed, as they shambled out of the gate of Hans van Ripper, and it was altogether such an apparition as is seldom to be met with in broad daylight.

LESSON LXXVI.

CHARLES DICKENS'S RAVEN.

Charles Dickens was fond of keeping ravens in his youth, and some of his experiences are related in the preface to "Barnaby Rudge." His first pet slept in a stable, generally on horseback. He terrified a Newfoundland dog by his tricks, and often walked off unmolested with the dog's dinner. He was increasing in intelligence when, in an evil hour, his stable was newly painted. He observed the workmen closely, saw that they were careful of their pigments, and immediately decided to outwit them. While they were at dinner one day, he began to eat the white lead they had left behind. Alas! this youthful folly resulted in death.

Who was Charles Dickens? Have you ever read "Barnaby Rudge"? Which of Dickens's pets is described in the preface? Where did the raven sleep? How did he frighten the dog? What do you understand by "increasing in intelligence"? How did the raven lose his life? Is white lead poisonous?

1. *Tell in your own words the story of Charles Dickens's pet raven.*

2. *Write a similar story, telling of the experiences of one of your own pets.*

Construct your sentences so that there can be no doubt as to the antecedent of each pronoun.

Be careful to set qualifying phrases or clauses as near as possible to the words they modify.

LESSON LXXVII.

INTERROGATIVE PRONOUNS.

1. Who gave me this book?   Henry.
2. Which of the boys gave me this book?   Henry.
3. Here are two books.   Which will you take?
4. What is in the box?   Wood.

What is the answer to the first question?   Which word in the question represents Henry?   It is therefore what part of speech? Which word in the second question represents Henry?

What does the pronoun *which* in the third sentence represent?

What does the pronoun *what* represent in the fourth question?

The pronouns *who, which,* and *what,* when used to ask questions, are called INTERROGATIVE PRONOUNS.

The interrogative pronouns (*who, which,* and *what*) are not changed in form to indicate person, gender, and number.

Who is used in asking questions referring to persons (first question).

Which is used in asking questions referring to persons (second question) or things (third question).

What is used in asking questions referring to things (fourth question).

The interrogative *who* shows by its form what case it is in; thus, —

> *Nom.*   Who saw the book?
> *Poss.*   Whose book is it?
> *Obj.*   By whom was the book seen?

Which and *what* are never in the possessive case, and they have the same forms both in the nominative and in the objective.

Point out the interrogative pronouns in the following sentences, tell the case of each, and give the reason: —

1. Which is the lovelier, — the lily, or the rose?
2. Who knows the errors of his thoughts?
3. Who shall nerve heroic boys
    To hazard all in freedom's fight? — EMERSON.
4. And what is so rare as a day in June? — LOWELL.
5. Which is the wind that brings the rain? — STEDMAN.
6. What flower is this that greets the morn,
    Its hues from heaven so freshly born? — HOLMES.
7. Who shall rise and cast away,
    First, the burden of the day?
    Who assert his place, and teach
    Lighter labor, nobler speech,
    Standing firm, erect, and strong,
    Proud as freedom, free as song? — BAYARD TAYLOR.

LESSON LXXVIII.

RELATIVE PRONOUNS.

1. I met a man who helped me.
2. The dog which was shot had bitten the boy.
3. I gave the picture to a boy that I liked.
4. We return to the books that we enjoy.
5. The boy read what he had written.

What man did I meet? By what words is the noun *man* modified?

What dog had bitten the boy? By what words is the noun *dog* modified?

Expressions like the following are called clauses : —

> *who helped me* (1st sentence)
> *which was shot* (2d sentence)
> *that I liked* (3d sentence)
> *that we enjoy* (4th sentence)
> *what he had written* (5th sentence).

If we rewrite the first sentence thus, *I met a man, and he helped me,* we see that the pronoun *he* stands for the noun *man :* so also the word *who* in the first sentence stands for *man,* or for *and he.*

In like manner we may rewrite the second sentence thus, *The dog had bitten the boy, and it was shot.* Here the pronoun *it* stands for *dog,* and it is clear that *which* stands for *dog,* or for *and it.*

The words *who, which, that,* and *what,* are pronouns because they represent nouns. They are called *relative* pronouns because they relate to a preceding noun or pronoun.

Who is used to relate to persons, and *which* to relate to animals and things, when an additional fact is stated and when they have the sense of *and he, and she, and it, and they, for he,* etc.

That relates to persons or things, and is to be preferred : —

1. When the clause which it introduces simply limits or defines the antecedent, as in the third and fourth sentences.

2. When the antecedent includes both persons and things; as, *The boys and the dogs that surrounded us made a great noise.*

3. After the superlative degree; as, *It was the biggest trout that we caught.*

4. Generally, after *all, any, each, every, no, same,* or *very;* as, *All that I had I gave him.*

5. Where the propriety of *who* or *which* is doubtful.

What represents things only, and has no antecedent expressed. It has a double relation in the sentence, — as the object of a verb or preposition, and as the subject or object of the verb in the clause it introduces.

A relative pronoun, because it connects the clause it introduces to the principal clause, is properly a CONJUNCTIVE PRONOUN.

DECLENSION OF RELATIVES.

Nom.	who	which
Poss.	whose	whose
Obj.	whom	which

That and *what* are not modified to indicate case.

Mention the relative pronouns in the following sentences, state the antecedent of each, read the clause that it introduces, and tell what case the relative is in and why: —

1. The willow which bends to the tempest often escapes better than the oak which resists it. — SCOTT.

2. They never fail, who die
   In a great cause ! — BYRON.

3. Nature never did betray the heart that loved her.
   WORDSWORTH.

4. A gentle stream, whose murm'ring wave did play.
   SPENSER.

5. Give plenty of what is given to you.— PHŒBE CARY.

6. He who would search for pearls must dive below.
   DRYDEN.

7. The wand'ring streams that shine between the hills,
   The grots that echo to the tinkling rills. — POPE.

8. We should rejoice if those who rule our land
Be men who hold its many blessings dear.

COLERIDGE.

9. To every man give that which most he needs;
Do that which he can never do for you. — SCHEFER.

10. O holy Night! from thee I learn to bear
What man has borne before. — LONGFELLOW.

11. He that lacks time to mourn lacks time to mend.

HENRY TAYLOR.

12. There is a tide in the affairs of men,
Which, taken at its flood, leads on to fortune.

SHAKESPEARE.

13. Thoreau, who has a strange faculty of finding what
the Indians have left behind them, first set me on the
search; and I afterwards enriched myself with some very
perfect specimens, so rudely wrought that it seemed
almost as if chance had fashioned them. — HAWTHORNE.

14. Who would not be tempted to frequent irritation
if he could enjoy that gift for which the poet so foolishly
prayed, the gift of seeing himself as others saw him, and
recognize his infinitesimal importance in the eyes of his
fellows? — A. P. RUSSELL.

15. 　　　I hear a voice you cannot hear,
　　　　　Which says I must not stay;
　　　I see a hand you cannot see,
　　　　　Which beckons me away. — TICKELL.

16. The flowers our mothers and sisters used to love
and cherish, those which grew beneath our eaves and by
our doorstep, are the ones we always love best. — HOLMES.

LESSON LXXIX.

PUNCTUATION. — THE RELATIVE CLAUSE.

A relative clause which simply explains its antecedent is separated from the rest of the sentence by a comma, or commas; thus, —

His plan, which was original, was full of genius.

Cherish true patriotism, which has its root in benevolence.

If the relative clause restricts the meaning of the antecedent, no comma is used; thus, —

It was only a few discerning friends who perceived the dawn of his future eminence.

No faculty lives within us which the soul can spare.

Justify the use or omission of the comma in the following sentences. Write the sentences from dictation.

1. Books, which are the repositories of knowledge, are an indispensable part of the furniture of a house.

2. Storms do not rend the sail that is furled.

3. He who reads in a proper spirit can scarcely read too much.

4. We must be courteous to a man as to a picture, which we are willing to give the advantage of a good light.

EMERSON.

5. I count him a great man who inhabits a higher sphere of thought, into which other men rise with difficulty and labor. — EMERSON.

6. He that is good at making excuses is seldom good for anything else. — FRANKLIN.

7. The subtle spider that from overhead,
  Hung like a spy on human guilt and error,
 Suddenly turned, and up its slender thread
  Ran with a nimble terror. — HOOD.

8. They are never alone that are accompanied with noble thoughts.

9. He was a man whom nothing could turn aside from the path which duty pointed out.

LESSON LXXX.

THE RIGHT WORD IN THE RIGHT PLACE.

Study carefully the use of the following words, and construct sentences of your own to show that you understand the meaning of each word: —

EAGER.	A shrewd trader is eager for profit.
EARNEST.	A lawyer is earnest in his pleading.
PERMANENT. DURABLE.	Durable materials should be united with graceful architecture in that which is designed to be permanent.
ECONOMICAL. FRUGAL. PARSIMONIOUS.	We must not conclude that, because one is frugal and economical, one must be also parsimonious and niggardly.
HAUGHTY. ARROGANT.	Arrogant manners often accompany a haughty carriage.
DILIGENT. INDUSTRIOUS.	They were industrious in their pursuits, and diligent in their researches.
SORROW. GRIEF.	You feel sorrow while your friend is ill, grief when he dies.

LESSON LXXXI.

ADJECTIVE PRONOUNS.

1. We looked at many houses, but few houses seemed suitable.

2. We looked at many houses, but few seemed suitable.

3. We called both boys, but neither boy came.

4. We called both boys, but neither came.

What noun is used twice in the first sentence? How many times does the same noun occur in the second sentence? What part of speech is *few* in the first sentence? How is it used in the second sentence? Of what noun does it take the place?

What part of speech are *both* and *neither* in the third sentence?

In place of what word is *neither* used in the fourth?

Adjectives like *many, few, both,* and *neither,* when they take the place of the nouns which they qualify, or are used instead of them, are called ADJECTIVE PRONOUNS.

The principal adjective pronouns are *all, any, another, both, each, either, enough, few, former, latter, last, little, many, much, neither, none, one, other, some, same, such, this, that, these, those.*

When they accompany the noun, they are parsed as adjectives ; when they represent the noun, they are parsed as pronouns.

Mention the adjective pronouns in the following sentences, and state the noun which each represents : —

1. That which made these men, and men like these, cannot die.

2. Known to me well are the faces of all.

3. For many are called, but few are chosen.

4. There is a calm for those who weep.

5. He that plants trees loves others besides himself.

6. The mountain and the squirrel
   Had a quarrel,
   And the former called the latter, " Little Prig."

7.   Have love, not love alone for one;
           But man as man thy brother call;
        And scatter, like the circling sun,
           Thy charities on all. — SCHILLER.

LESSON LXXXII.

COMPOSITION.

HOW SEEDS GROW INTO PLANTS.

Plant a handful of beans in moist earth. Keep them in a very warm place, and examine one every day.

Study carefully the following hints, and make a record of what you observe.

First Day. After soaking the beans in water for a few hours, break one open and notice its parts. The thick seed leaves are called *cotyledons*. These are inclosed in a covering or coat. At the upper end they are connected with a stemlet called the *radicle*. Above this you will see a tiny bud or plumule.

Second Day. Dig up one of the sprouting seeds. Take a needle and carefully separate the parts. You will probably find the upper end of the radicle bent over, and you will notice the wrinkled leaves of the plumule.

Third Day. Dig up another bean. Split it open, and see if the stem or radicle is growing. How do the tiny leaves of the plumule look?

Fourth Day. Dig up a fourth bean, and see how the plantlet is getting ready for life in two worlds, — the atmosphere above and the soil beneath. Measure the young leaflets and the tiny roots.

Fifth Day. Probably your beans are now above the ground. The skin has become a small dry husk, and the two thick seed leaves are turning green.

Sixth Day. The tiny wrinkled leaves- have grown greener and larger. They are heart-shaped; and between their stems is a little bud that will soon shoot up, and put out other leaves.

Seventh Day. For a week, the plant has been living on the food stored up in the thick seed leaves. Now it has long fibrous roots and green leaves ; henceforth it can get its food from the soil and the air.

LESSON LXXXIII.

HOW TO PARSE PRONOUNS.

To parse a pronoun, state : —

1. *Class* — personal, interrogative, relative (conjunctive), or adjective, and why.
2. *Gender* — masculine, feminine, or neuter, and why.
3. *Person* — first, second, or third, and why.
4. *Number* — singular or plural, and why.
5. *Case* — nominative, possessive, or objective, and why.

MODEL FOR ORAL EXERCISE.

Who is this youth? Surely he has never gone down into the depths! I know all the aspects of those who have passed through the dark valley. By what right is he among us? — HAWTHORNE.

WHO is an interrogative pronoun because it is used in asking a question; it is of the masculine gender and singular number because its antecedent, *youth*, is masculine and singular; it is in the nominative case because it is the attributive complement of the verb *is*.

HE is a personal pronoun because it shows by its form that it is of the masculine gender, third person, singular number, and nominative case. It is the subject of the verb *has gone*.

I is a personal pronoun because it shows by its form that it is of the first person, singular number, nominative case. It is here of the masculine gender because the speaker is a male, and it is the subject of the verb *know*.

THOSE is an adjective pronoun because it stands for the noun *persons*, which it would limit if expressed; it is here of the masculine gender because it denotes persons of the male sex; it is of the third person because it denotes those spoken of; it is of the plural number because it denotes more than one; it is in the objective case because it is the object of the preposition *of*.

WHO is a relative pronoun because it introduces the clause *who have passed through the dark valley;* it is of the masculine gender, third person, plural number, because its antecedent, *those*, is of the masculine gender, third person, plural number; it is in the nominative case because it is the subject of the verb *have passed*.

HE is a personal pronoun because it shows by its form that it is of the masculine gender, third person, singular number. It is in the nominative case because it is the subject of the verb *is*.

Us is a personal pronoun because it shows by its form that it is of the first person, plural number, objective case.   It is the object of the preposition *among*.

A shorter method of oral parsing is suggested in lesson on parsing nouns.

The form given in Lesson LXV. for a written parsing exercise will be available here, except that one more column will be needed for person.

Parse the pronouns in the following sentences : —

1. He met with a great many strange adventures, which would be well worth your hearing if I had leisure to narrate them as minutely as they deserve.

2. O sweet is the new violet, that comes beneath the
        skies,
    And sweeter is the young lamb's voice to me that
        cannot rise,
    And sweet is all the land about, and all the flowers
        that blow,
    And sweeter far is death than life to me that long
        to go. — TENNYSON.

3. Continue thou in the things which thou hast learned and hast been assured of, knowing of whom thou hast learned them. — BIBLE.

4.   And but for those vile guns,
    He would himself have been a soldier.

SHAKESPEARE.

5. How happy is he born or taught,
    That serveth not another's will ;
    Whose armor is his honest thought,
    And simple truth his utmost skill. — WOTTON.

6. Our acts our angels are, or good or ill,
   Our fatal shadows that walk by us still.— FLETCHER.

7. And then the brook noted that none of these lived
to themselves alone. The tree gave its fruit to the birds,
and afforded quiet, shaded resting places for their nests.
The birds brooded and fed their little ones. The rabbits
and squirrels were busy carrying home food to their families. The elder, which bloomed beside her, gave its blossoms to make tea for a sick child, as she learned from the
talk of two little girls who came for them. She was rest-
less, they said, and it would soothe her to sleep. All were
busy, all contented. — CHILDREN'S HOUR.

LESSON LXXXIV.

KINDS OF SENTENCES.

1. Harold bought an interesting book.
2. Harold bought a book that interested him.
3. Harold bought a book, and his mother read
it to him.

By what is the noun *book* modified in the first sentence?
In the second? How do the sentences differ in form?
Point out the principal clause of the second sentence.
Point out the modifying clause.

How many clauses make up the third? Is one a
principal and the other a modifying clause, or are they of
equal importance? By what are they connected?

A sentence like the first, which consists of a single
statement, is called a SIMPLE SENTENCE.

A sentence like the second, which contains a clause that modifies some other word in the sentence, is called a COMPLEX SENTENCE.

A sentence like the third, which consists of two or more clauses of equal importance connected by a conjunction, is called a COMPOUND SENTENCE.

State if each of the following sentences is simple, complex, or compound. In the case of complex and compound sentences point out the clauses.

1. Men have done brave deeds,
   And bards have sung them well.

2. How can we expect a harvest of thought who have not had a seedtime of character?— THOREAU.

3. The toll gatherer lived with his family in a house on the bridge.

4. The streams were full of trout then, and the moose and the elk left their broad tracks on the sands of the river. — WARNER.

5. Only he can be trusted with gifts who can present a face of bronze to expectations. — THOREAU.

LESSON LXXXV.

COMPOSITION.

PLANT GROWTH.

Plant in warm, moist earth six seeds each, of the pea, the corn, the squash, the morning-glory. Examine one every day, and study carefully the various changes. Write down exactly what you see as you watch the growth of your seedlings.

From the record of your observations give an account of how seeds grow into plants. *Describe:* —

1. The swelling of the seed.
2. The bursting of the outer covering.
3. The form and color of the first leaves.
4. The growth of the stem, of the root.
5. The appearance of the second leaves.
6. The young plant.

Remember that ideas only slightly connected in sense should not be crowded into one sentence.

LESSON LXXXVI.

PUNCTUATION. — THE COMMA.

A comma is placed after each phrase or clause in a series of phrases or clauses alike in grammatical construction; thus, —

This lovely land, this glorious liberty, these benign institutions, are ours to enjoy, ours to preserve.

The same vigor of thought, the same form of expression, the short sentences, have been developed.

A parenthetical word, phrase, or clause is separated from the rest of the sentence by commas; thus, —

True eloquence, indeed, does not consist in mere speech.
Speak for, not against, the principles of love and peace.
There were, surely, always pretenders in science.

Words, phrases, and clauses used out of the natural order are usually separated from the rest of the sentence by commas; thus, —

In believing attainment possible, you will make it so.
On these plains, thousands of cattle range.

Explain the use of the comma in the following sentences. Write the sentences from dictation.

1. A form more fair, a face more sweet,
   Ne'er hath it been my lot to meet.

2. On that plain, in rosy youth, they had fed their father's flocks.

3. There, where a few torn shrubs the place disclose,
   The village preacher's modest mansion rose.

4. Of all the solitary insects I have ever remarked, the spider is the most sagacious.

5. Next to Washington, Greene was the ablest commander in the Revolutionary army. — J. T. HEADLEY.

6. Concentration is the secret of strength in politics, in war, in trade. — EMERSON.

7. Dead silence succeeded the bellow of the thunder, the roar of the wind, the rush of the waters, the moaning of the beasts, the screaming of the birds.

8. When there was any extraordinary power of performance, when great national movements began, when heroes existed, the human soul was in earnest. — EMERSON.

9. Natural history may, I am convinced, take a profound hold upon practical life by its influence over our finer feelings. — HUXLEY.

10. The great make us feel, first of all, the indifference of circumstances. — EMERSON.

11. Modern times, with all their boasted progress, have never produced as strong a man as Samson, as meek a man as Moses, as wise a man as Solomon.

12. Beyond all wealth, honor, or even health, is the attachment we form to noble souls. — DR. ARNOLD.

LESSON LXXXVII.

REVIEW.— NOUNS AND PRONOUNS.

1. Express in your own words the chief distinctions between common and proper nouns. Apply your explanation to the nouns *city* and *Rome.*

2. From the selection "The Blue Jays," Lesson LXXII., select examples of collective, abstract, and verbal nouns.

3. The plural of nouns is usually formed by adding *s* or *es* to the singular. Explain the following plurals : *loaves, mice, cities, teeth, knives.*

4. Write the plural of *box, pencil, piano, gulf, ox, poppy, journey.*

5. State the gender of the following nouns : *countess, tiger, tree, founder, island.*

6. Explain the term *objective case.* Distinguish between predicate nominative and objective complement.

7. Mention the different classes of pronouns, and illustrate each.

8. What is the difference in use between *my* and *mine ?* Give illustrations.

9. Are the possessive forms of pronouns spelled with an apostrophe ? Illustrate.

10. What is the peculiar use of absolute possessive pronouns ? Illustrate.

11. Mention the compound personal pronouns, and tell how each is formed.

12. Write sentences containing *who* as a relative, *who* as an interrogative, *which* as a relative, *which* as an interrogative.

LESSON LXXXVIII.

KINDS OF ADJECTIVES.

There was *an English* poet who speaks of *the dim, religious* light transmitted through *painted* glass. I have always admired *this* richly *descriptive* phrase. — HAWTHORNE.

What word does each adjective in the above sentence modify?

Adjectives like *English, dim, religious, painted,* and *descriptive,* that qualify or describe a noun or pronoun, are called QUALIFYING or DESCRIPTIVE ADJECTIVES.

Adjectives like *an, the,* and *this,* that limit the meaning of a noun or pronoun, are called LIMITING ADJECTIVES.

Descriptive adjectives are sometimes derived from other parts of speech; as, proper adjectives from proper nouns, *French* from *France, American* from *America,* etc.

Participles are sometimes used as adjectives; as, —

The *frightened* deer fled from the *pursuing* hunter.

Such words may be called DESCRIPTIVE ADJECTIVES or PARTICIPIAL ADJECTIVES.

Two words are sometimes joined together by a hyphen to form one descriptive adjective; as, —

The *star-spangled* banner in triumph shall wave
O'er the land of the free and the home of the brave.

I fetched my *sea-born* treasures home.

Such adjectives are sometimes called COMPOUND ADJECTIVES.

Limiting adjectives are divided into four classes : —

1. Articles: a and an, *indefinite;* the, *definite.*

2. Numeral adjectives: (*a*) Those indicating definite number; as, *four* girls, *both* men, the *third* chair, etc. This class is sometimes subdivided into *Cardinal*, as *one, two, three, four*, etc., and *Ordinal*, as *first, second, third, fourth*, etc. (*b*) Those indicating number, but indefinite, as *any* man, a *few* friends, *all* boys, *no* child, *many* flowers, etc.

3. Distributive adjectives: *each* hand, *every* paper, *either* river, *neither* book, etc.

4. Demonstrative adjectives: *this* pen, *that* desk, *these* readers, *those* spellers.

Limiting adjectives (except articles) may be used instead of the nouns which they limit. They are then called ADJECTIVE PRONOUNS.

Mention the adjectives in the following sentences. State to what class each belongs, and what word it modifies.

1. A quiet, quaint, and ancient town
    Among the green Alsatian hills.

2. How inspiring are the odors that breathe from the upland turf, from the rock-hung flower, from the hoary and solemn pine!

3. And there, too, was the bluster of the wind, and the chill and watery clouds, and the blazing sun, all taking their turns to make Hercules uncomfortable.

4.   Naught he heard
    But the strange twittering of a strange green bird
    Within an Indian ship. — WILLIAM MORRIS.

5. He saw at a distance the lordly Hudson, far, far below him, moving on its silent but majestic course, with the reflection of a purple cloud, or the sail of a lagging bark, here and there sleeping on its glassy bosom, and at last losing itself in the blue highlands. — IRVING.

6. A little child,
   A little meek-faced, quiet, village child,
   Sat singing at her cottage door at eve
   A low, sweet sabbath song. — THOMAS WESTWOOD.

7. I love to hear thine earnest voice,
   Wherever thou art hid,
   Thou testy little dogmatist,
   Thou pretty Katydid! — HOLMES.

8. I see the convent's gleaming wall
    Rise from its grove of pine,
   And towers of old cathedrals tall,
    And castles by the Rhine. — LONGFELLOW.

9. A shining Hour, with golden plumes, was laden
    with a deed
   Of generous sacrifice a child had done for one in
    need. — MRS. GORDON.

10. The riches of the Commonwealth
    Are free, strong minds and hearts of health ;
    And more to her than gold or grain,
    The cunning hand and cultured brain. — WHITTIER.

LESSON LXXXIX.

THE RIGHT WORD IN THE RIGHT PLACE.

1. Mark Twain told a funny story.
2. My umbrella has a queer handle.
3. Puss is an odd name for a boat.

Which adjective means amusing? Which means unusual?
Which means to differ in some odd way from the ordinary?
Which is derived from a word meaning twisted?

Separate the following words into groups, according to their meaning : —

queer	good	lovely
odd	elegant	pretty
funny	majestic	splendid
bright	exquisite	delicious
awful	grand	delightful
severe	handsome	pleasant
horrid	beautiful	real
superb	excellent	magnificent

Which of these words are properly applied to large objects?

Which of these words do you apply to things pleasing to the senses?   Which refer to unpleasant objects?

Which of these words are properly applied to flowers?   To fruit?   To articles of dress?   To buildings?   To mountains?   To pictures?   To music?

Which express fear?   Love?   Reverence?   Which describe habits?   Character?

Illustrate by original sentences the exact use of real, awful, splendid, lovely, delicious, horrid, funny, queer, odd.

Complete the following sentences by inserting for the blanks appropriate words : —

1. He heard the —— thunder of battle.
2. The camel is an —— looking animal.
3. Yesterday was a —— day.
4. She has a —— headache.
5. The oriental nations have —— customs.
6. He told a —— story.
7. This chocolate is ——.
8. The book has a —— cover.

9. They have moved into a —— house.

10. Aunt Harriet brought home from Europe a —— lace collar.

11. Marjorie is a —— child.

12. Her mother is a very —— woman.

13. She is a very —— companion.

14. The scenery of the Yosemite Valley is ——.

15. The Alps are ——.

16. The pine is a —— tree.

17. We saw many —— cathedrals.

18. The sunset was ——.

19. The cook makes —— bread.

20. The music of the opera was ——.

21. Tiffany's exhibit at the Chicago Fair was ——.

22. The display of silver was very ——.

23. Jackanapes is an —— title for a book.

24. We met a —— tramp.

25. Try to keep your writing desk in —— order.

LESSON XC.

STUDY OF A POEM.

LITTLE BY LITTLE.

"Little by little," an acorn said,
As it slowly sank in its mossy bed,
"I am improving every day,
Hidden deep in the earth away."
Little by little each day it grew;
Little by little it sipped the dew;
Downward it sent out a thread-like root;
Up in the air spread a tiny shoot.

Day after day, and year after year,
Little by little the leaves appear;
And the slender branches spread far and wide,
Till the mighty oak is the forest's pride.

Far down in the depths of the dark-blue sea
An insect train works ceaselessly:
Day by day they are building well,
Each one alone in his little cell.
Moment by moment, and day by day,
Never stopping to rest or to play.
Rock upon rock they are rearing high,
Till the top looks out on the sunny sky,
And the summer sunbeams gayly smile
On the buds and flowers of a coral isle.

"Little by little," said a thoughtful boy,
"Moment by moment, I'll well employ,
Learning a little every day,
And not misspending my time in play;
And still this rule in my mind shall dwell:
'Whatever I do, I will do it well.'
Little by little, I'll learn to know
The treasured wisdom of long ago;
And one of these days, perhaps, will see
That the world will be the better for me."

Where did the acorn sleep? What did it sip? What did it
send down into the earth? What sprung up into the air? What
appeared day after day? What spread far and wide? How are
coral islands built? What lessons did the boy learn from the
acorn and the coral polyp? What rule did he adopt? How
may we learn wisdom? Will a good and studious boy grow into

a worthy and wise man?　Will the world be better because he lived?

Write a composition on " The Acorn and the Boy."

1.　Tell how the acorn grew into an oak tree.　Describe the bursting of the shell, the growth of the root and stem, the appearance of the leaves, the development of the branches.

2.　Tell how a boy may grow into a useful man.　Describe his progress in school, the habits he forms, the work he is planning to do, his influence on those around him.

LESSON XCI.

COMPARISON OF ADJECTIVES.

1.　William caught a large bass, James a larger one, but Harry's was the largest.

2.　We thought the road through the woods short, we found the path across the field shorter, but the walk along the beach was the shortest.

What is added to the adjective *large,* in the first sentence, to enable us to express our comparison of James's fish and William's?　Of Harry's and James's and William's?

What is added to the adjective *short* to enable us to express the comparison of the field path with the wood road?　Of the beach walk with both the other ways?

The annexing of *er* and *est* to adjectives to indicate different degrees of quality or quantity is called COMPARISON OF ADJECTIVES.

Adjectives like *large* and *short,* which simply express the quality or quantity of an object without reference to any other, are said to be of the POSITIVE DEGREE.

Adjectives like *larger* and *shorter*, which denote that the object possesses the property in a greater or less degree compared with one or more, are said to be in the COMPARATIVE DEGREE.

Adjectives like *largest* and *shortest*, which denote that the object possesses the property in the highest or lowest degree of all that are considered, are said to be in the SUPERLATIVE DEGREE.

Most adjectives of one syllable (and some of more than one) form the comparative by adding *er*, and the superlative by adding *est*, to the positive.

Write sentences, using the following adjectives in the comparative or the superlative degree. Form the comparative or superlative by annexing er *or* est.

CAUTION. — In annexing *er* or *est* to the positive degree of an adjective, observe the rules for spelling that relate to final letters ; thus, *large, larger; happy, happiest.*

kind	high	bright
fair	narrow	strong
happy	long	gentle
brave	pure	strange
noble	slight	cold

Adjectives, particularly most of those of more than one syllable, are also compared by means of the adverbs *more* and *most*, and *less* and *least;* thus, —

Positive,	An ambitious man.
Comparative,	A more ambitious man.
Superlative,	The most ambitious man.

Positive,	An expensive trip.
Comparative,	A less expensive trip.
Superlative,	The least expensive trip.

Select eight of the following adjectives, form the comparative of each by the use of more *or* less, *and use it in a sentence. Form the superlative of each of the remaining seven by the use of* most *or* least, *and use each in a sentence.*

patient	peaceful	fragrant
curious	blithesome	gracious
beautiful	gorgeous	graceful
fantastic	drowsy	pleasant
steadfast	solemn	stately

Commit to memory the comparatives and superlatives of the following adjectives, which are said to be compared irregularly, and be prepared to write them : —

POSITIVE.	COMPARATIVE.	SUPERLATIVE.
good	better	best
bad	worse	worst
ill		
much	more	most
many		
little	less	least
fore	former	foremost
		first
hind	hinder	hindermost
far	farther	farthest
near	nearer	nearest
		next
late	later	latest
	latter	last
old	older	oldest
	elder	eldest

Point out the adjectives in the following sentences. Give the degree of comparison. Tell what each modifies.

1. Youngest of all was he of the men who came in the Mayflower.

2. Our debts and our sins are always greater than we think for. — FRANKLIN.

3. Next to the lightest heart, the heaviest is apt to be most playful. — HAWTHORNE.

4. A blue smoke went curling up from the chimney, and was almost the pleasantest part of the spectacle to Ulysses. — TANGLEWOOD TALES.

5. He that is greatest among you, let him be servant unto the least. — BIBLE.

6. They are poor
   That have lost nothing : they are poorer far
   Who, losing, have forgotten : they most poor
   Of all, who lose, and wish they might forget.

7. Though home is a name, a word, it is a strong one: a stronger than magician ever spoke, or spirit answered to, in strongest conjuration. — DICKENS.

8. But our love was stronger by far than the love
   Of those who were older than we,
   Of many far wiser than we. — POE.

9.   Our sincerest laughter
         With some pain is fraught ;
   Our sweetest songs are those that tell of saddest thought. — SHELLEY.

10. There purer streams through happier valleys flow,
    And sweeter flowers on holier mountains blow.
                              PIERPONT.

LESSON XCII.

COMPOSITION. — COMPARISON.

EXERCISES IN THE USE OF ADJECTIVES.

I. *Write sentences about the following objects. In what respects are they alike? How do they differ? Which do you like best? Why?*

A leaf and a flower.	A watch and a clock.
A sled and a boat.	A pencil and a pen.

2. *Study the following substances, and write sentences describing their qualities and important uses.*

Gold and iron.	Cotton and wool.
Wheat and coffee.	Leather and rubber.

3. *Study the following animals, and compare them with respect to their size, habits, and value to mankind.*

The horse and the camel.	The dog and the fox.
The bee and the butterfly.	The parrot and the canary.

LESSON XCIII.

STUDY OF A DESCRIPTION.

THE VAN TASSEL HOUSE.

It was one of those spacious farmhouses, with high-ridged but lowly-sloping roofs, built in the style handed down from the first Dutch settlers; the low projecting eaves forming a piazza along the front capable of being closed up in bad weather. Under this were hung flails, harness, various utensils of husbandry, and nets for fishing in the neighboring river. Benches were built along the sides for summer use; and a great spinning wheel at one end and a churn at the other, showed the various uses to which this important porch might be devoted.

From this piazza the wandering Ichabod entered the hall, which formed the center of the mansion and the place of usual residence. Here, rows of resplendent pewter, ranged on a long dresser, dazzled his eyes. In one corner stood a huge bag of wool ready to be spun; in another, a quantity of linsey-woolsey just from the loom. Ears of Indian corn, and strings of dried apples and peaches, hung in gay festoons along the wall, mingled with the gaud of red peppers; and a door left ajar gave him a peep into the best parlor, where the claw-footed chairs and dark mahogany tables shone like mirrors. Andirons, with their accompanying shovel and tongs, glistened from their covert of asparagus tops; mock oranges and conch shells decorated the mantelpiece; strings of various-colored birds' eggs were suspended above it; a great ostrich egg was hung from the center of the room; and a corner cupboard, knowingly left open, displayed immense treasures of old silver and well-mended china. — IRVING.

After studying carefully the foregoing description, write out from memory : —

1. What Ichabod saw as he approached the Van Tassel house.

2. What he noticed after entering the house.

Avoid closing sentences and clauses with short and unimportant words.

LESSON XCIV.

ADJECTIVE PHRASES.

1. The trees *along the road* have been trimmed.
2. We reached the fence *across the pasture.*
3. A field *of clover* attracted a swarm *of bees.*

What trees have been trimmed? By what phrase is the noun *trees* limited? By what is the noun *fence* limited? What kind of field is mentioned? What words qualify the noun *field?* What kind of swarm is mentioned? What words qualify the noun *swarm?*

Expressions like *along the road, across the pasture, of clover, of bees,* are called PHRASES. Because such phrases are introduced by prepositions, they are called PREPOSITIONAL PHRASES.

When they perform, as in the sentences above, the office of an adjective, and qualify or limit a noun, they are called ADJECTIVE PHRASES.

Point out the prepositional adjective phrases in the following sentences, and mention the nouns which they limit: —

1. The apples are ripe in the orchard,
     The work of the reaper is done,
   And the golden woodlands redden
     In the light of the dying sun. — WINTER.

2. Ideas are the great warriors of the world. — GARFIELD.

3. April cold with dropping rain
   Willows and lilacs brings again,
   The whistle of returning birds,
   And trumpet lowing of the herds. — EMERSON.

4. Order is the sanity of the mind, the health of the body, the peace of the city, the security of the state.

SOUTHEY.

5. A man's own good breeding is the best security against other people's ill manners. — LORD CHESTERFIELD.

6. Mirth and cheerfulness are but the reward of innocence of life.

7. Dreams are the bright creatures of poem and legend, who sport on earth in the night season, and melt away in the first beam of the sun. — DICKENS.

8. And cradled there in the scented hay,
   In the air made sweet by the breath of kine,
   The little child in the manger lay,
   The child that would be king one day
   Of a kingdom not human but divine.

LONGFELLOW.

An adjective phrase may be sometimes substituted for an adjective ; thus, —

1. Country roads are often muddy.
   Roads in the country are often muddy.
2. I noticed an interesting item.
   I noticed an item of interest.
3. The prize was a scientific book.
   The prize was a book on science.

Rewrite the following sentences, changing each adjective into an equivalent adjective phrase : —

1. It was a summer evening.
2. Their knell was rung by fairy hands.
3. He climbed the tower by the wooden stairs.

4. The boy seemed almost lifeless.
5. The world still wants light-hearted men.
6. Speechless they gazed upon the sky.
7. The northern hurricane swept across the prairie.
8. Build up heroic lives.
9. The oak trees bent before the fury of the wind.
10. Heavenly blessings fall upon thy head.

LESSON XCV.

HOW TO PARSE ADJECTIVES.

To parse an adjective, state : —

1. *Class* — descriptive (proper or participial), or limiting (article, numeral, distributive, or demonstrative).
2. *Degree of Comparison* — positive, comparative, or superlative.
3. *Use* — the noun which it modifies, or the verb which it completes and the noun or pronoun to which it relates.

MODEL FOR EXERCISE.

I learned this night how fragrant the English elder is while in bloom. — BURROUGHS.

THIS is a demonstrative adjective, and limits the noun *night.*

FRAGRANT is a descriptive adjective, positive degree, completes. the verb *is,* and relates to the noun *elder.*

THE is a definite article, and limits the noun *elder.*

ENGLISH is a proper adjective, and qualifies the noun *elder.*

Parse the adjectives found in the exercises arranged for Lessons LXXXVI., XCIV.

LESSON XCVI.

DIARIES AND JOURNALS.

To keep a diary, make notes of what happens during each day, putting down every trifling event in the order of its occurrence.

To keep a journal, select the incidents that seem to you worth remembering, and add to the account your own thoughts and feelings.

MODEL FROM JOHN GREENLEAF WHITTIER.

Margaret Smith's Journal.

MAY 14, 1678.

I was awakened this morning by the pleasant voice of my cousin. She had thrown open the window looking toward the sunrising, and the air came in soft and warm, and laden with the sweets of flowers and green-growing things.

When we went below, we found on the window a great bunch of flowers of many kinds, very fresh, and glistening with the dew.

APRIL 24, 1679.

A vessel from London has just come to port, bringing Rebecca's dresses for the wedding, which will take place about the middle of June. Uncle Rawson has brought me a long letter from Aunt Grindall, with one also from Oliver, pleasant and lively, like himself. No special news from abroad that I hear of. My heart longs for Old England more and more.

It is supposed that the freeholders have chosen Mr.

Broadstreet for their governor. The vote, uncle says, is exceedingly small, very few people troubling themselves about it.

Keep a diary for a week, telling exactly what happened Sunday, Monday, Tuesday, Wednesday, Thursday, Friday, Saturday.

Select the more important incidents, and write three pages of a journal.

LESSON XCVII.

CHOICE OF WORDS.

Study the words in each of the following pairs till you think that you understand their meaning. Then use each of the words so as to show that you can discriminate between them.

SPECIMEN. SAMPLE.	A cabinet of minerals contains specimens : a sample of any one of them is evidence of the quality of the whole.
NECESSITY. NEED.	There is no necessity for deception. I have no need to beg.
BALANCE. REMAINDER.	A balance was struck, and the remainder of the estate divided.
OCCASION. OPPORTUNITY.	Her beauty was the occasion of the war. Seize the opportunity that offers.
THIEF. ROBBER.	He came like a thief in the night. An organized band of robbers infested the place.

LESSON XCVIII.

KINDS OF ADVERBS.

An adverb is a word used to modify the meaning of a verb, an adjective, or another adverb (Lesson XLIII.).

Adverbs are divided, according to their use in the sentence, into four classes, — *simple, interrogative, conjunctive,* and *modal.*

A simple adverb is one used to modify directly the meaning of a verb, an adjective, or an adverb. A simple adverb may express time, place, degree, or manner.

I will go now.   The work is very useful.
I am here.   We marched rather slowly.

An interrogative adverb is one used to ask a question with reference to time, place, or manner.

When shall we three meet again ?
Why do you not attend school more regularly ?
How did you work the last example ?

Point out the adverbs that are used in the above sentences to ask questions.

A conjunctive adverb is one used to introduce an adverbial clause, and connect it to the word which it modifies.

The old moon laughed and sung a song
As they rocked in the wooden shoe.

What words in the principal clause does the clause, *as they rocked in the wooden shoe,* modify? What kind of word is *as ?* What kind of sentence do the two lines make ?

10

By what clause are the verbs *rock* and *sing* modified? What word introduces the dependent clause? What kind of sentence do the lines make?

A modal adverb is one used to change or modify the meaning of an entire sentence, rather than to modify a single word.

> The tender grace of a day that is dead
> Will never come back to me. — TENNYSON.

> We can not all be masters, nor all masters
> Can not be truly followed. — SHAKESPEARE.

Read the quotation from Tennyson, omitting the word *never*. Read it again, putting the word *never* in its place. What does the word *never* do?

Read the lines from Shakespeare, omitting the word *not*. Read them again as printed above. What does the word *not* do?

Ideas of time, place, manner, etc., are sometimes expressed by several words taken together, making a PHRASE ADVERB.

> We are going by and by.
> We learned that long ago.

The words *yes* and *no*, and some other words and phrases of like meaning, are abridged forms for entire sentences, and are called RESPONSIVES.

Mention all the adverbs in the following sentences, and tell to which class each belongs, and why: —

1. Oh! brightly, brightly glow thy skies
   In summer's sunny hours! — THURSTON.

2. I knew the spot upon the hill
    Where checkerberries could be found ;
  I knew the rushes near the mill
    Where pickerel lay that weighed a pound. — FIELD.

3. When the moon shone, we did not see the candle :
  So doth the greater glory dim the less.
SHAKESPEARE.

4. Tenderly, gently, by his own
    He knew and judged another's heart. — WHITTIER.

5.   Swiftly, swiftly flew the ship,
      Yet she sailed softly too :
    Sweetly, sweetly blew the breeze,
      On me alone it blew. — COLERIDGE.

6.   When Freedom from her mountain height
      Unfurled her standard to the air,
    She tore the azure robe of night,
      And set the stars of glory there. — DRAKE.

7.   It is an ancient Mariner,
    And he stoppeth one of three :
    " By thy long beard and glittering eye,
    Now wherefore stopp'st thou me ?" — COLERIDGE.

Write ten sentences, each containing one of the following, used as an interrogative adverb : how, when, where, why.

Write ten sentences, each containing one of the following, used as a conjunctive adverb : as, why, when, where, whence, whereby, wherefore, whereon, while, whenever.

Write ten sentences, using in each one of the following modal adverbs : —

Of affirmation : *surely, verily, yes, truly, positively.*

Of negation : *no, not, never, nowise, nay.*

Of doubt : *perhaps, probably, possibly, haply, perchance.*

Of cause : *why, hence, whence, wherefore, consequently, therefore.*

CAUTION. — Certain adverbs may be of different classes, according to their use in the sentence.

LESSON XCIX.

SIMPLE ADVERBS.

Simple adverbs are divided into four classes, — of *time*, of *place*, of *degree*, of *manner*.

Adverbs of *time* are such as answer the questions, When? How long? How often?

> He is going away to-morrow.
> I shall always remember you.
> We use this book frequently.

Adverbs of *place* are such as answer the questions, Where? Whither? Whence?

> Bring the pencil here.
> Go forth, little book.

Adverbs of *degree* are such as answer the questions, How much? In what degree? To what extent?

> The journey was very delightful.
> His health is greatly improved.
> The story is partly true.

Adverbs of *manner* are such as answer the questions, How? In what way?

> The steamer moved slowly away.
> We were needlessly alarmed.

Construct sentences illustrating the use of the following words :—

ADVERBS OF TIME.

to-day	now	never
formerly	hereafter	then
recently	always	lately

ADVERBS OF PLACE.

there	somewhere	around
abroad	whither	away
elsewhere	backward	whence

ADVERBS OF DEGREE.

greatly	equally	so
very	partly	sufficiently
entirely	mostly	somewhat

ADVERBS OF MANNER.

gently	hopefully	fast
carefully	silently	somehow
thoughtfully	softly	otherwise

Point out and classify the adverbs in Lesson LXIV. Tell what words they modify, in each case naming the part of speech.

LESSON C.

COMPOSITION. — A LETTER.

HIGHAM BY ROCHESTER, KENT,
June 23, 1861.

MY DEAR WILKIE:—

I shall remain in town on Thursday, and return with you on Friday. We can settle our train when we meet on Wednesday.

The country is most charming, and this place very pretty. I am sorry to hear that the hot east winds have taken such a devastating blow into No. 12 Harley Street. They have been rather surprising, if anything in weather can be said to surprise.

I don't know whether anything remarkable comes off in the air to-day, but the bluebottles (there are nine in this room) are all banging their heads against the window glass in the most astonishing manner. I think there must be a competitive examination somewhere, and these nine have been rejected.

Ever affectionately,

CHARLES DICKENS.

TO MR. WILKIE COLLINS.

P.S.— I reopen this to state that the most madly despondent bluebottle has committed suicide, and fallen dead on the carpet.

You may imagine yourself living at No. 12 Harley Street. Write a letter to Charles Dickens, telling him about the city in June. Describe the weather, the shops, the parks, and the people.

LESSON CI.

FORMS OF ADVERBS.

A few adverbs are roots (not formed from simple words) ; as, *ill, well, off, not, now.*

Some adverbs are formed from other words by various changes, as *once, twice,* etc., from *one, two,* etc. ; *abed, betimes, to-day, underground, perchance,* etc.

Many are formed by the adding of a suffix ; as, *homeward, backward, likewise, alway, straightway, besides.*

The greater number of adverbs are formed by means of the suffix *ly,* meaning " in the manner of."

This suffix *ly* is a softened form of the word *like,* still found in a few words ; as, *childlike, warlike, Godlike,* etc.

Adverbs are formed from adjectives in four ways ; viz., —

1. By adding *ly* to the adjective ; as, —

> The prisoner stood up in a hopeless way.
> The prisoner stood up hopelessly.

In this way many adverbs are formed from participial adjectives ; as, *falteringly, decidedly,* etc.

2. When the adjective ends in *le,* drop the *le* before annexing *ly;* thus, —

> The case was settled in an equitable manner.
> The case was settled equitably.
>
> The old miser died a miserable death.
> The old miser died miserably.

3. When the adjective ends in *ic,* add *al* before annexing *ly;* thus, —

> His speech seemed to act like magic words.
> His speech seemed to act magically.

4. Many words are used either as adjectives or as adverbs without changing the form ; thus, —

He is the best boy.	He behaves best.
We have traveled a long way.	We have traveled long.

Write sentences containing the following words used as adjectives.   Write sentences containing adverbs formed from these words.

sudden	visible	comic
noble	joyous	sympathetic
courageous	angry	terrible
frantic	contemptible	happy
stammering	prophetic	energetic

Tell whether the Italicized words in the following sentences are used as adjectives or adverbs, and why : —

1. He is an *early* riser.
2. They arrived *early*.
3. He went *yonder*, toward the tree.
4. *Yonder* house is his home.
5. Do not run so *fast*.
6. That is a *fast* train.
7. He is *no* idler.
8. I was entertained *well*.
9. The boy is always *well*.
10. You should study *better*.
11. Are you not *better*?
12. He has a *hard* life, with *little* pleasure.
13. He labors *hard*, and rests *little*.
14. Do not stay so *long* away.
15. The way was *long*.

LESSON CII.

COMPARISON OF ADVERBS.

A few adverbs may be compared like adjectives and in the same three ways : —

1. Regularly, by annexing *er* and *est :* —

POSITIVE.	COMPARATIVE.	SUPERLATIVE.
soon	sooner	soonest
late	later	latest

2. By means of the adverbs *more* and *most* and *less* and *least :* —

POSITIVE.	COMPARATIVE.	SUPERLATIVE.
steadily	more steadily	most steadily
harshly	less harshly	least harshly
severely	more severely	most severely

3. Irregularly, by change of word : —

POSITIVE.	COMPARATIVE.	SUPERLATIVE.
well	better	best
ill	worse	worst
much	more	most
little	less	least
forth	further	furthest
far	farther	farthest

Write sentences, using adverbs in the positive degree, and other sentences, using the same adverbs in the comparative or superlative degree.

LESSON CIII.

ADVERBIAL PHRASES.

1. Behind the cloud the starlight lurks,
Through showers the sunbeams fall.

2. The wave is breaking on the shore,
The echo (is) fading from the chime.

Where does the starlight lurk? By what is the verb *lurks* modified? What kind of phrase is *through showers?* Why? By what is the verb *is breaking* modified? What phrase modifies the verb (*is*) *fading?*

Phrases such as *behind the cloud, through showers, on the shore, from the chime,* used like adverbs, are called ADVERBIAL PHRASES.

An adverbial phrase is sometimes preceded by an adverb, which modifies the phrase, or some part of it; as, —

They softly lie and sweetly sleep
Low in the ground.

Mention the adverbial phrases in the following sentences, and tell what each modifies : —

1. Pleasantly under the silver moon, and under the silent, solemn stars, ring the steel shoes of the skaters on the frozen sea, and voices, and the sound of bells.

2. When the weather is fair and settled, the mountains are clothed in blue and purple, and print their bold outlines on the clear evening sky.

3. On one side of the church extends a wide, woody dell, along which raves a large brook among broken rocks and trunks of fallen trees.

4. The glory of the sunset heaven
    On land and water lay, —
    On the steep hills of Agawam,
    On cape, and bluff, and bay. — WHITTIER.

5. Above the pines the moon was slowly drifting,
    The river ran below;
    The dim Sierras, far beyond, uplifting
    Their minarets of snow. — BRET HARTE.

6. With exquisite taste, simplicity, and pathos he has narrated the fabulous traditions of early ages, and given to them that appearance of reality which only a master hand could impart.

ADVERBS CHANGED TO PHRASES.

An adverb may sometimes be changed to an equivalent adverbial phrase; thus, —

1. The visitors were treated kindly.
    The visitors were treated with kindness.
2. When will you return?
    At what time will you return?

Rewrite the following sentences, changing the adverbs in Italics to equivalent adverbial phrases: —

1. Then speak at once, and *fearlessly*.
2. *Gently* the breeze tosses the curls of his hair.
3. *Firmly* and *honestly* make your mark.
4. *Sadly* rose the morning of the year.
5. Thirty nobles saddled *speedily*.
6. The next wave dashed the ship *violently* upon the rocks.
7. *Vainly* did they turn to go.

8. *Silently*, under cover of night, the troops withdrew.
9. The man walked *hurriedly* down the street.
10. She called *loudly* for aid.

LESSON CIV.

HOW TO PARSE ADVERBS.

To parse an adverb, state : —

1. *Class* — whether simple, interrogative, conjunctive, or modal. If simple, state whether of time, of place, of degree, or of manner.
2. *Degree of Comparison* — whether positive, comparative, or superlative. Many adverbs cannot be compared.
3. *Use* — the word it modifies, the question it asks, the clause it introduces, or the sentence whose meaning it modifies.

MODEL FOR ORAL OR WRITTEN EXERCISE.

1. Why do the people cheer so loudly?
2. They always cheer when the Governor passes.

WHY is an interrogative adverb, and is used to ask a question.
So is an adverb of degree, and modifies the adverb *loudly*.
LOUDLY is an adverb of manner, positive degree, and modifies the verb *cheer*.
ALWAYS is an adverb of time, and modifies the verb *cheer*.
WHEN is a conjunctive adverb; it introduces the clause *when the Governor passes*, and modifies the verbs *cheer* and *passes*.

Parse the adverbs in Lesson XCIII.

LESSON CV.

PUNCTUATION. — THE COMMA.

Words or phrases contrasted are separated by commas; thus, —

Strong proofs, not a loud voice, produce conviction.
Language is not made, but grows.

Expressions denoting persons or things addressed are separated from the rest of the sentence by commas; thus, —

Go to the ant, thou sluggard; consider her ways.
Charge, Chester, charge! On, Stanley, on!
My Lords, I could not have said less.

Words and phrases in apposition are separated from each other and from the rest of the sentence by commas, unless they may be regarded as a proper name or a single phrase; thus, —

"An elm," says the poet Holmes, "is a little forest on a single stem."
Cortes, the conqueror of Mexico, was a brave man.
I spoke with the man himself.
He himself led the troops.

Justify the use of the comma in the following sentences. Write the sentences from dictation.

1. Industry, and not mean savings, produces wealth.
2. The carriage, as well as the horse, was very much injured.
3. Continued exertion, and not hasty efforts, leads to success.
4. Here Washington, our first President, lies buried.
5. False delicacy is affectation, not politeness.

5. There is no terror, Cassius, in your threats.

6. I come to bury Cæsar, not to praise him.

SHAKESPEARE.

7. Ring out, wild bells, to the wild sky ! — TENNYSON.

8. Where are the flowers, the fair young flowers that
   lately sprung and stood
   In brighter light and softer airs, a beauteous sister-
   hood ? — BRYANT.

9. Now the bright morning star, day's harbinger,
   Comes dancing from the East, and leads with her
   the flowery May. — MILTON.

10. Under her great leader, William of Orange, Hol-
land advanced to a glorious triumph.

11. Homer, the greatest poet of antiquity, is said to
have been blind.

12. Learning is the ally, not the adversary, of genius.

LESSON CVI.

STUDY OF SELECTION.

"I'LL FIND A WAY, OR MAKE IT."

It was a noble Roman,
   In Rome's imperial day,
Who heard a coward croaker
   Before the castle say,
" They're safe in such a fortress :
   There is no way to shake it ! "
" On, on," exclaimed the hero :
   " I'll find a way, or make it ! "

Is Fame your aspiration?
  Her path is steep and high;
In vain he seeks her temple,
  Content to gaze and sigh.
The shining throne is waiting;
  But he alone can take it
Who says with Roman firmness,
  " I'll find a way, or make it!"

Is Learning your ambition?
  There is no royal road:
Alike the peer and peasant
  Must climb to her abode.
Who feels the thirst for knowledge,
  In Helicon may slake it,
If he has still the Roman will
  " To find a way, or make it!"

JOHN G. SAXE.

Read the first stanza. What two persons are represented as speaking? What does the noble Roman say?

Read the second stanza. How is the path to the Temple of Fame described? Will the man who gazes and sighs ever reach it? For whom is the throne of Fame waiting?

Read the third stanza. Is there a royal road to Learning? Must the poor and the rich alike climb to her abode? What do you understand by " I'll find a way, or make it " ?

Tell in your own words the story of the noble Roman, and apply his motto to the efforts of —

    1. Boys who wish to become men of action.
    2. Boys who wish to become men of thought.

LESSON CVII.

REVIEW. — ADJECTIVES AND ADVERBS.

1. What is an adjective?

2. How are adjectives classified? How are they compared? Point out and classify the adjectives in the selection entitled, "I'll Find a Way, or Make it."

3. What is a cardinal numeral? An ordinal numeral? Illustrate.

4. Write a sentence in which an adjective in the predicate modifies the subject.

5. Define an adverb. How are adverbs classified? How are they compared?

6. Write four sentences to illustrate the different classes of adverbs.

7. Write a sentence in which an adverb modifies a verb. An adjective. Another adverb.

8. Parse the Italicized words in the following sentences : —

1. *When* shall we three meet again?
2. The lowing herd winds *slowly* o'er the lea.
3. *Truly* the world does move.
4. The rain is falling *where* they lie.
5. She looks *cold.*
6. The sky is *blue.*
7. Name the *seven* wonders of the world.
8. Lo ! *while* we are gazing, in *swifter* haste
   Stream *down* the snows, *till* the air is *white.* — BRYANT.
9. Books that you may carry to the fire, and hold *readily* in your hand, are the *most useful,* after all.

LESSON CVIII.

VERBS AND VERBALS.

1. Dogs bark.
2. Grass is green.
3. The picture hangs over the mantel.

The verb *bark* in the first sentence asserts an action of dogs.

The verb *is* in the second sentence asserts a condition of grass.

The verb *hangs* in the third sentence asserts a position of picture.

A verb asserts something, usually an action, a condition, or a position, of its subject.

4. The name of the girl reading is Helen.
5. We found a child resting in a hammock.
6. The box, filled with gold coins, was given to the minister.
7. To escape was his only thought.

The word *reading* assumes an action, but does not assert it.

The word *resting* assumes, but does not assert, the position of the child.

The word *filled* assumes, but does not assert, a condition of the box.

To escape expresses an action in a general way, but does not assert it of any particular object.

Words used like *reading, resting, filled,* and *to escape,* — to assume the action, condition, or position of a subject, or to express it in a general way, — are called VERBALS.

Verbals are divided into two classes according to their forms, — *participles* and *infinitives.*

11

Verbals commonly ending in *ing* are PRESENT PARTICIPLES, as *reading*, *resting;* those commonly ending in *ed* or *en* (and some others) are PAST PARTICIPLES, as *filled.*

A participle with its complement is called a PARTICIPIAL PHRASE ; as, *resting in a hammock, filled with gold coins.*

Verbals commonly preceded by the preposition TO, as, *to escape*, are INFINITIVES, or VERBS IN THE INFINITIVE MODE.

An infinitive with its complement is called an INFINITIVE PHRASE ; as, *to launch the boat was a long task.*

Mention the verbs, participles, and infinitives in the following sentences : —

1. He had learned to speak the truth, to ride, to shoot, to do with little sleep and less food. — MOTLEY.

2. To think is to speak low; to speak is to think aloud. — MAX MÜLLER.

3. He struggled against the stream for a little, and then drifted with the current, lamenting, but no longer resisting.

4. Keep plodding, 'tis wiser than sitting aside,
   And dreaming and sighing, and waiting the tide.

5. A drowsy, dreamy influence seems to hang over the land, and to pervade the very atmosphere.

6. Startled at the stillness broken by reply so aptly
         spoken. — POE.

7. He went through life bearing the load of a people's sorrows upon his shoulders, with a smiling face. — MOTLEY.

8. Then shook the hills with thunder riven !
   Then rushed the steed to battle driven !
   And louder than the bolts of heaven
       Far flashed the red artillery ! — CAMPBELL.

9. Irving came amongst us, bringing the kindest sympathy, the most artless, smiling good will. — THACKERAY.

10. They are like those little nooks of still water which border a rapid stream, where we may see the straw and bubble riding quietly at anchor, or slowly revolving in their mimic harbor, undisturbed by the rush of the passing current. — IRVING.

LESSON CIX.

TRANSITIVE AND INTRANSITIVE VERBS.

1. Snow protects plants.
2. Washington defended our country.
3. The boys will see the mountains.

Snow protects what? Could we say snow protects, and not say it protects something? Washington defended what? Could Washington defend, and not defend something? What will the boys see? Can any one see, and not see something? What kind of complement is *plants? Country? Mountains?*

Verbs like *protects, defended,* and *will see,* which require an object to complete their meaning, are called TRANSITIVE VERBS.

4. The horses run.
5. The rain fell gently.
6. The train will stop here.

What is asserted of horses? Of rain? Of train? Do the horses run anything? Will the train stop anything? Do these verbs require objects to complete their meaning?

Verbs like *run, fell,* and *will stop,* which are used so as not to require an object to complete their meaning, are called INTRANSITIVE VERBS.

Most intransitive verbs make a complete assertion, as in the fourth, fifth, and sixth sentences.

A few intransitive verbs require an attributive complement; as, —

> 7. Henry is a big boy.
> 8. Mary looks sad.
> 9. The velvet feels smooth.

What word in the seventh sentence explains the subject? What word qualifies the subject in the eighth? What word in the ninth describes the subject?

Verbs like *is, looks, feels,* followed by an attributive complement, are called INCOMPLETE INTRANSITIVES.

The principal incomplete intransitives are *be, become, appear, seem, feel, look,* etc.

A few verbs may be transitive used in one sense, and intransitive used in another; as, —

> *Trans.* The man runs a factory.
> *Intrans.* The man runs away.
> *Trans.* The girl stopped me.
> *Trans.* The girl spoke a few words.
> *Intrans.* The girl stopped and spoke to me.

Tell of each verb in the following sentences whether it is transitive or intransitive: —

1. The poet lived in a quaint old house near the river.
2. Very delicious was their fragrance in the morning breeze.
3. Water cooleth the brow and cooleth the brain,
   And maketh the faint one strong again. — JOHNSON.
4. Talent is something, but tact is everything.

> JEFFREY.

5. Absence destroys trifling intimacies, but it invigorates strong friendships.

6. Pomona loves the orchard;
   And Liber loves the vine;
   And Pales loves the straw-built shed
   Warm with the breath of kine. — MACAULAY.

7. The boy critic loves the story; grown up, he loves the author who wrote the story. — THACKERAY.

8. Now the wild, white horses play,
   Champ and chafe and toss in the spray.

   MATTHEW ARNOLD.

9. They heard the clarion's iron clang,
   The breeze which through the roses sang. — CROLY

10. The fairest action of our human life
    Is scorning to revenge an injury. — CAREW.

11. Only the actions of the just
    Smell sweet, and blossom in the dust. — SHIRLEY.

12. Oft in the stilly night
    Ere slumber's chain has bound me,
    Fond memory brings the light
    Of other days around me. — MOORE.

13. Triumphal Arch that fill'st the sky
    When storms prepare to part,
    I ask not proud Philosophy
    To teach me what thou art. — CAMPBELL.

14. I am monarch of all I survey,
    My right there is none to dispute;
    From the center all round to the sea
    I am lord of the fowl and the brute. — COWPER.

LESSON CX.

THE MODES OF VERBS.

1. James writes a letter.
2. James wrote a letter.
3. James will write a letter.

Each of the verbs above asserts an action of James as a fact.

A verb used like *writes, wrote,* or *will write,* to assert something as a fact, is said to be in the INDICATIVE MODE.

4. James may write a letter.
5. James can write a letter.
6. James must write a letter.

The verb *may write* asserts the possibility or contingency of James writing, but does not assert a fact.

The verb *can write* asserts the ability of James to write.

The verb *must write* asserts the obligation or necessity resting on James to write.

A verb used like *may write, can write, must write,* — to assert possibility, contingency, ability, obligation, or necessity, — is said to be in the POTENTIAL MODE.

7. James would write if he knew how.

The verb *would write* asserts the contingency or possibility of James writing : the condition is expressed by *knew.* The idea that the sentence conveys is, that James does not know how.

A verb used like *knew* in a clause — to assert something as merely thought of, as conditioned or doubtful, or which implies that the contrary is true — is said to be in the SUBJUNCTIVE MODE.

The clause containing the subjunctive mode is never used alone, but always limits a principal clause.

8. James, write a letter.

The verb *write* in the eighth sentence expresses a command.

A verb used like *write*, to express a command, is said to be in the IMPERATIVE MODE.

We see that, in the example above, the same verb may be used to assert the action in different manners. The manner of asserting is called the MODE OF THE VERB.

The use of the various modes in interrogative and exclamatory sentences will be considered in a later lesson.

State whether the verbs in the following sentences are in the indicative, potential, subjunctive, or imperative mode, and why.

1. The night-blooming cereus blooms and fades in a single night.

2. If you do this in earnestness and sincerity, it may possibly repair the mischief which your avarice has occasioned. — TANGLEWOOD TALES.

3. Live truly, and thy life shall be
   A great and noble creed. — BONAR.

4. Had there been only one child at the window of Tanglewood, gazing at ·this wintry prospect, it would perhaps have made him sad. — TANGLEWOOD TALES.

5. If ever I should wish for a retreat, whither I might steal from the world and its distractions, and dream quietly away the remnant of a troubled life, I know of none more promising than this little valley. — IRVING.

6. Part thy blue lips, northern lake !
   Moss-grown rocks, your silence break ! — WHITTIER.

7. Grief may bide an evening guest;
  .   But joy shall come with early light. — BRYANT.
8. Dreary are the years when the eye can look no
     longer
  With delight on nature, or hope on human kind.

                                        BRYANT.

9. He determined to revisit the scene of the last evening's gambol, and, if he met with any of the party, to
demand his dog and gun. — IRVING.

10. When a man can look upon the simple wild rose,
and feel no pleasure, his taste has been corrupted.

                                        BEECHER.

*In the foregoing sentences, state whether the verbs are
transitive or intransitive. Tell the objects of the transitive
verbs and the attributive complements of the intransitive
verbs.*

LESSON CXI.

THE TENSES OF VERBS.

  1. I laugh now.
  2. I laughed yesterday.
  3. I shall laugh to-morrow.

The verb *laugh* represents the action as taking place in the
present time.

A verb used to represent something as occurring at the present
time is said to be in the PRESENT TENSE.

The verb *laughed* represents the action as taking place at some
past time. The idea of time conveyed by *laughed* is not limited
to yesterday. It extends to any time in the past; as, *I laughed a
minute ago; I laughed ten years ago.*

A verb used to represent something as having occurred in the past is said to be in the PAST TENSE.

The verb *shall laugh* represents the action as future. The idea conveyed by *shall laugh* is not limited to to-morrow. It extends to any time in the future ; as, *I shall laugh in five minutes,* or *I shall laugh five years from now.*

A verb used to express something that will occur in the future is said to be in the FUTURE TENSE.

4. I have laughed to-day.
5. I had laughed yesterday.
6. I shall have laughed before to-morrow.

The verb *have laughed* represents the action as completed at the present time.

A verb used to represent an action as having been completed or perfected at the present time is said to be in the PRESENT PERFECT TENSE.

The verb *had laughed* represents the action as being completed before some past time which is mentioned.

A verb used to represent an action as completed before some past time mentioned is said to be in the PAST PERFECT TENSE.

The verb *shall have laughed* declares that the action will be completed before some definite time in the future : that time must be stated or implied. Of course, such definite time need not be to-morrow. We could say, *I shall have laughed before five minutes elapse,* or *I shall have laughed before I die.* In the last sentence, the future time is indefinite and implied, and may be very remote.

A verb used to represent an action as having taken place before some definite time in the future is said to be in the FUTURE PERFECT TENSE.

We see from the preceding six examples that the same verb may be used to express the action as taking place at different times.

That form or variation of the verb that expresses the time of the action is called TENSE.

As there are three divisions of time, — the present, the past, and the future, — so there are three primary or simple tenses, — the *present,* the *past,* and the *future.*

The three compound or perfect tenses are the *present perfect* the *past perfect,* and the *future perfect.*

Tell the tense of each verb in the following sentences : —

1. Next Christmas, I shall have been at school four years.

2.   I had a thing to say,
   But I will fit it with some better time.

                                   SHAKESPEARE.

3. Before the letter reaches him, he will have left the country.

4.   The scouts had parted on their search,
       The castle gates were barred. — SCOTT.

5.   Breathes there a man with soul so dead,
       Who never to himself hath said,
          This is my own, my native land ? — SCOTT.

6. Pomona was the especial patroness of the apple orchard.

7.   So the little coral workers,
          By their slow but constant motion,
       Have built up those pretty islands
          In the distant dark-blue ocean.

8.   From sunrise unto sunset,
          All earth shall hear thy fame :
       A glorious city thou shalt build,
          And name it by thy name. — MACAULAY.

9. The clanging sea fowl came and went,
The hunter's gun in the marshes rang;
At nightfall from a neighboring tent
A flute-voiced woman sweetly sang.

WHITTIER.

Tell the tense of each verb in exercise, Lesson CIX., and in exercise, Lesson CX.

LESSON CXII.

CHOICE OF WORDS.

Construct sentences to illustrate the use of the following words: —

SUFFER. ALLOW. PERMIT.	He was suffered to remain for some time unmolested, then he was allowed a hearing, and finally permitted to depart.
ACCOMPLISH. EXECUTE.	Nothing satisfactory was accomplished, though the commander's orders were strictly executed.
PERFORM.	You can best perform that duty.
ACHIEVE.	Some are born great; some achieve greatness.
RIDICULE. DERIDE.	We ridicule what offends our taste; we deride what seems to merit our scorn.
ACQUIRE. OBTAIN.	He acquired honor, reputation, and fortune; but we cannot know the efforts he made to obtain them.
PERSEVERE. PERSIST.	Persevere in spite of discouragement; persist in spite of opposition.

LESSON CXIII.

PUNCTUATION. — THE COMMA.

Place a comma where a word is understood, unless the connection is very close; thus, —

Curiosity allures the wise; vanity, the foolish; and pleasure, both.

Labor brings pleasure; idleness, pain.

Place a comma after a subject and its modifiers, only when it is necessary to prevent ambiguity; thus, —

The best monuments of the virtuous are their actions.

He who teaches, often learns himself.

A quotation closely connected in grammatical construction is separated from the rest of the sentence by a comma; thus, —

Then the first sound went forth, "They come, they come."

It hurts a man's pride to say, "I do not know."

I say to you, "You are not an honest man."

The members of a compound sentence are usually separated by a comma when one of them expresses the condition upon which the other statement is made; thus, —

Make up your mind to do a thing, and you will surely do it.

Fill your heart with goodness, and you will find that the world is full of good.

Justify the use of the comma in the following sentences. Write the sentences from dictation.

1. Plants are formed by culture; men, by education.
2. The Greeks excelled in poetry; the Romans, in jurisprudence.
3. War is the law of violence; peace, the law of love.
4. Worth makes the man; the want of it, the fellow.

POPE.

5. Ignorance is the curse of God; knowledge, the wing wherewith we fly to heaven. — SHAKESPEARE.
6. The rolling rock leaves its scratches on the mountain; the river, its channel in the soil; the animal, its bones in the stratum; the fern and leaf, their modest epitaph in the coal. — EMERSON.
7. It is customary to say, " Take care of the small sums, and the large will take care of themselves."

SUMNER.

8. A dewdrop falling on the wild sea wave
   Exclaimed in fear, " I perish in this grave."

TRENCH.

9. An old French sentence says, " God works in moments." — EMERSON.
10. He who pursues pleasure only, defeats the object of his creation.

LESSON CXIV.

COMPOSITION.

MECHANIC ART IN THE ANIMAL CREATION.

Spiders are geometricians, as are also bees, whose cells are so constructed, as, with the least quantity of material, to have the largest-sized spaces and the least possible loss of interstices. The mole is a meteorologist; the nautilus is a navigator, for he raises and lowers his sails, casts and weighs anchor, and performs other nautical evolutions; while the whole tribe of birds are musicians. The beaver may be called a builder or architect; the marmot is a civil engineer, for he not only constructs houses and aqueducts, but also drains to keep them dry; caterpillars are silk spinners; wasps are paper manufacturers; the indefatigable ants are day laborers; the monkey, a ropedancer; dogs are hunters; pigs, scavengers; and the torpedo and eel are electricians.

Find out all you can concerning the habits and work of some animal; then write a composition, combining the ideas you have gathered: —

1. By observation.
2. By conversation.
3. By reading.

Here is a thoughtful boy's account of what he saw on the window : —

HOW WASPS BUILD THEIR NESTS.

One spring day, a wasp came between the blind and the window, and after much buzzing began to build. She first laid down, beneath the under edge of the upper sash, a patch of paper about a third of an inch in diameter; then, standing on this, she raised cup-shaped edges all about her, increasing outward and downward, like the cup of an acorn, and then drawing together a little, until a little house was made just about the size and shape of a white-oak acorn, except that she left a hole in the bottom, where she might go in and out.

Then she began at the top, and laid another cover of paper over the first, just as far away as the length of her legs made it easy for her to work. Now it was clear that she made the first shell as a frame or a scaffold on which she might stand to make the second. She would fly away, and after a few minutes come back, with nothing that could be seen, either in her feet or in her jaws. But she at once set to laying her paper stuff, which came out of her mouth, upon the edge of the work she had done before. As she laid the material, she walked backward, building and walking, until she had laid a patch a little more than an eighth of an inch wide and half or three-quarters of an inch long. When laid, the pulp looked like wet brown paper, which soon dried to an ashen gray and still resembled coarse paper. As she laid the material, she occasionally went over it again, putting a little now here and there in the thin places; generally the work was well done the first time.

So the work went on. The second paper shell was about as large as a pigeon's egg; then a third was laid as large as a hen's egg; then another still larger. After a time, the wasp seemed to go inside to get her material, and it appeared that she was taking down the first house, and putting the paper on the outside. If so, she did not bring out pieces and patch them together as a carpenter, saving of work, would do; but she chewed the paper up, and made fresh pulp of it, just as the first was made.

Compare your account with that of the young naturalist, and then rewrite your composition, trying to express simply and accurately the information you have acquired.

LESSON CXV.

REGULAR AND IRREGULAR VERBS.

PRESENT TENSE.	PAST TENSE.	PAST PARTICIPLE.
laugh	laughed	laughed
call	called	called
break	broke	broken
draw	drew	drawn

What is added to the present tense of the verb *laugh* to form the past tense? What is added to the present tense to form the past participle?

How are the past tense and past participle of the verb *call* formed from the present tense?

A verb whose past tense and past participle are formed by annexing *ed* to the present tense is called a REGULAR VERB.*

Is the past tense of *break* formed by adding *ed* to the present? How is the past participle formed? Are the past tense and past participle of *draw* formed regularly?

A verb whose past tense and past participle are not formed by annexing *ed* to the present tense is called an IRREGULAR or STRONG VERB.

Form the past tense and past participle of : —

smile	talk	refer
bestow	imply	charge
reform	gather	authorize
transact	respect	prosper
destroy	invite	discover

* *Regular verbs* are by some grammarians called *weak verbs.*

Learn the past tense and past participle of each of the following irregular verbs : —

PRESENT.	PAST.	PAST PART.	PRESENT.	PAST.	PAST PART.
be (am)	was	been	lay	laid	laid
begin	began	begun	leave	left	left
blow	blew	blown	lie	lay	lain
break	broke	broken	rise	rose	risen
choose	chose	chosen	run	ran	run
come	came	come	say	said	said
do	did	done	see	saw	seen
draw	drew	drawn	set	set	set
drive	drove	driven	sit	sat	sat
eat	ate	eaten	sing	sang	sung
fall	fell	fallen	slay	slew	slain
fly	flew	flown	steal	stole	stolen
freeze	froze	frozen	take	took	taken
give	gave	given	tear	tore	torn
go	went	gone	throw	threw	thrown
grow	grew	grown	wear	wore	worn
know	knew	known	write	wrote	written

For a full list of irregular verbs, see p. 329.

A number of verbs conjugated regularly, are sometimes spelled in an abbreviated form, with *t* instead of *ed;* as, *spelt, spilt,* etc.

A few verbs have two forms, — the regular and the irregular. Such verbs are called REDUNDANT ; as, —

	PRESENT.	PAST.	PAST PART.
Reg.	light	lighted	lighted
Irreg.	light	lit	lit

A REDUNDANT VERB is one whose past tense or past participle is formed regularly as well as irregularly.

12

A DEFECTIVE VERB is one that lacks either the past tense or the past participle, or both.

The defective verbs have no present participle, and the auxiliaries *may, can, must* are never used as infinitives.

LIST OF DEFECTIVE VERBS.

PRESENT.	PAST.	PRESENT.	PAST.
beware	——	shall	should
can	could	will	would
may	might	wis	wist
must	——	wit	——
ought	——	wot	——
——	quoth		

Beware is used only in the imperative and in the infinitive (and the tenses compounded with it; as, *should* [*to*] *beware*, etc.).

Do and *will* as auxiliaries have only the present and past tenses; *have* as an auxiliary uses all its principal parts. As principal verbs, they have all the forms.

Meseems, methinks, are used in present and past tenses only: the prefix *me* is the dative of the pronoun [*to me*]; as if, *It seems to me*, etc. These are idiomatic.

Wis and *wist* are rarely found except in old authors.

Wit and *wot* are ancient, the form *to wit* being now used only as an infinitive, meaning *namely*, or *that is to say*.

Worth (an old verb meaning *to be, to become, to happen*) is now used only in such expressions as, *Woe worth the day*, etc., in which the verb is in the imperative mode and the noun in the dative; as if, *Woe be to the day*. — WEBSTER.

Quoth is used only in the past indicative and in the first and third persons, the subject always following the verb; as, *Quoth he.*

LESSON CXVI.

THE RIGHT WORD IN THE RIGHT PLACE.

1. Howard learned to skate last winter.
2. My brother will teach me to skate next winter.

Which verb signifies past time? Which refers to future time? Do you notice any other difference in the meaning of *learned* and *will teach?*

Which verb signifies to receive instruction?

Which signifies to give instruction?

Complete the following sentences : —

1. Miss Pratt —— us to sketch from nature.
2. What have you —— to draw from the cast?
3. Carl has —— to play the violin.
4. Alice is —— to speak French.
5. Who —— your Sunday-school class last sabbath?
6. John Stuart Mill —— to read Latin when he was younger than any of you.
7. Robert Louis Stevenson —— to compose by imitating good sentences.
8. Ruskin is said to —— —— to draw by playing with a key on the carpet.

Construct sentences illustrating the use of the following words : —

teach	will teach	will learn
taught	have taught	may learn
teaching	learn	is learning
are teaching	learned	are learning
can teach	have learned	can learn

Explain the meaning of the verbs teach *and* learn *in each of the following quotations :* —

1.   Little monitor, by thee
        Let me learn what I should be;
        I'll learn the round of life to fill,
        Useful and progressive still.

2. One lesson, Nature, let me learn of thee! — ARNOLD.

3. New occasions teach new duties; Time makes
        ancient good uncouth;
   They must upward still, and onward, who would
        keep abreast with Truth. — LOWELL.

LESSON CXVII.

STUDY OF SELECTION.

A SENSITIVE DOG.

I formerly possessed a large dog, who, like every other dog, was much pleased to go out walking. He showed his pleasure by trotting gravely before me with high steps, head much raised, moderately erected ears, and a tail carried aloft, but not stiffly. Not far from my house a path branches off to the right, leading to the hothouse, which I used often to visit for a few moments, to look at my plants. This was always a great disappointment to the dog, as he did not know whether I would continue my walk; and the sudden and complete change of expression which came over him as soon as my body swerved in the least toward the path — and I sometimes tried this as an experiment — was laughable.

His look of dejection was known to every member of the family, and was called his " hothouse face." This consisted in the head drooping much, the whole body sinking a little and remaining motionless, the ears and tail falling suddenly down ; but the tail was by no means wagged. With the falling of his ears and of his great chaps, the eyes became much changed in appearance, and I fancied they looked less bright. His aspect was that of piteous, hopeless dejection ; and it was the more laughable as the cause was so slight. Every detail in his attitude was in complete opposition to his former joyous yet dignified bearing, and I can explain it in no other way except through the principle of contrast. — CHARLES DARWIN.

What does Mr. Darwin tell us about his dog? How did the dog show pleasure? How did he show disappointment? Do you think the dog enjoyed going for a walk with his master? Did he like to go to the hothouse?

Why did the family laugh at the dog's hothouse face? Notice the contrast in the attitudes of the head, body, ears, tail. How did the expression of the dog's eyes change? Is the appearance of a happy dog exactly opposite to that of an unhappy dog? How does Mr. Darwin explain the changes?

WRITTEN EXERCISES.

1. *Describe the appearance of a cat when threatened with danger.*

HINTS.

How does the cat show terror and anger? Have you ever seen a cat arch its back, erect its hair, open its mouth and spit? Does a cat ever look like a tiger? Does it growl? Does it crouch as if ready to spring? How do the claws show anger? The ears? The eyes?

2. *Describe the appearance of a cat that wishes to gain your friendship.*

HINTS.

Notice the cat's manner. Describe the hair, the ears, the mouth. Does the cat sometimes purr? Does the cat show intelligence? Affection? Fidelity?

3. *Write a story about "A Brave Cat." In your account mention : —*

1. How the cat dozed before the fire. 2. What it did when a strange dog came into the room. 3. What changes you noticed in the appearance of the dog and the cat. 4. The retreat of the dog.

LESSON CXVIII.

HOW TO FORM THE TENSES.

1. I walk.	I give.
2. I walked.	I gave.
3. I will walk	I will give
(or I shall walk).	(or I shall give).
4. I have walked.	I have given.
5. I had walked.	I had given.
6. I shall have walked	I shall have given
(or I will have walked).	(or I will have given).

Is *walk* a regular, or an irregular verb? Why? What is the past tense and the past participle?

Is *give* a regular, or an irregular verb? Why? Name the past tense. Name the past participle.

In what tense is the verb *walk* in the first line? In what tense is the verb *give* in the first line?

How is the past tense of the verb *walk* formed? Of the verb *give?*

In what tense are the verbs in the third line? How is it formed? What part of each verb is used? What new word (auxiliary) is used to help form the tense?

In what tense are the verbs in line four? What part of the verbs *walk* and *give* is used in forming this tense? What auxiliary (or helping) word is used?

In what tense are the verbs in line five? What part of the verbs *walk* and *give* is used to form this tense? What auxiliary is used?

In what tense are the verbs in line six? What part of the verbs *walk* and *give* is used to form this tense? What auxiliaries are used to form this tense?

A verb when used alone in its *simple* or *root* form is in the PRESENT TENSE.

The PAST TENSE of regular verbs is formed by annexing *ed* to the root.

The FUTURE TENSE is formed by prefixing *shall* or *will* to the simple or root form of the verb.

The PRESENT PERFECT TENSE is formed by prefixing *have* to the past participle of the verb.

The PAST PERFECT TENSE is formed by prefixing *had* to the past participle of the verb.

The FUTURE PERFECT TENSE is formed by prefixing *will have* or *shall have* to the past participle of the verb.

Write sentences, using each of the following verbs in all the tenses of the indicative mode: —

plant	write	touch
begin	study	lose
spend	blow	notice
bloom	finish	find

Write sentences, using each of the following verbs in all the tenses of the potential mode : —

go	laugh	run
play	try	destroy
possess	continue	come

LESSON CXIX.

PERSON AND NUMBER OF THE VERB.

PRESENT TENSE.

SINGULAR.	PLURAL.
1. I give.	We give.
2. Thou givest.	You give.
3. He gives.	They give.

In the preceding lessons on verbs, only the pronoun *I* (first person, singular number) has been used as a subject. You will now observe what changes take place in the verb to agree with subjects of other persons and numbers.

In the sentences, in what persons and numbers is the root form of the verb unchanged? What is added to the first person singular to form the second person singular? What is added to the first person singular to form the third person singular?

The pronouns *she* or *it,* or a *singular noun,* may be used in place of *he* in all the tenses, and a *plural noun* may take the place of *they.*

PAST TENSE.

SINGULAR.	PLURAL.
1. I gave.	We gave.
2. Thou gavest.	You gave.
3. He gave.	They gave,

In what person and number of the past tense is the verb changed? How is the change made?

FUTURE TENSE.

SINGULAR.

1. I shall give.   I will give.
2. Thou wilt give.   Thou shalt give.
3. He will give.   He shall give.

PLURAL.

1. We shall give.   We will give.
2. You will give.   You shall give.
3. They will give.   They shall give.

In which person and number of the future tense is the verb changed? Does the change occur in the principal verb, or in the auxiliary verb? The auxiliary verb is sometimes called the SIGN.

PRESENT PERFECT TENSE.

SINGULAR.	PLURAL.
1. I have given.	We have given.
2. Thou hast given.	You have given.
3. He has given.	They have given.

What change occurs in the second person singular? In the third person singular?

PAST PERFECT TENSE.

SINGULAR.	PLURAL.
1. I had given.	We had given.
2. Thou hadst given.	You had given.
3. He had given.	They had given.

In what person and number is the verb changed in the past perfect tense? What is the change?

FUTURE PERFECT TENSE.

SINGULAR.

1. I shall or will have seen.
2. Thou wilt or shalt have seen.
3. He will or shall have seen.

PLURAL.

1. We shall or will have seen.
2. You will or shall have seen.
3. They will or shall have seen.

State in what person and number, and in what part of the auxiliary, the change occurs.

Write sentences, using each verb in the tense, person, and number indicated.

1. study, pres. perf., 1st, sing.
2. choose, fut. perf., 2d, sing.
3. know, past perf., 3d, plu.
4. take, past, 1st, sing.
5. find, pres., 2d, plu.
6. violate, fut., 3d, sing.
7. carry, fut. perf., 1st, sing.
8. freeze, fut. perf., 3d, plu.
9. speak, fut. perf., 2d, sing.
10. consist, pres., 3d, plu.
11. ring, pres. perf., 2d, plu.
12. sing, past perf., 1st, plu.
13. prefer, past, 3d, sing.
14. eat, pres. perf., 1st, sing.
15. do, past perf., 1st, plu.

LESSON CXX.

PUNCTUATION.

DASH, PARENTHESIS, QUOTATION MARKS, AND HYPHEN.

Place a dash (—) where a sentence breaks off abruptly, or when there is a sudden turn in the thought; thus, —

Was there ever — but I scorn to boast.

The dash is sometimes used before a statement of particulars; thus, —

I see in this world two heaps, — one of happiness, and the other of misery.

An expression occurring in the body of a sentence, and nearly or quite independent of it in meaning, may be inclosed in a parenthesis ( ); thus, —

Are you still (I fear you are) far from being comfortably settled?

Expressions and passages belonging to another, when introduced into one's own composition, should be inclosed in quotation marks (" "); thus, —

Let us always remember this ancient proverb, "Know thyself."

A quotation within a quotation requires only single marks (' '); thus, —

He replied, "Your version of the Golden Rule must be, 'Do as you are done by.'"

The apostrophe(') is used to denote the omission of a letter or letters, and as a sign of the possessive case; thus, —

> Not in Fancy's maze he wander'd long,
> But stoop'd to truth, and moraliz'd his song.

The hyphen (-) is used to separate the parts of a compound word, and at the end of a line when one or more syllables of a word are carried to the beginning of the next; thus, —

> Short swallow-flights of song.

The hyphen should never be used at the end of a line to divide a syllable: the part of the word carried forward to the next line must be one or more whole syllables.

Give reasons for the use of the marks of punctuation in the following sentences. Write the sentences from dictation.

1. But next day (such are the rapid changes in high-lands) broke blue and shining.

2. I told him (it is the way of society) that we should be glad to see him. — STOCKTON.

3. He gave to misery (all he had) a tear ;
   He gained from Heaven ('twas all he wished) a
       friend. — GRAY.

4. Isabel and I (she is my cousin, and is seven years old, and I am ten) are sitting together on the bank of the stream. — MITCHELL.

5. Animals are such agreeable friends ! — they ask no questions, they pass no criticisms. — GEORGE ELIOT.

6. But " Ivanhoe " and " Quentin Durward " ! — oh for a half holiday and a quiet corner, and one of those books again ! — THACKERAY.

7. "Time is the warp of life," said he, " oh tell
    The young, the fair, the gay, to weave it well!"

MARSDEN.

8. 'Tis good to give a stranger a meal, or a night's lodging. — EMERSON.

9. Every man's, and boy's, and girl's head carries snatches of his (Burns's) songs. — EMERSON.

10. The honest man, tho' ne'er sae poor,
    Is king o' man for a' that. — BURNS.

11. The old oaken bucket, the iron-bound bucket,
    The moss-covered bucket, which hangs in the well.

WOODWORTH.

12. No one minds what Jeffrey says, — it is not more than a week ago that I heard him speak disrespectfully of the Equator. — SYDNEY SMITH.

LESSON CXXI.

COMPOSITION.

A NIGHTINGALE'S MISTAKE.

A nightingale made a mistake!
   She sang a few notes out of tune;
Her heart was ready to break,
   And she hid from the moon.
She wrung her claws, poor thing,
   But was far too proud to weep:
So she tucked her head under her wing,
   And pretended to be asleep.

A lark, arm in arm with a thrush,
  Came sauntering up to the place;
The nightingale felt herself flush,
  Though feathers hid her face.
She knew they had heard her song,
  She felt them snigger and sneer,
She thought that this life was too long,
  And wished she could skip a year.

"O nightingale!" cooed a dove;
  "O nightingale! what's the use?
You bird of beauty and love,
  Why behave like a goose?
Don't skulk away from our sight
  Like a common, contemptible fowl;
You bird of joy and delight,
  Why behave like an owl?

"Only think of all you have done,
  Only think of all you can do;
A false note is really fun
  From such a bird as you!
Lift up your proud little crest,
  Open your musical beak;
Other birds have to do their best,
  You need only speak!"

The nightingale shyly took
  Her head from under her wing,
And giving the dove a look,
  Straightway began to sing.

There was never a bird could pass,
The night was divinely calm,
And the people stood on the grass
To hear that wonderful psalm.

The nightingale did not care,
She only sang to the skies;
Her song ascended there,
And there she fixed her eyes.
Of the people who stood below
Very little she knew;
So clear did the sweet sound flow,
That the angels listened too. — INGELOW.

WRITTEN EXERCISE.

*After studying carefully "A Nightingale's Mistake,"
make an outline by answering the following questions: —*

1. How did the nightingale feel when she realized that she
had sung a few notes out of tune?

2. What did she think of life when she thought her mistake
had been noticed by a lark and a thrush?

3. How did the dove try to comfort the nightingale?

4. What was the result of the dove's argument?

*With the outline before you, try to express in prose every
thought of the poem.*

*Compare your story with the original, and improve your
work by adding new sentences.*

*Read your composition four times to correct errors in
grammar, spelling, punctuation, and capitalization.*

LESSON CXXII.

THE INDICATIVE MODE.

In the preceding lessons on tenses and person and number, all the verbs are in the indicative mode.

The formation of the various tenses of the indicative mode is further shown below. Root means the simple or present tense form of the verb. Past T. means the past tense form of the verb. Past P. means the past participle.

PRESENT TENSE.

SINGULAR.	PLURAL.
1. I (Root).	We (Root).
2. Thou (Root) est.	You (Root).
3. He (Root) s.	They (Root).

PAST TENSE.

SINGULAR.	PLURAL.
1. I (Past T.).	We (Past T.).
2. Thou (Past T.) st.	You (Past T.).
3. He (Past T.).	They (Past T.).

FUTURE TENSE.

SINGULAR.	PLURAL.
1. I shall or will (Root).	We shall or will (Root).
2. Thou wilt or shalt (Root).	You will or shall (Root).
3. He will or shall (Root).	They will or shall (Root).

PRESENT PERFECT TENSE.

SINGULAR.	PLURAL.
1. I have (Past P.).	We have (Past P.).
2. Thou hast (Past P.).	You have (Past P.).
3. He has (Past P.).	They have (Past P.).

PAST PERFECT TENSE.

SINGULAR.	PLURAL.
1. I had (Past P.).	We had (Past P.).
2. Thou hadst (Past P.).	You had (Past P.).
3. He had (Past P.).	They had (Past P.).

FUTURE PERFECT TENSE.

SINGULAR.

1. I shall or will have (Past P.).
2. Thou wilt or shalt have (Past P.).
3. He will or shall have (Past P.).

PLURAL.

1. We shall or will have (Past P.).
2. You will or shall have (Past P.).
3. They will or shall have (Past P.).

Read through the above conjugation, substituting the present tense of some verb wherever the word *Root* occurs, the past tense of the same verb wherever *Past T.* occurs, and the past participle of the same verb wherever *Past P.* occurs.

The pronoun of the second person plural, *you*, is now generally used for the second person singular, *thou*, and with it the verb in the plural form. Thus we say, *You have given*, or *You will have given*, instead of *Thou hast given*, or *Thou wilt have given*, to one person, or to a number.

Shall in the first person is simply future in its meaning; it simply foretells. In the second and third persons, it promises or threatens. *Will* in the first person promises or threatens, and in the second and third simply foretells.

I shall go, or *we shall go*, means that it is our expectation, without any particular desire or will, to go.

I will go, or *we will go*, means that the speaker intends to go, even in spite of opposition.

You will go, or *he will go*, means that the person spoken to or of will in the future go; but

You shall go, or *he shall go*, means that the speaker intends to help or threaten the person spoken to or of to go.

Write the conjugation of the following verbs in the indicative mode: —

choose	forsake
fade	fly
go	spend
run	put
flow	succeed

LESSON CXXIII.

CHOICE OF WORDS.

1. I shall be very glad to see you.
2. You will be late at school.
3. The teacher will not excuse us.

Mention the verbs, and state the time each expresses. Name the subjects, and state the person of each.

1. I will meet you at half-after eight.
2. You shall have my book to-morrow.
3. Henry shall not use my knife again.

What does the speaker promise in the first sentence? In the second and third, what does the speaker control? What verb expresses the determination of the speaker?

To express futurity, use *shall* in the first person, and *will* in the second and third.

To express promise, purpose, determination, obligation, or inevitable action which the speaker means to control, use *will* in the first person, and *shall* in the second and third.

Write three sentences, using shall *to express simple future action.*

I shall go to the park to-morrow.

Write three sentences, using will *to make a promise.*

I will meet you at the south gate.

Write three sentences, using shall *to express inevitable action over which the speaker has control.*

He shall not see my rabbits.

Explain the use of shall *and* will *in the following examples : —*

I will die ere she shall grieve. — WITHER.

The pound of flesh which I demand of him
Is dearly bought, is mine, and I will have it.

.   .   .   .

I stand for judgment; answer, shall I have it?

SHAKESPEARE.

This child I to myself will take;
She shall be mine, and I will make
   A lady of my own.

.   .   .   .

The stars of midnight shall be dear
To her; and she shall lean her ear
In many a secret place
Where rivulets dance their wayward round,
And beauty born of murmuring sound
   Shall pass into her face. — WORDSWORTH.

In corresponding cases, *should* and *would* are used in the same manner as *shall* and *will*.

Copy the following sentences, filling the blanks with the proper words : —

1. I —— be pleased to accept your kind invitation.
2. I think you —— enjoy playing tennis.
3. He said he —— be sorry to lose the ball.
4. I —— not lend him my skates.
5. You —— not be selfish.
6. The teacher —— be obeyed.
7. Every boy —— read " Plutarch's Lives."
8. Henry Clay said, " I —— rather be right than be President."
9. In speaking of the Indians, Lincoln said he —— not rest until they had justice.
10. You —— have heard the Hamelin people
   Ringing the bells till they rocked the steeple.

In which of the above sentences does the verb **express the** determination of the speaker?

Which verbs express obligation?

Which verbs express simple future action?

Construct six original sentences illustrating the correct use of should.

Explain the use of would *and* should *in the following quotations :* —

I.   A dreary place would be this earth,
            Were there no little people in it;
        The song of life would lose its mirth,
            Were there no children to begin it.

WHITTIER.

2.   Teach me half the gladness,
            That thy brain must know,
        Such harmonious madness
            From my lips would flow,
    The world should listen then as I am listening now.

SHELLEY.

3. A man should never be ashamed to own he has been in the wrong, which is but saying in other words that he is wiser to-day than he was yesterday. — POPE.

LESSON CXXIV.

THE POTENTIAL MODE.

The potential mode has four tenses. They are, with their auxiliaries or signs, —

Present Tense: may, can, or must.

Past Tense: might, could, would, or should.

Present Perfect Tense: may have, can have, must have.

Past Perfect Tense: might have, could have, would have, should have.

The forms of the verb in the first and third persons singular, and the first, second, and third persons, plural, are the same, and may be summarized thus : —

Present Tense, —
  I, he, we, you, or they
    may, can, or must (Root).
Past Tense, —
  I, he, we, you, or they
    might, could, would, or should (Root).
Present Perfect Tense, —
  I, he, we, you, or they
    may have, can have, or must have (Past P.).
Past Perfect Tense, —
  I, he, we, you, or they
    might have, could have, would have, or should have (Past P.).

In the second person singular, *st* is added to the auxiliaries ; thus, —

Present Tense, —
  Thou mayst, canst, or must (Root).
Past Tense, —
  Thou mightst, couldst, wouldst, or shouldst (Root).
Present Perfect Tense, —
  Thou mayst have, canst have, or must have (Past P.).
Past Perfect Tense, —
  Thou mightst have, couldst have, wouldst have, or shouldst have (Past P.).

Write out a conjugation of two or more verbs (selected by teacher) in the potential mode, using the form given in Lesson CXVIII.

LESSON CXXV.

CHOICE OF WORDS.

1. May I speak to Grace?
2. Can you play the piano?

Which verb **asks** permission? Which inquires concerning ability?

Write ten sentences showing your power to discriminate between the following words : —

may	might
can	could

Explain each use of may, can, might, *and* could *in the following quotations : —*

1. We may build more splendid habitations,
    Fill our rooms with paintings and with sculptures ;
    But we cannot
    Buy with gold the old associations. — LONGFELLOW.

2. How little thou canst tell
    How much in thee is good or well ! — CLOUGH.

3. We might all of us give far more than we do without being a bit the worse.

4. When Duty whispers low, Thou must,
    The youth replies, I can. — EMERSON.

5. One could wander for miles through this forest without meeting a person.

6. When I turned again to look for the bird, I could not see it.

7.   I found this,
      That of goods I could not miss
      If I fell within the line. ―― EMERSON.

8. One impulse from a vernal wood
        May teach you more of man,
      Of moral evil and of good,
        Than all the sages can. ― WORDSWORTH.

LESSON CXXVI.

COMPOSITION. ― DESCRIPTION.

THE SPARROW.

The sparrows are all meek and lowly birds. They are of the grass, the fences, the low bushes, the weedy wayside places. Theirs are the quaint and lullaby songs of childhood. The whitethroat has a timid, tremulous strain, that issues from the low bushes, or from behind the fence where its cradle is hid. The song sparrow modulates its simple ditty as softly as the lining of its own nest.

What pretty nests, too, the sparrows build! Can anything be more exquisite than a sparrow's nest under a grassy or mossy bank? What care the bird has taken not to disturb one straw, or spear of grass, or thread of moss!

BURROUGHS.

Study John Burroughs's account of sparrows. Note what he says of their haunts, of their songs, of their nests. Write a similar description of the robin.

1. Tell where you have seen robins.
2. Describe the robin's song.
3. Tell what you can of the robin's nest.

LESSON CXXVII.

THE VERB BE.

INDICATIVE MODE.

PRESENT TENSE.

SINGULAR.	PLURAL.
1. I am.	We are.
2. Thou art.	You are.
3. He is.	They are.

PAST TENSE.

SINGULAR.	PLURAL.
1. I was.	We were.
2. Thou wast.	You were.
3. He was.	They were.

FUTURE TENSE.

SINGULAR.	PLURAL.
1. I shall or will be.	We shall or will be.
2. Thou wilt or shalt be.	You will or shall be.
3. He will or shall be.	They will or shall be.

PRESENT PÉRFECT TENSE.

SINGULAR.	PLURAL.
1. I have been.	We have been.
2. Thou hast been.	You have been.
3. He has been.	They have been.

PAST PERFECT TENSE.

SINGULAR.	PLURAL.
1. I had been.	We had been.
2. Thou hadst been.	You had been.
3. He had been.	They had been

FUTURE PERFECT TENSE.

SINGULAR.

1. I shall or will have been.
2. Thou wilt or shalt have been.
3. He will or shall have been.

PLURAL.

1. We shall or will have been.
2. You will or shall have been.
3. They will or shall have been.

POTENTIAL MODE.

PRESENT TENSE.

SINGULAR.	PLURAL.
1. I may be.	We may be.
2. Thou mayst be.	You may be.
3. He may be.	They may be.

PAST TENSE.

SINGULAR.	PLURAL.
1. I might be.	We might be.
2. Thou mightst be.	You might be.
3. He might be.	They might be.

PRESENT PERFECT TENSE.

SINGULAR.	PLURAL.
1. I may have been.	We may have been.
2. Thou mayst have been.	You may have been.
3. He may have been.	They may have been.

PAST PERFECT TENSE.

SINGULAR.	PLURAL.
1. I might have been.	We might have been.
2. Thou mightst have been.	You might have been.
3. He might have been.	They might have been.

In the present and present perfect tenses of the potential mode, the auxiliaries *can* and *must* may be used instead of *may*. In the past and past perfect tenses, the auxiliaries *could, would*, and *should*, may be used instead of *might*.

Compare the conjugation of the verb be *with that of* give *in Lesson CXIX., and of the models in Lessons CXXII. and CXXXIV.*

Be prepared to recite any tense of the verb be, *using either auxiliary in the potential mode as directed, or to give any person and number of any tense.*

LESSON CXXVIII.

THE PROGRESSIVE FORM OF VERBS.

INDICATIVE MODE.

TENSE.	SIMPLE FORM.	PROGRESSIVE FORM.
Present.	I write.	I am writing.
Past.	I wrote.	I was writing.
Future.	I shall write.	I shall be writing.

Pres. Per.	I have written.	I have been writing.
Past Per.	I had written.	I had been writing.
Fut. Per.	I shall have written.	I shall have been writing.

Verbs like *am writing, was writing, shall be writing,* etc., which represent the action as continuing at the time indicated by the verb, are said to be in the PROGRESSIVE FORM.

What is the difference in meaning between *I write* and *I am writing? I wrote* and *I was writing?* Compare each simple form with its corresponding progressive.

If the word *writing* were omitted from each of the above verbs, you would have remaining the different tenses of what verb?

Writing is the present participle of the verb *write* (see Lesson CVIII.).

The present participle of any verb is formed by annexing *ing* to its present tense or root.

The progressive form of a verb in any tense is formed by adding its present participle to the verb *be* in that tense.

Write the potential mode, progressive form, of the verb write.

Write the numbers and tenses of the following verbs as indicated below.

	VERB.	MODE.	FORM.	TENSE.	NUMBER.
1.	Break	Indicative	Simple	Past Per.	Singular
2.	Burn	"	Progressive	Future	Plural
3.	Buy	Potential	Simple	Present	Singular
4.	Build	Indicative	Simple	Fut. Per.	Plural
5.	Cut	Potential	Progressive	Past	Singular
6.	Bleed	"	Simple	Pres. Per.	Plural
7.	Draw	Indicative	Progressive	Pres. Per.	Singular
8.	Drive	"	Simple	Fut. Per.	Plural
9.	Dwell	Potential	Simple	Past Per.	Singular
10.	Bring	"	Progressive	Past	Plural

LESSON CXXIX.

STUDY OF SELECTION.

EVANGELINE.

Fair was she to behold, that maiden of seventeen sum-
mers.

Black were her eyes as the berry that grows on the thorn
by the wayside,

Black, yet how softly they gleamed beneath the brown
shade of her tresses!

. . . .

Fairer was she when, on Sunday morn, while the bell
from its turret

Sprinkled with holy sounds the air, as the priest with his
hyssop

Sprinkles the congregation, and scatters blessings upon
them,

Down the long street she passed, with her chaplet of beads
and her missal,

Wearing her Norman cap, and her kirtle of blue, and the
earrings

Brought in the olden time from France, and since, as an
heirloom,

Handed down from mother to child, through long generations.

But a celestial brightness — a more ethereal beauty —

Shone on her face and encircled her form, when, after
confession,

Homeward serenely she walked with God's benediction
upon her. — LONGFELLOW.

How old was Evangeline? What color were her eyes? With what does the poet compare them? What color was her hair? What did she wear on Sunday? When was she most beautiful? Is beauty of expression more attractive than beauty of features? What do you understand by the last line? Is nobility of character the greatest personal charm?

Write an account of some person you know, describing the strongest points of individuality, — height, form, features; peculiarities of dress, manner, gait, speech, and expression; occupation, habits, traits of character; influence, usefulness.

LESSON CXXX.

CHOICE OF WORDS.

Construct sentences to illustrate the use of the following words: —

APOLOGY. EXCUSE.	An apology is dictated by a sense of justice; an excuse is offered in extenuation of a fault.
CONDUCT. BEHAVIOR.	Good conduct will include right behavior as a part of it.
EFFORT. ENDEAVOR. STRUGGLE.	Effort is a putting forth of strength, physical or mental; endeavor is prolonged effort; struggle is effort exerted against opposition.
PERIL. DANGER. JEOPARDY.	Peril implies destruction; danger implies loss; jeopardy applies to things of value, as well as to persons.

LESSON CXXXI.

ACTIVE AND PASSIVE VOICE.

1. The grocer sells strawberries.
2. The boy will bring the book.
3. The trolley car killed a man.

In the first sentence, the verb *sells* represents the subject *grocer* as doing something to the object *strawberries*. In like manner, the verb *will bring* expresses that its subject *boy* acts and the object *book* does not. The verb *killed* represents its subject *car* as acting on the object *man*.

A transitive verb like *sells*, *will bring*, or *killed*, that represents its subject as acting on an object, is said to be in the active voice, and is called a TRANSITIVE ACTIVE VERB.

We may rewrite the sentences, making the object of each verb stand in the place of the subject.

4. Strawberries are sold by the grocer.
5. The book will be brought by the boy.
6. A man was killed by the trolley car.

Although the form of the sentences seems much changed, we know that the facts are not.

In both the first and fourth sentences, the *grocer* acts, the *strawberries* receive the action. In the first sentence, the object receives the action; in the fourth, the subject receives it. In the same manner, by comparing the second and fifth sentences and the third and sixth, we find that, in the second and third, the subject acts; in the fifth and sixth, the subject receives the action. Because the subjects in such sentences as the fourth, fifth, and sixth, are represented not as acting but as being passive, their predicates are called PASSIVE VERBS.

A verb like *are sold, will be brought,* or *was killed,* which represents its subject as receiving the action, is said to be in the passive voice, and is called a TRANSITIVE PASSIVE VERB.

The passive form of the verb represents the subject as receiving that which is done.

In the first three sentences above, those having active transitive verbs for predicates, the actors, *grocer, boy, car,* are more prominent than the objects. In the other three sentences, those having passive transitive verbs for predicates, the objects become more prominent and the actors less so.

In the sentence, —

The British hanged Nathan Hale as a spy,

the actors, *the British,* are more prominent. By making the predicate passive, we may avoid mentioning them, —

Nathan Hale was hanged as a spy.

All active transitive verbs may take the passive transitive form.

A few intransitive verbs, when they have united to them a preposition, may take the passive form; as, *They had been laughed at, He is well thought of.*

The passive form of a verb in any tense is formed by adding its past participle to the verb *be* in that tense.

Rewrite the following sentences, changing the verbs in the active transitive form to the passive transitive form, and those in the passive transitive form to the active transitive form : —

    1. Pharaoh and his host pursued them.
    2. The lightning shattered the oak.

3. One bad example spoils many good precepts.

4. Shall we gather strength by irresolution and inaction? — PATRICK HENRY.

5. Our buskins on our feet we drew.

6.   What scenes of woe
Are witnessed by that red and struggling beam!

7. Ambition breaks the ties of blood, and forgets the obligations of gratitude. — SCOTT.

8. Deep in the grove, beneath the secret shade,
A various wreath of odorous flowers she made;
Gay mottled pinks, and jonquils sweet, she chose,
The violet blue, sweet thyme, and flaunting rose.

COLLINS.

9. A poor man served by thee shall make thee rich;
A sick man helped by thee shall make thee
   strong;
Thou shalt be served thyself by every sense
Of service which thou renderest.

MRS. BROWNING.

LESSON CXXXII.

THE EMPHATIC FORM OF VERBS.

INDICATIVE MODE.

PRESENT TENSE.

SINGULAR.	PLURAL.
1. I do write.	We do write.
2. Thou dost write.	You do write.
3. He does write.	They do write.

PAST TENSE.

SINGULAR.	PLURAL.
1. I did write.	We did write.
2. Thou didst write.	You did write.
3. He did write.	They did write.

What is the difference between the simple form *I write* and the emphatic form *I do write?* Between *I wrote* and *I did write?* What form of the principal verb *write* is used with *do* and *did* to make the emphatic form?

The auxiliary *do* is used with the root of a verb to form the PRESENT TENSE EMPHATIC, and the auxiliary *did* to form the PAST TENSE EMPHATIC.

The emphatic form can be used only in these two tenses.

Write sentences, using the following verbs in each of the three forms, — simple, progressive, and emphatic: —

believe	choose
pursue	control
judge	drown
estimate	understand
publish	dispose

LESSON CXXXIII.

COMPOSITION.

A MORNING INCIDENT.

[Scene: Morning on the bridge cars at the hour when the better class of money-seekers, both employer and employed, are on their way from Brooklyn homes to New York offices.]

Just before the bell rang to start the train, a frail man, evidently a German, came panting into the car, carrying a large bundle of overcoats carefully pinned in a piece of black muslin. The linings of the coats were folded out-side, and were of shining silk. The man carrying the coats wore a thin cotton coat, in which he shivered as the cold air swept through the open door.

The brakeman, a frowning giant, bounded into the car, and in a voice loud enough to attract everybody's atten-tion, shouted, "Get along out of here with your bundle. Can't have ye blocking up the whole car!" In sheer fright the poor bewildered man looked about. Language spoke to deaf ears; but the gesture said, "Go!" It could not mean that he must leave the car; for how would he ever get over to New York with the coats, if not allowed to ride — they were so heavy! Bending under the heavy load, he went out on the platform, casting an appealing glance backward as he went through the door. He crossed to the front platform of the car behind, and holding the coats lengthwise, so that the only glimpse to be seen was the dented and shabby hat and the brown, misshapen boots, with the strained wrists, and grimy, thin hands, he took his position against the door frame. Some smothered remark from the tyrant in blue coat and brass buttons brought the white, frightened face in sight; but the tighter clutching of the hands and the shrinking out of sight of the rest of the man behind the satin-lined coats was the only result.

At this point, a new actor appeared on the scene. From about the center of the car, a magnificent specimen of American manhood stood up leisurely. From the top of the shining silk hat to the toes of the shining boots was written righteous prosperity. One gloved hand held the paper he had been reading, with a grasp that told of the muscular power that years of healthful living had preserved and developed. He glanced neither to right nor left, but, with flashing eyes fastened on the brakeman's back, went through the door, and, standing directly in front of the tailor, tapped him gently on the shoulder, saying pleasantly, " My friend, put your bundle on this gate," at the same time pointing to the closed gate on the inner side of the car platform. A frightened glance was flashed into the speaker's face, and then at the scowling brakeman; but the tailor did not move. Crowding the paper into his pocket, the new actor in this quickly moving drama took the bundle of coats, and, with a kindly " Stand here " to the tailor, rested them on the gate. The tailor, with a face of smiles and relief, took his place beside the bundle. The new protector, with his silk-lined coat thrown back, a rather set look in his face, the tips of the fingers of one hand inside of his trousers' pockets, faced the cowed and silenced brakeman, his whole attitude bringing to mind the now historical sentence in the annals of New York politics, " Well, what are you going to do about it ? "

At the New York end of the bridge, the tailor and his friend were the last to leave the platform. As they parted at the head of the stairs, the gloved hand touched the rim of the silk hat to the little bent man who was going down the stairs. A face radiant answered the salute; but the burdened hands made its return impossible. Was it imagination ? The air seemed eloquent with these words : —

> " The Holy Supper is kept indeed
> In whatso we share with another's need."

WRITTEN EXERCISES.

After reading thoughtfully the above extract, try to describe some similar incident that you have witnessed.

If you do not recall a kind deed, write a brief newspaper article on one of the following subjects: —

Almost an Accident.

A Frightened Horse.

A Careless Wheelman.

An Hour in a Railway Station.

How we Caught a Burglar.

The Effects of a Recent Storm.

HINTS.

1. Choose a point of view.

2. Forecast the whole story before you begin to write.

3. Remember that your story should be probable, and should have a purpose.

4. Relate particulars, not merely because they occurred at a certain time, but because they grew out of preceding particulars.

LESSON CXXXIV.

AUXILIARY VERBS.

Verbs like *do, did, have, may, might,* etc., when prefixed to a principal verb to form compound tenses, are called AUXILIARY VERBS. They are as follows, and as auxiliaries have the form of only the present and past tenses, except *be*, which is used as an auxiliary in all its parts.

Present.	do	have	shall	will	may	can	must
Past.	did	had	should	would	might	could	——

Be, do, and *have* are also principal verbs, and take others before them in their compound tenses ; as, —

I shall be early.

You may have an apple.

He may have done wrong.

They have had a sail.

A verb is made to deny by using it with the word *not;* as, —

I will give.   I will not give.

The negative *not* is placed after the verb in the simple form ;
as, —   He thought not;

and after the first auxiliary in the compound forms ; as, —

You did not look.

They would not stop.

We are not going.

Write sentences illustrative of the uses of the auxiliary verbs.

LESSON CXXXV.

INTERROGATIVE SENTENCES.

INDICATIVE MODE.

TENSE.	COMMON FORM.	PROGRESSIVE FORM.
Present.	Do you write?	Are you writing?
Past.	Did you write?	Were you writing?
Future.	Will you write?	Will you be writing?
Pres. Per.	Have you written?	Have you been writing?
Past Per.	Had you written?	Had you been writing?
Fut. Per.	Shall you have written?	Shall you have been writing?

POTENTIAL MODE.

TENSE.	COMMON FORM.	PROGRESSIVE FORM.
Present.	Can you write?	Can you be writing?
Past.	Could you write?	Could you be writing?
Pres. Per.	Can you have written?	Can you have been writing?
Past Per.	Could you have written?	Could you have been writing?

By comparing the above forms with declarative sentences in Lesson XI., you will see that in interrogative sentences, the verb is used in both the common and the progressive form.

1. When the verb has an auxiliary, the subject is placed between the auxiliary and the verb.

2. When the verb has more than one auxiliary, the subject is placed after the first auxiliary.

3. In the present and the past indicative, the emphatic instead of the common form of the verb is generally used. The simple form of the verb is sometimes used in interrogative sentences in the present and past tenses ; as, —

Seest thou a man diligent in his business?

When an interrogative sentence is negative, the negative is placed immediately after the subject ; as, —

Is it not excellent to have the strength of a giant?
Are you not going to the mountains this summer?

Only the indicative and potential modes can be used in interrogative sentences.

In the following exercises, change the interrogative sentences into declarative sentences, and the declarative into interrogative : —

1. See you yon light on the southern headland?
2. The maple on the hillside has lost its bright green.
3. Can you hear the roaring of the breakers?
4. 'Tis liberty alone that gives the flowers of fleeting life their luster and perfume.
5. Was there ever a better charity sermon preached in the world than Dickens's "Christmas Carol"?

6. I would not enter on my list of friends
The man who needlessly sets foot upon a worm.
COWPER.

7. Know ye the land where the cypress and myrtle
Are emblems of deeds that are done in their clime?
BYRON.

8. In this past year's diary, is there any precious day noted on which you have made a new friend? — THACKERAY.

9. Stillest streams oft water fairest meadows.

10. All the kings of the nations lie in glory,
Cased in cedar, and shut in a sacred gloom.
INGELOW.

11. Down swept the chill winds from the mountain peak.
LOWELL.

12. Are the blossoms singing? Or is all this humming sound the music of bees? — BEECHER.

13. Who is losing? who is winning? are they far, or
come they near?
Look abroad, and tell us, sister, whither rolls the
storm we hear. — WHITTIER.

LESSON CXXXVI.

THE SUBJUNCTIVE MODE.

The subjunctive mode is that form of a verb used in a subordinate clause to express something merely thought of as conditional or doubtful, and generally to imply that the contrary is true ; as, —

If I were you, I would try to do better.
Though he slay me, yet will I trust him.

The subjunctive mode is generally preceded by the conjunctions *if, though, lest,* etc. The sign is omitted when the verb stands before the subject ; as, —

Were I in his place, *for,* If I were in his place.

The subjunctive mode is sometimes used in the expression of a strong desire ; thus, —

I wish I were at home.

Oh that he were here!

Notice, however, that these sentences express a wish for something not to be attained.

The subjunctive mode is not used to express a mere uncertainty ; thus we say, —

If he is here, ask him to come to me; *not,* If he be here.

If he was sick, he surely did not go ; *not,* If he were sick.

This mode, as its name indicates, is always dependent on another verb, expressed or implied ; but every tense of the indicative and the potential mode may be used in conditional clauses.

The forms peculiar to the subjunctive are found only in the present tense of active verbs and the present and past tenses of the verb *be,* and of verbs in the passive voice.

Observe the forms of the verbs as given below in the subjunctive and the indicative. Notice in which persons, numbers, and tenses the two modes differ.

THE VERB *HEAR.*

SUBJUNCTIVE MODE.		INDICATIVE MODE.	
PRESENT TENSE.		PRESENT TENSE.	
SINGULAR.	PLURAL.	SINGULAR.	PLURAL.
1. If I hear.	If we hear.	I hear.	We hear.
2. If thou hear.	If you hear.	Thou hearest.	You hear.
3. If he hear.	If they hear.	He hears.	They hear.

PAST TENSE.		PAST TENSE.	
SINGULAR.	PLURAL.	SINGULAR.	PLURAL.
1. If I heard.	If we heard.	I heard.	We heard.
2. If thou heard.	If you heard.	Thou heardest.	You heard.
3. If he heard.	If they heard.	He heard.	They heard.

THE VERB *BE*.

SUBJUNCTIVE MODE.		INDICATIVE MODE.	
PRESENT TENSE.		PRESENT TENSE.	
SINGULAR.	PLURAL.	SINGULAR.	PLURAL.
1. If I be.	If we be.	I am.	We are.
2. If thou be.	If you be.	Thou art.	You are.
3. If he be.	If they be.	He is.	They are.

PAST TENSE.		PAST TENSE.	
SINGULAR.	PLURAL.	SINGULAR.	PLURAL.
1. If I were.	If we were.	I was.	We were.
2. If thou wert.	If you were.	Thou wast.	You were.
3. If he were.	If they were.	He was.	They were.

When the verb is placed before the subject, the *if* is omitted ; as, Were I sure, I would tell you.

Explain the use of the subjunctive in the following sentences : —

1. If he were more courteous, I should like him better.

2. Should it rain, I will not go.

3. I wish that my mother were here.

4. If he be diligent, he will succeed.

5. If he had been wise, he would have accepted the offer.

6. If it were ever so fine, I would not buy it.

7. Beware, lest thou be led into temptation.

8. Let him that thinketh he standeth take heed lest he fall.

9. Oh that thou wert my brother!

10. Oh had I the wings of a dove!

11. If it were done when 'tis done, then 'twere well It were done quickly.

12. Were gold more abundant, it would be of less value.

LESSON CXXXVII.

THE IMPERATIVE MODE.

Verbs in the imperative mode are used only in imperative sentences, and are always in the second person and the present tense.

The form is the same for both the singular and the plural number.

That form is the simple or root form of the verb (see Lesson CXXII.).

The subject of a verb in the imperative mode is usually the pronoun *you*, either expressed or understood. *Thou* and *ye* are used in solemn and emphatic forms.

Write ten sentences, using the following verbs in the imperative mode : —

rest	ring
stand	praise
make	hide
think	sweep
come	count

LESSON CXXXVIII.

STUDY OF A DESCRIPTION.

THE GARRET OF THE GAMBREL-ROOFED HOUSE.

It has a flooring of laths with ridges of mortar squeezed up between them, (which if you tread on you will go to — the Lord have mercy on you! — where *will* you go to?) the same being crossed by narrow bridges of boards, on which you may put your feet, but with fear and trembling. Above you and around you are beams and joists, on some of which you may see, when the light is let in, the marks of the conchoidal clippings of the broadax, showing the rude way in which the timber was shaped as it came, full of sap, from the neighboring forest. It is a realm of darkness and thick dust, and shroud-like cobwebs, and dead things they wrap in their gray folds. For a garret is like a seashore, where wrecks are thrown up, and slowly go to pieces. There is the cradle which the old man you just remember was rocked in ; there is the ruin of the bedstead he died on, and that ugly slanting contrivance used to put under his pillow in the days when his breath came hard ; there is his old chair with both arms gone, symbol of the desolate time when he had nothing earthly left to lean on ; there is the large wooden reel which the deacon sent the minister's lady, who thanked him graciously, and twirled it smilingly, and in fitting season bowed it out decently to the limbo of troublesome conveniences. And there are old leather portmanteaus, like stranded porpoises, their mouths gaping in gaunt hunger for the food with which they used to be gorged to repletion; and the old brass andirons, waiting until time shall revenge them on their paltry substitutes, and they shall have their own again, and bring with them the forestick and backlog of ancient days; and the empty churn with its idle dasher, and the brown, shaky old spinning wheel, which was running, it may be, in the days when they were hanging Salem witches. — HOLMES.

WRITTEN EXERCISE.

Give a similar description of a room you have seen.

1. Locate the room.

2. Describe its general appearance.

3. Reproduce the various objects by homely illustrations and familiar comparisons.

4. Choose one of the things in which you are most interested, and write out its history.

LESSON CXXXIX.

SOME VERBS ALIKE IN SOUND.

PRESENT.	PAST.	PRES. PART.	PAST PART.
lay	laid	laying	laid
lie	lay	lying	lain
set	set	setting	set
sit	sat	sitting	sat
raise	raised	raising	raised
rise	rose	rising	risen
see	saw	seeing	seen
saw	sawed	sawing	sawed *or* sawn

Lay is a transitive verb, and requires an object.

Lie, meaning to rest, is intransitive, and does not require an object.

Present.
{ Lay the scythe on the grass.
Let the scythe lie on the grass.

Past.
{ He laid the scythe on the grass.
The scythe lay on the grass.

Pres. P.
{ He is laying the scythe on the grass.
The scythe is lying on the grass.

Past P.
{ He has laid the scythe on the grass.
The scythe has lain on the grass.

Set is a transitive verb, and requires an object.

Sit is an intransitive verb, and does not require an object.

Present.
{ I set a chair by the window.
I sit in the chair.

Past.
{ I set a chair by the window.
I sat in the chair.

Pres. P.
{ I am setting a chair by the window.
I am sitting in the chair.

Past P.
{ I have set a chair by the window.
I have sat in the chair.

Raise, meaning to lift, is regular and transitive.

Rise, meaning to ascend, is irregular and intransitive.

See, meaning to perceive, is irregular and transitive.

Saw, meaning to cut, is regular or irregular and transitive.

1. *Write eight sentences discriminating between* raise *and* rise. *Follow the form given above for* lay *and* lie.

2. *Write eight sentences discriminating between* see *and* saw *in each tense.*

Copy the following sentences, filling the blanks with suitable words : —

1. Lake Ontario —— between New York and Canada.
2. The rain —— —— the dust.
3. I found a horseshoe —— in the road.
4. Mother has —— down to rest.
5. The snow will not —— long on the ground.
6. Do not leave your hat —— on a chair.
7. Many poets have been —— to rest in Westminster.
8. Will you —— aside your work?
9. The autumn leaves —— scattered on the ground.
10. The men are —— a concrete pavement.

Copy and complete the following sentences : —

1. We —— and talked until the night,
   Descending filled the room.
2. The Arab's foe, having ever broken bread with him, may safely —— beneath his tents.
3. The robin —— on her nest.
4. On Arbor Day our class —— out two trees.
5. Where do you —— in church?
6. You may —— the table for four.
7. Still —— the schoolhouse by the road,
   A ragged beggar sunning.
8. The hilt of his sword was —— with gems.
9. The sun was —— as we turned homeward.
10. Slowly and disconsolately little Marygold —— down.
11. He goes on Sunday to the church,
    And —— among his boys.
12. Robert has been —— traps for partridges.

LESSON CXL.

THE AGREEMENT OF THE VERB.

PERSON AND NUMBER.

In Lessons CXIX., CXXII., and CXXVII., you have seen that a verb changes its form on account of the person and number of its subject.

1. *Est,* or some contraction of it, is usually annexed to a verb, or to one of its auxiliaries, when the subject is in the second person singular; as, *Thou hearest, Thou mayst go.*

2. *S* is usually annexed to a verb in the present tense of the indicative mode, when the subject is in the third person singular; as, *The child reads.*

3. *Has* as an auxiliary is used only in the third person singular of the present perfect tense; as, *He has listened.*

4. The verb *be* has seven different forms in the present and past tenses of the indicative mode: *I am, thou art, he is, we are, I was, thou wast, we were.*

A verb must agree with its subject in person and number.

When the subject is a collective noun standing for many considered as one whole, the verb must be in the singular; as, —

> The army invades the country.
> A committee of three was appointed.

When the subject is a collective noun standing for many considered as individuals, the verb must be in the plural; as, —

> The audience were much pleased.
> The committee were unanimous.

In the following sentences explain the agreement of the verbs with their subjects. Point out the objects of the prepositions.

1. Congress has adjourned.
2. Neither precept nor discipline is so forcible as example.
3. Many blessings has the world derived from those whose origin was humble.
4. Neither Charles nor Henry knows his lesson.
5. Not only the father, but the son also, was involved in the disaster.
6. The long row of poplars was luxuriantly green.
7. Star after star appears on high.
8. There is Concord, and Lexington, and Bunker Hill — and they will remain forever. — WEBSTER.
9. The mansion, with its groves and gardens, extends over a large area.
10. Continued exertion, and not hasty efforts, leads to success.
11. His praise, ye winds, that from four quarters blow,
    Breathe soft or loud. — MILTON.
12. Every house was burned; and every man, woman, and child was killed.
13. The seasons, each in its turn, cheer the soul.
14. The sleigh, as well as the horses, was much injured.
15. The roses and myrtles bloomed unchilled on the verge of the avalanche. — MACAULAY.
16. The joyful parents, with Perseus and Andromeda, repaired to the palace, where a banquet was spread for them, and all was joy and festivity. — BULFINCH.

LESSON CXLI.

TWO OR MORE SUBJECTS.

1. Maud and Estelle are reading.
2. Maud or Estelle is reading.

What are the subjects of the verb *are reading?* Is each
subject singular, or plural? Is the verb singular, or plural in form?
By what are the subjects connected? Does this conjunction
make us consider the two subjects together, or separately? Taken
together, have they a singular significance, or a plural significance?

**When a verb has two or more subjects connected by *and*, it
must agree with them in the plural number.**

Several singular subjects, though connected by *and*, if preceded
by *each*, *every*, or *no*, take a verb in the singular ; as, —

Every flower and every shrub was torn from its place.

When the several subjects connected by *and* denote only one
person or thing, the verb is singular ; as, —

The hue and cry of the country pursues him.
The philosopher and poet was banished from his
country.

In the second sentence at the head of the lesson, by what
are the subjects connected? Does this conjunction make us
consider the subjects together, or separately? Is the verb singular,
or plural in form?

**When a verb has two or more singular subjects connected by
or or *nor*, it must agree with them in the singular number.**

If two or more subjects connected by *or* or *nor* differ in person or number, the verb should generally agree with the one next to it ; as, —

Either my uncle or my cousins are coming.

When a singular and a plural subject are used, the plural should be placed last.

It is better, however, to avoid such constructions, and by repeating the verb, avoid misunderstanding ; as, —

Either my uncle is coming, or my cousins are.

Mention the subjects of the verbs in the following sentences, and tell why each verb is of the singular or plural form : —

1. Every tree and every shrub is beginning to send forth green leaves.
2. Each day and each hour brings its own duties.
3. The stone and the flower hold locked up in their recesses the three great known forces, — light, heat, electricity. — ROBERT HUNT.
4. A hundred eager fancies and busy hopes fill his brain.
5. Nor eye nor listening ear an object finds.
6. What wonderful advancement have science and invention made in this century !
7. One or more persons were injured.
8. The cheerful light, the vital air,
   Are blessings widely given. — BARBAULD.
9. Seasons return, but not to me returns
   Day, or the sweet approach of even or morn.

MILTON.

LESSON CXLII.

HOW TO PARSE VERBS.

To parse a verb, state: —

1. *Form* — regular or irregular, and why.
2. *Class* — transitive or intransitive, and why. If transitive, state whether it is in the active or the passive voice.
3. *Inflection:* —
   (*a*) *Mode* — indicative, potential, subjunctive, or imperative, and why,
   (*b*) *Tense* — present, past, future, present perfect, past perfect, or future perfect, and why.
   (*c*) *Person and Number* — whether it is in the first, second, or third person, and in the singular or plural number, and why.
4. *Syntax* — its agreement with its subject.

MODEL FOR PARSING VERBS.

1. The fields were devastated by the war.
2. If our general were in command, we could win the battle.

WERE DEVASTATED is a regular verb because it forms its past tense and past participle by annexing *ed*. Principal parts, *devastate, devastated, devastated*. It is transitive; in the passive voice because it represents its subject *fields* as receiving the action; in the indicative mode, it simply declares something; in the past tense, it represents something which occurred in the past; in the third person plural number, to agree with its subject *fields*.

WERE is an irregular verb because it does not form its past

tense and past participle by annexing *ed.* Principal parts, *be* or *am, was, been.* Intransitive, it has not an object; in the subjunctive mode, it is used in a conditional clause to express something which is merely thought of; it has the form of the past subjunctive, but denotes present time; in the third person and singular number, to agree with its subject *general.*

COULD WIN is an irregular verb because it does not form its past tense and past participle by annexing *ed.* Principal parts, *win, won, won.* It is transitive, and in the active voice because it represents its object *battle* as receiving the action; in the potential mode, it expresses a possibility; it has the form of the past potential, but denotes present time; in the first person and plural number, to agree with its subject *we.*

ABBREVIATED MODEL. — WERE DEVASTATED is a verb, regular, transitive, passive, indicative, past, and in the third plural, to agree with its subject *fields.*

Parse the verbs in Lesson CXXXVIII.

LESSON CXLIII.

STUDY OF SELECTION.

GRANDFATHER'S CHAIR.

The chair in which Grandfather sat was made of oak, which had grown dark with age, but had been rubbed and polished till it shone as bright as mahogany. It was very large and heavy, and had a back that rose high above Grandfather's white head. This back was curiously carved in openwork, so as to represent flowers and foliage, and other devices, which the children had often gazed at, but could never understand what they meant. On the very tiptop of the chair, over the head of Grandfather himself, was the likeness of a lion's head, which had such a savage grin that you would almost expect to hear it growl and snarl.

The children had seen Grandfather sitting in this chair ever since they could remember anything. Perhaps the younger of them supposed that he and the chair had come into the world together, and that both had always been as old as they were now. At this time, however, it happened to be the fashion for ladies to adorn their drawing-rooms with the oldest and oddest chairs that could be found. It seemed to Cousin Clara that, if these ladies could have seen Grandfather's old chair, they would have thought it worth all the rest together. She wondered if it were not even older than Grandfather himself, and longed to know all about its history. — HAWTHORNE.

Try to imagine the chair described by Hawthorne. What kind of wood was it made of? Why did it look dark? Why did it shine like mahogany? How high was the back of the chair? What is meant by "curiously carved in openwork"? Were the flowers cut clear through the back of the chair? What do you understand by foliage? Where was the carved lion's head? How do you know that it looked very much like a live lion? Why did the younger children think that the chair had come into the world with their grandfather? Do ladies sometimes buy old furniture for their parlors? Have you ever seen an old clock? A curious claw-footed table? A spinning wheel?

WRITTEN EXERCISES.

Describe an old clock. Use, if you wish, the following hints : —

The clock stands in the hall at the top of the stairway. It is made of mahogany almost black with age. It is eight feet high. It has a glass door. You can see the pendulum, the white face, the black figures, the bluish steel hands. There are pink flowers painted on the corners of the face, and green leaves. The glass door is hung with brass hinges, and has a brass scroll-work keyhole. The old clock has witnessed many scenes of joy and sorrow.

Describe other objects you have seen. A bureau. A table. A writing desk. A book. A spinning wheel.

First try to give a picture of the whole. Then describe the material, shape, size, ornamentation, use, age, owners, associations.

LESSON CXLIV.

PARTICIPLES.

Participles may be classified either with reference to *form* or the *time* denoted by them.

According to *form*, participles are either *simple* or *compound*.

According to *time*, participles are either *present, past,* or *past perfect.*

The participles of the verb *write* are, —

Simple.	writing written
Compound.	being written having written having been written having been writing

The compound participles are formed by the use of the auxiliary participles of the verbs *be* and *have*.

As in the formation of the tenses of the verb (see Lesson

CXVIII.) the use of the auxiliary *be* with the past participle makes the passive form, so the use of the same auxiliary with the present participle makes the progressive form.

The same participles may be again classified; as, —

	ACTIVE.	PASSIVE.
Present.	writing	being written
Past.	written	written
Past Perfect.	having written having been writing	having been written

As intransitive verbs have no passive form, so the participles of intransitive verbs form no participles of the passive form.

A participle may be modified, like a verb, by an adverb, by an adverbial phrase, or by an adverbial clause; thus,—

1. *By an adverb.*

The mountain streams went babbling by.

2. *By an adverbial phrase.*

The flush of life may well be seen
Thrilling back over hills and valleys.

3. *By an adverbial clause.*

The boat sank lying where we saw it yesterday.

A transitive participle is one that requires an objective complement.

The objective complement of a participle may be a noun or pronoun; thus, —

1. *A noun.*

The child is happy gathering flowers.

2. *A pronoun.*

Hearing me call, he came to my rescue.

An intransitive participle is one that does not require an object. An incomplete intransitive participle requires an attributive complement, which may be either a noun, a pronoun, or an adjective; thus, —

1. *A noun.*

Having become President, he took the oath of office.

2. *An adjective.*

The cherries being ripe, we picked them.

A participle with its modifiers or complements is called a PAR- . TICIPIAL PHRASE.

A participle (or participial phrase) may be used as a noun or as an adjective; thus, —

As a noun, a participle may be : —

1. The subject of a verb.

Listening to music is a charming diversion.

2. The attributive complement of a verb.

A sorrow's crown of sorrow is remembering happier things.

3. The objective complement of a verb.

Kittens enjoy playing with a ball.

4. The object of a preposition.

He takes no pleasure in gazing at the stars.

As an adjective, a participle may : —

1. Limit a noun.

Truth, crushed to earth, shall rise again.

2. Limit a pronoun.

I found him sleeping at his post.

3. Be an attributive complement.

She is graceful, and her manner winning.

Mention the participles in the following sentences, and tell whether each is simple or compound, transitive or intransitive, passive or active, present, past, or perfect.

State how each participle is used in the sentence in which you find it.

1. Walking is a healthful exercise.

2. The robin and the bluebird piping loud
   Filled all the blossoming orchards with their glee.

3. Round the beautiful valley,
       Towering aloft in the sky,
   Stand the mountains like giants,
       Grim and rocky and high. — MILLER.

4. By the wayside, on a mossy stone,
       Sat a hoary pilgrim sadly musing ;
   Oft I marked him sitting there alone,
       All the landscape like a page perusing.

   RALPH HOYT.

5. And thou, O River of To-morrow, flowing
       Between thy narrow adamantine walls ;
   I hear the trumpets of the morning blowing,
       I hear thy mighty voice, that calls and calls.

   LONGFELLOW.

6. I heard him walking across the floor
   As he always does, with a heavy tread.

7. Sweet is the air with the budding haws; and the
       valley stretching for miles below
   Is white with blossoming cherry trees, as if just
       covered with lightest snow. — LONGFELLOW.

LESSON CXLV.

INFINITIVES.

Infinitives are classified as *simple* or *compound, active* or *passive, present* or *present perfect.*

The simple form of the infinitive is the root of the verb to which the word *to* is prefixed. The other infinitives are all compound.

The other classifications of the infinitive of the verb *write* are : —

	ACTIVE.	PASSIVE.
Present.	{ to write { to be writing	to be written
Present Perfect.	{ to have written { to have been writing	to have been written

As in the formation of the passive and progressive forms of the verb and of participles (Lessons CXXVIII. and CXXXI.), the auxiliary verbs *be* and *have* are used in making the compound forms.

The auxiliary *be* with the past participle makes the passive form ; with the present participle, the progressive form of the infinitive.

Intransitive verbs form no passive infinitive.

Infinitives take the same modifiers and complements as verbs ; thus, —

The modifiers of an infinitive may be : —

1. *An adverb.*

Resolve to study diligently.

2. *A phrase.*

I expect to start at five o'clock.

3. *A clause.*

> We intend to go when our friends arrive.

The objective complement of an infinitive may be : —

1. *A noun.*

> We are commanded to love our enemies.
> He comes to break oppression.

2. *A pronoun.*

> I shall invite him to accompany me.

3. *A clause.*

> I promised to ask what was the matter with the
> child.

The attributive complement of an infinitive may be : —

1. *A noun.*

> They urged him to become a candidate for the
> office.

2. *A pronoun.*

> It did not seem to be he.

3. *An adjective.*

> I believe the location to be desirable.
> You will find her to be brave and true.

An infinitive with its modifiers or complements is called an
INFINITIVE PHRASE (see Lesson CVIII.).

The verbs *bid, dare, feel, hear, let, make, need,* and *see,* and their
participles and infinitives, take an infinitive after them without the
preposition *to ;* thus, —

> Let us walk.
> Make her study her lessons.
> See him throw the ball.

An infinitive (or infinitive phrase) may be used as a noun, an adjective, or an adverb ; thus, —

An infinitive used as a noun may be : —

1. *The subject of a verb.*

     To watch is his duty.

2. *The object of a verb.*

     The boy learns to read.

3. *The attributive complement of a verb.*

     All we want is to be let alone.

4. *In apposition with a substantive.*

     Delightful task ! to rear the tender thought.

5. *The object of a preposition.*

     There is nothing left but to submit.

An infinitive used as an adjective may : —

1. *Limit a noun.*

     You have my permission to speak.

2. *Be the attributive complement of a verb.*

     The best way to prosper is to keep out of debt.

An infinitive used as an adverb may modify : —

1. *A verb.*

     And fools who came to scoff remained to pray.

2. *An adjective.*

     They are afraid to speak.
     He was quick to reply.

Mention the infinitives and infinitive phrases in the following sentences, and state how each is used: —

1. To be frightened is not pleasant.
2. It is easier to pull down than to build.
3. I'll learn the round of life to fill.
4. In the schoolroom while we stay,
   There is work enough to do.
5. Mary has gone to visit her little friend.
6. Have you been invited to go to the picnic?
7. Beautiful feet are they that go
   Swiftly to lighten another's woe.
8. Teach me to feel another's woe,
   To hide the fault I see. — POPE.
9. Let man, who hopes to be forgiven,
   Forgive and bless his foe. — SADI.
10. To persevere in one's duty and to be silent is the best answer to calumny. — WASHINGTON.
11. It is always safe to learn, even from our enemies; seldom safe to instruct, even our friends.
12. In woods and glens I love to roam
    When the tired hedger hies him home,
    Or by the woodland pool to rest
    When pale the star sleeps on its breast. — WHITE.
13. To gild refined gold, to paint the lily,
    To throw a perfume on the violet,
    To smooth the ice, or add another hue
    Unto the rainbow, or with taper light
    To seek the beauteous eye of heaven to garnish,
    Is wasteful and ridiculous excess. — SHAKESPEARE.

LESSON CXLVI.

HOW TO PARSE VERBALS.

To parse an infinitive or a participle, state: —

1. From what verb it is formed.
2. Its *Form* — simple or compound.
3. Its *Class* — intransitive or transitive, active or passive.
4. Its *Use* — the part that it, or the phrase of which it forms a part, performs in the sentence.

Model for parsing infinitives and participles.

1. To doubt would be disloyalty.
2. The sun, darting its rays through the window, awoke me.
3. The road, after winding through the forest, leads to a swiftly flowing river.
4. Truth, crushed to earth, shall rise again.

To DOUBT is a simple intransitive infinitive, active, and the subject of the verb *would be.*

DARTING, formed from the verb *dart*, is a simple transitive participle ; and the phrase *darting its rays through the window,* is used as an adjective to modify the noun *sun.*

WINDING is a simple intransitive participle, active ; and the participial phrase *winding through the forest,* is used as a noun, and is the object of the preposition *after.*

CRUSHED is a simple transitive participle, passive ; and the participial phrase *crushed to earth,* is used as an adjective to modify the noun *truth.*

Parse the participles and infinitives in Lesson CXXXIII.

LESSON CXLVII.

REVIEW.

1. Distinguish between a verb and a verbal. Illustrate.

2. Into what two classes are verbals divided? Illustrate each.

3. Distinguish between transitive and intransitive verbs. Classify the verbs in the selection entitled " Mechanic Art in the Animal Creation," Lesson CXIV.

4. Write a sentence having a transitive verb, a subject, and an object. Can you change the verb to the passive voice? How? .

5. What is an auxiliary verb? Mention three verbs that may be used as either independent or auxiliary verbs.

6. How is the indicative mode of verbs used? The potential? The subjunctive? The imperative?

7. Name the tenses of the indicative mode. The potential. The subjunctive. The infinitive. How is each tense formed?

8. How are participles classified? Name the classes, and illustrate each.

9. How are infinitives classified? How may they be modified? How used?

10. What verbs may be followed by the infinitive without the preposition *to?*

11. When is a verb said to be in the progressive form? Of what two parts does it consist? How does the progressive form differ from the passive voice?

12. Write the subjunctive mode, progressive form, of the verb *read.*

LESSON CXLVIII.

COMPOSITION.

WORD PICTURES.

Between broad fields of wheat and corn
Is the lowly home where I was born ;
The peach tree leans against the wall,
And the woodbine wanders over all.

There is the barn ; and, as of yore,
I can smell the hay from the open door,
And see the busy swallows throng,
And hear the pewee's mournful song.

Oh, ye who daily cross the sill,
Step lightly, for I love it still ! — READ.

Read the first four lines. Do you see a large house? Where are the fields of wheat and corn? Where is the peach tree? Does the woodbine improve the picture? Who lives in the house?

Read the remainder of the selection. Try to imagine the barn. Is the door closed, or open? Can you think of persons or animals not mentioned by the poet?

Write out a complete description of the scene, adding to the poet's word picture your own ideas.

WRITTEN EXERCISES.

Study carefully each of the following word pictures. Try to imagine the scene suggested. Write out a full description of what you see in your own mind, and add anything you like to the sketch. Perhaps you will think of a story.

1. Only a newsboy, under the light
    Of the lamp-post, plying his trade in vain;
    Men are too busy to stop to-night,
    Hurrying home through the sleet and the rain.

    PHŒBE CARY.

2. Down the chimney St. Nicholas came with a bound.
    He was dressed all in fur from his head to his foot,
    And his clothes were all tarnished with ashes and soot;
    A bundle of toys he had flung on his back,
    And he looked like a peddler just opening his pack.

    MOORE.

3. On the hearth of Farmer Garvin blazed the crackling
        walnut log;
    Right and left sat dame and goodman, and between
        them lay the dog,
    Head on paws, and tail slow wagging, and beside him
        on the mat,
    Sitting drowsy in the firelight, winked and purred the
        mottled cat. — WHITTIER.

4. Bright yellow, red, and orange,
        The leaves come down in hosts;
    The trees are Indian princes,
        But soon they'll turn to ghosts. — ALLINGHAM.

5. All the little boys and girls,
    With rosy cheeks and flaxen curls,
    And sparkling eyes, and teeth like pearls,
    Tripping and skipping, ran merrily after
    The wonderful music, with shouting and laughter.

    BROWNING.

LESSON CXLIX.

PREPOSITIONS.

A preposition is a word used to introduce a phrase, and show the relation of its object to the word which the phrase modifies; as,—

Heaven lies about us in our infancy.

In this sentence, *about* is a preposition introducing the phrase *about us*, and showing the relation between *us* and *lies*, — lies *about* us, not *around* us, or *over* us. *Us* is the object of the preposition *about*, and is in the objective case. The entire phrase is an element in the sentence. *About* is an element in the phrase. *In* is also a preposition introducing the phrase *in our infancy*, and showing the relation between *infancy* and *lies*. *Infancy* is the object of the preposition *in*, and is in the objective case.

A phrase introduced by a preposition is called a PREPOSITIONAL PHRASE.

1. If it performs the office of an adjective, it is called an ADJECTIVE PHRASE.

2. If it performs the office of an adverb, it is called an ADVERBIAL PHRASE.

A prepositional phrase may modify : —

1. *A noun.*

The house on the hill has been blown down.

2. *A pronoun.*

Which of you saw the yacht race?

3. *An adjective.*

It is good for nothing.

4. *A verb.*

I stood on the bridge at midnight.

Our echoes roll from soul to soul.

5. *An adverb.*

You acted inconsistently with your professions.

6. *A participle.*

The clustered spires of Frederick stand
Green-walled by the hills of Maryland.

I met him coming through the rye.

A preposition may take for its object : —

1. *A noun.*

We rise by the things that are under our feet.

2. *A pronoun.*

Come unto me, and I will give you rest.

3. *A participle.*

There was much excitement over the reading of
the will.

4. *An infinitive.*

He was about to write a letter.

5. *An adverb of place or time.*

The odor of gas comes from below.
It was not till then that I knew.

6. *An adverbial phrase.*

The diver came up from under the water.

7. *A clause.*

This will depend on who the commissioners are.

A preposition is parsed by stating : —

1. That the word is a preposition.
2. That the phrase introduced is an adjective or an adverbial phrase, and what the phrase modifies.

MODEL FOR PARSING.

Among them all, none braver marched against the foe.

AMONG is a preposition. It introduces the adjective phrase *among them all*, which modifies the adjective pronoun *none*.

AGAINST is a preposition. It introduces the adverbial phrase *against the foe*, which modifies the verb *marched*.

Parse the prepositions in the following sentences : —

1. Beside a pleasant dwelling ran a brook,
   Scudding along a narrow channel paved
   With green and yellow pebbles.

2. Lightly and brightly breaks away
   The morning from her mantle gray,
   And the noon will look on a sultry day. — BYRON.

3. Bregenz, that quaint city
   Upon the Tyrol shore,
   Has stood above Lake Constance
   A thousand years and more. — PROCTER.

4. They are slaves who dare not be
   In the right with two or three. — LOWELL.

5. The valley of Chamouni is a place where a traveler loves to linger for days and even for weeks.

6. General Thomas was indeed the " Rock of Chickamauga," around and against which the wild waves of battle dashed in vain. — GARFIELD.

7. Whose heart hath ne'er within him burned,
　　As home his footsteps he hath turned
　　　From wandering on a foreign strand? — SCOTT.

Write fifteen sentences containing not fewer than fifteen of the prepositions in the following list, and be prepared to state what each phrase modifies : —

above	below	since
across	beneath	through
after	beside	toward
against	between	under
along	from	unto
among	over	upon
around	past	within
before	round	without

Construct sentences in which the following expressions are correctly used : —

attend to	need of
bestow upon	notice of
boast of	profit by
call on	provide for, with, against
change for	regard for
convenient to, *or* for	smile at, upon
dependent on, upon	taste of, for
die of, *or* by	think of, on
difficulty in	worthy of
fell from	wait on, at, for

LESSON CL.

KINDS OF PHRASES.

Phrases, according to *form*, are classified as : —

1. *Prepositional* (phrases introduced by a preposition).

   A statue of marble stood in the public square.

   But yesterday the word of Cæsar might have stood against the world.

2. *Participial* (phrases introduced by a participle).

   Having written his letter, he sealed it.

   A tree stripped of its leaves was no obstruction to the view.

3. *Infinitive* (phrases introduced by an infinitive).

   He was born to be great.

   A few baskets of peaches, to be sent to market, stood in the yard.

Phrases, according to *office*, are classified as : —

1. *Substantive.*

   To relieve the poor is our duty.

   He spends much time in reading Scott's novels.

2. *Adverbial.*

   He came early in the morning.

   The lowing herd winds slowly o'er the lea.

3. *Adjective.*

   A tree, dead at the top, stands in front of the house.

   The pitch of the musical tone depends upon the rapidity of vibration.

A phrase made up of two or more phrases, one of which is modified by the other or others, is called a COMPLEX PHRASE.

> Then read from the treasured volume
> The poem of thy choice,
> And lend to the rhyme of the poet
> The beauty of thy voice.

The phrase *to the rhyme of the poet* is a complex phrase, because the phrase *of the poet* modifies the word *rhyme*. The phrases in the first, second, and fourth lines, and the phrase *of the poet,* are simple phrases.

> Over the river and through the wood
> To grandfather's house we go.

The phrase making up the first line, composed of two phrases joined by the conjunction *and,* is called a COMPOUND PHRASE.

Point out and classify the phrases in the following sentences : —

1. Under the spreading chestnut tree
   The village smithy stands.
2. To pay as you go is the safest way to fortune.
3. A life of beauty lends to all it sees
   The beauty of its thought. — WHITTIER.
4. Now the bright morning star, day's harbinger,
   Comes dancing from the east. — MILTON.
5. Here jasmines spread their silver flower,
   To deck the wall, or weave the bower.
6. The night wind with a desolate moan swept by,
   And the old shutters of the turret swung
   Creaking upon their hinges. — WILLIS.
7. For a man to be proud of his learning is the greatest ignorance.

8. In shimmering lines, through the dripping pines,
   The stealthy morn advances;
   And the heavy sea fog straggles back
   Before those bristling lances. — ALDRICH.

9. There's a dance of leaves in that aspen bower;
   There's a twitter of wind in that beechen tree;
   There's a smile on the fruit, and a smile on the
   flower,
   And a laugh from the brook that runs to the sea.
   BRYANT.

10. Full many a gem of purest ray serene
    The dark, unfathomed caves of ocean bear;
    Full many a flower is born to blush unseen
    And waste its sweetness on the desert air.
    GRAY.

LESSON CLI.

WORDS EXPANDED INTO PHRASES.

1. I saw a treeless plain.
2. I saw a plain without a tree.

What word in the first sentence modifies *plain ?*
What phrase fulfills the same office in the second sentence?
Do both sentences express the same idea?

Rewrite the following sentences, expanding the Italicized words into equivalent phrases. State whether the phrases are substantive, adjective, or adverbial, and why.

1. *Here* General Custer fell.
2. Industry is *commendable*.
3. A *wealthy* man has great advantages,

4. I will return *immediately.*
5. Here is a *four-leaved* clover.
6. *Where* did you find it?
7. He was a *learned* man.
8. Those children are *homeless.*
9. His journey was *very long.*
10. It was a *cloudless* day.

LESSON CLII.

PHRASES CONTRACTED INTO WORDS.

1. He opposed us with violence.
2. He opposed us violently.

Do these sentences express the same idea?

What adverb in the second sentence is equivalent to the phrase *with violence?*

Rewrite the following sentences, contracting the Italicized phrases into equivalent words. State whether the new words are substantives, adjectives, or adverbs.

1. The transaction was *according to law.*
2. *In this place* I will remain.
3. *In a short time* the work will be completed.
4. His conceit was *not to be borne.*
5. *On this spot* Garfield fell.
6. The groves were the *first temples of God.*
7. The egotism of the man was *not to be tolerated.*
8. The lady spoke *with great precision.*
9. These drawings were made *with extreme accuracy.*
10. *At this place* the President took the oath of office.

LESSON CLIII.

COMPOSITION.

Ask your teacher to take you and your companions to some place of interest in your neighborhood. Then make an outline by asking and answering questions similar to those in Lesson XX. Expand each topic of the outline into a paragraph. Try to make your story brief, clear, complete, and interesting.

If you have visited one of the following places, you may write from memory an account of what you saw.

The County Jail.	The Mill.
The Public Library.	The Poorhouse.
The Newspaper Pressroom.	The Foundry.
The Telephone Exchange.	The Shipyard.

LESSON CLIV.

CONJUNCTIONS.

A conjunction is a word used to connect words, phrases, clauses, or sentences.

A coördinate conjunction is one that connects elements of equal rank. These elements may consist of: —

1. Two or more independent members, or clauses, used to form a compound sentence ; as, —

> Without economy none can be rich, and with it few
>> can be poor.
> We have met tne enemy and they are ours.

2. Two or more subordinate clauses that have a common dependence ; as, —

> Millions of creatures walk the earth unseen
> Both when we wake and when we sleep.

3. Phrases having the same relation ; as, —

> Up the mountain and through the glen he took his
> silent way.

4. Words of the same class (and generally in the same form) that have a common relation to some other word ; as, —

> Her eyes are bright and blue.
> Honor thy father and thy mother.
> Sweep up the hearth, and mend the fire, and put the
> kettle on.

The principal coördinate conjunctions are *and, or, nor, because, but, therefore.*

A subordinate conjunction is one that introduces a clause, and connects it to a principal sentence ; as, —

> If he were studious, he would excel.

Among the conjunctions most frequently used are *if, unless, since, after, before, till, until, though, although, except, for, that.*

Certain conjunctions and adverbs are sometimes used in pairs as connectives, and when so used they are called CORRELATIVES. Among these are the following : —

Both — and: Both the house and its furniture were insured.

Either — or: Either ability or inclination was wanting.

Neither — nor: Neither the captain nor the passengers were saved.

Whether—or: It has not been decided whether we shall have Monday or Tuesday for a holiday.

If—then: If Julia comes, then you can go to the concert.

Though—yet: Though I am old, yet I am strong.

So—that, with a finite verb to express a consequence:—

The summer and autumn had been so wet
That in winter the corn was growing yet.

As—as, with adjectives or adverbs, to denote equality:—

The water was as bright and pure as liquid diamonds.

'Tis as easy now for the heart to be true
As for grass to be green, or skies to be blue.

As—so, to express equality or proportion:—

As the hart panteth after the water brooks, so panteth my soul after thee, O God.

So—as: So I take care of my arms, as you of your pens and your inkhorn.

Such—as: Nature ever faithful is
To such as trust her faithfulness.

Such—that: The Bible is such that a child can understand it.

Not only—but also: I confess I did once aspire to be queen, not only of Palmyra, but also of the East.

(*But* and *but even* are often used in the second member.)

A copulative conjunction denotes an addition, a cause, a consequence, or a supposition.

The Rhine and the Rhone rise in Switzerland.

A disjunctive conjunction is one which, while it joins two terms together, disconnects their meaning.

God bids the ocean roar, or bids its roaring cease.
He sowed little, but reaped much.

Point out the conjunctions in the following sentences. State the class to which each belongs and the office it performs.

1. With him lay dead both hope and pride.
2. A book's a book, although there's nothing in't.
3. His conduct was neither just nor wise.
4. Words that the heart did neither hatch nor harbor do sometimes fly from the tongue.
5. He will be as good as his word.
6. 　　　　　　　　Hannah the housemaid
Laughed with her eyes as she listened, but governed her tongue, and was silent.
7. As thy days, so shall thy strength be.
8. What recked the chieftain if he stood
On Highland heath or Holy rood? — SCOTT.
9. The coming and going of the birds is more or less a mystery and a surprise.
10. Give me such things as you have.
11. This is not written so carefully as it should be.
12. And the stars never rise but I feel the bright eyes
Of the beautiful Annabel Lee. — POE.
13. Neither the sunbeams, nor the birds, nor the red clouds which morning and evening sailed above him, gave the little tree any pleasure.
14. I do not know whether he is in Boston or in New York.

15. Bonaparte was the idol of common men, because he had in transcendent degree the qualities and powers of common men. — EMERSON.

16. In fact, there's nothing that keeps its youth,
    So far as I know, but a tree and truth ! — HOLMES.

17. Little birds are silent all the dark night through ;
    But when the morning dawneth, their songs are sweet and new.

18. The mind of the scholar, if you would have it large and liberal, should come in contact with other minds.

LESSON CLV.

SIMILES AND METAPHORS.

1. The warrior fought like a lion.
2. The warrior was a lion in the fight.

To what is the warrior compared in these sentences?

Do the words *lion* and *warrior* represent different classes of objects?

In which sentence is the comparison directly expressed by the word *like ?*

In which sentence is the comparison implied, and the warrior spoken of as if he were a lion?

A direct comparison between objects of different classes is called a *simile.*

As and *like* are the usual signs of a simile ; but *so, just so, similar to,* and many other expressions, may be used to express the comparison.

An implied comparison between two objects of different kinds is called a *metaphor.*

In the following sentences point out and explain the similes and the metaphors : —

1. His spear was like the mast of a ship.

2. Thou art my rock and my fortress.

3. Virtue is a jewel.

4. Webster was one of the brightest luminaries of the age.

5. A thing of beauty is a joy forever.

6. Pitt was the pilot who guided the ship of state through a stormy sea.

7. Black were her eyes as the berry that grows on the thorn by the wayside.

8. Necessity is the mother of invention.

9. The twilight hours like birds flew by.

10. My winged boat, a bird afloat,
Swims round the purple peaks remote.

11. Like sportive deer they coursed about.

HOOD.

12. Such a brow
His eyes had to live under, clear as flint.

BROWNING.

13. Poetry is
The grandest chariot wherein king thoughts ride.

SMITH.

14. Like winged stars the fireflies flash and glance
Pale in the open moonshine.

SHELLEY.

15. Books, like proverbs, receive their chief value from the stamp and esteem of ages through which they have passed.

LESSON CLVI.

REVIEW.

1. Define a preposition. Illustrate.

2. Define a conjunction. Illustrate.

3. Make a list of the correlative conjunctions, and write sentences to illustrate their use.

4. What kind of conjunction is used to connect elements of equal rank? Illustrate.

5. Mention ten coördinate conjunctions, and write a sentence to illustrate the use of each.

6. Distinguish between copulative and disjunctive conjunctions.

7. How are prepositions and conjunctions alike?

8. Point out the prepositions and conjunctions in the selection entitled " Grandfather's Chair," Lesson CXLIII.

9. When do you place a comma after a subject and its modifiers? Illustrate.

10. When do you separate the clauses of a compound sentence by a comma? Write three illustrations.

11. Construct five sentences containing quotations carefully introduced and properly punctuated.

12. Write sentences containing the following : —

  1. An adverbial phrase.

  2. Two phrases contrasted.

  3. A word and a phrase in apposition.

  4. A phrase out of its natural order.

  5. A series of phrases alike in grammatical construction.

  6. A parenthetical phrase separated from the rest of the sentence by commas.

17

LESSON CLVII.

SUBJECT AND PREDICATE.

A sentence is a collection of words so arranged as to express a thought (Lesson I.).

A sentence may be formed of two words, — a subject noun or pronoun and a predicate verb; as, —

Children play.   She sings.

| Children | play | | She | sings |

Either the subject or the predicate may be enlarged by modifiers; as, —

These little children play.

Children play earnestly.

Or both subject and predicate may be enlarged by modifiers; as, —

Some children play very roughly.

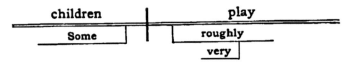

The predicate may be completed by : —

1. *An object.*

The boys caught trout.

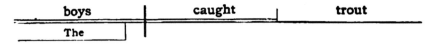

2. *An adjective.*

The steamer is swift.

steamer | is | swift
The

3. *A noun.*

The boys are students.

For explanation of diagrams, see pp. 346, 351, 356.

The simple subject (Lesson XVI.) is also called the GRAMMATI-CAL SUBJECT.

The simple predicate (Lesson XVII.) is also called the GRAM-MATICAL PREDICATE.

The modified subject (Lesson XVI.) is also called the LOGICAL SUBJECT.

The term LOGICAL PREDICATE is applied either to the modified predicate or to the complete predicate (Lesson XVII.).

State, with reference to each of the sentences in the exercise in Lesson CLIII., —

1. The logical subject.   2. The logical predicate.   3. The grammatical subject.   4. The grammatical predicate.

Enlarge the following sentences by supplying modifiers or complements. Mention the logical subjects and predicates of the enlarged sentences.

The wind blows.	The snow falls.
Children are playing.	The sun shines.
School was dismissed.	A valley lies.
Chestnuts ripen.	The rain fell.
The river runs.	The cricket is chirping.
We found violets.	The moon shone.
The pupils sang.	The sunlight fills.
The birds were singing.	The snow is falling.

LESSON CLVIII.

THE SUBJECT.

The grammatical subject of a sentence may be : —

1. *A noun.*

> The pen is mightier than the sword. — BULWER.
> The dew sparkles in the sunlight.

2. *A pronoun.*

> I will never forsake you.
> He is not content with his situation.

3. *An infinitive or an infinitive phrase.*

> To bear is to conquer our fate. — CAMPBELL.
> To be simple is to be great. — EMERSON.
> To be prepared for war is one of the most effectual means of preserving peace. — WASHINGTON.

4. *A participle or a participial phrase.*

> Plain living and high thinking are no more.
>
> WORDSWORTH.
>
> Buying goods on credit has caused him to fail.

5. *A clause.*

> Whate'er is best administered is best. — POPE.
> That he will succeed is evident.

Mention the grammatical subject of each of the following sentences, and tell to which of the foregoing classes it belongs.

1. The brilliancy of the light dazzled his eyes.
2. And now the earth hides itself under a veil of snow.
3. The fisherman, from his motionless boat, casts forth his nets, breaking the surface of the water.

4. The butterflies, powdered with sulphur, rest their velvety heads upon the hearts of the flowers.

5. The leaves of the willow are like new gold.

6. To be employed is to be happy.

7. Walking in the fields is agreeable.

8. Have you read "Robinson Crusoe"?

9. I am expecting a letter.

10. To learn in youth is less painful than to be ignorant in old age.

11. Ideas are the great warriors of the world.

12. Learn the luxury of doing good.

13. Honest labor bears a lovely face.

14. Dispatch is the soul of business.

15. To talk and to talk well are two different things.

16. To write well is an accomplishment.

17. There are two white daisies peeping through the green.

18. "What lovely flowers we'll have!" said they.

19. Playing tennis is a favorite pastime.

20. Dogs in their love for man play a part in nearly every tragedy.

LESSON CLIX.

COMPOSITION.

THE GREAT BATTLE OF HASTINGS.

There was one tall Norman knight who rode before the Norman army on a prancing horse, throwing up his heavy sword and catching it, and singing of the bravery of his countrymen. An English knight, who rode out from the English lines to meet him, fell by this knight's hand.

Another English knight rode out, and he fell too. But then a third rode out, and killed the Norman. This was the first beginning of the fight. It soon raged everywhere.

The English, keeping side by side in a great mass, cared no more for the showers of Norman arrows than if they had been showers of Norman rain. When the Norman horsemen rode against them, with their battle-axes they cut men and horses down. The Normans gave way. The English pressed forward. Duke William, the Norman commander, pretended to retreat. The eager English followed. Duke William's army turned again, and fell upon the English with great slaughter. The sun rose high, and sank, and the battle still raged. Through all the wild October day, the clash and din resounded in the air. In the red sunset and in the white moonlight, heaps upon heaps of dead men lay strewn all over the ground. Harold, the Saxon king, wounded in the eye by an arrow, was nearly blind. His brothers were already killed. At length Harold, the king, received a mortal wound, and dropped. The English broke and fled. The Normans rallied, and the day was lost. — DICKENS.

Study carefully Dickens's vivid description of the battle of Hastings. Try to imagine, and then describe, some historic scene with which you are familiar.

If you cannot think of any picturesque event, you may write on one of the following subjects : —

PAUL REVERE'S RIDE.

The time. The signal light. The movements of the British. The ride to Medford. Lexington. The result.

THE CHARTER OAK.

The tyrant Andros. The precious document lying on the table. The candles blown out. In the darkness the charter disappears. The hollow oak becomes famous in American history.

THE CAPTURE OF QUEBEC.

The situation at Quebec. Condition of armies. Both commanders wounded. General Wolfe's last words. Effect of battle upon French and English claims.

LESSON CLX.

EXERCISE. — SIMILES AND METAPHORS.

Point out and explain the similes and metaphors in the following sentences : —

1. Adversity is the grindstone of life.
2. Gravity is the ballast of the soul,
Which keeps the mind steady. — FULLER.
3. The lion is the desert's king. — STEDMAN.
4. My only defense is the flag of my country, and I place myself under its folds. — POINSETT.
5. Lovely flowers are the smiles of God's goodness.

WILBERFORCE.

6. Like a spear of flame the cardinal flower
Burned out along the meadow. — EDDY.
7.   Weariness
Can snore upon the flint. — SHAKESPEARE.
8. And the cares that infest the day
Shall fold their tents like the Arabs,
And as silently steal away. — LONGFELLOW.

LESSON CLXI.

MODIFIERS OF THE SUBJECT.

The grammatical subject of a sentence may be modified by : —

1. *An adjective.*

    The silent organ loudest chants
    The master's requiem. — EMERSON.

2. *A possessive noun.*

    Man's inhumanity to man
    Makes countless thousands mourn. — BURNS.

3. *A noun in apposition.*

    In arms the Austrian phalanx stood,
    A living *wall*, a human *wood*.

4. *A possessive pronoun.*

    Their loss is our victory.
    His heart is large, his hand is free.

5. *A participle.*

    Heaped in the hollow of the grove,
    The autumn leaves lie dead. — BRYANT.

    There in his noisy mansion, skilled to rule,
    The village master taught his little school.
    GOLDSMITH.

6. *An infinitive.*

    The question to be decided is difficult.

7. *A phrase.*

    Full many a gem of purest ray serene
    The dark, unfathomed caves of ocean bear.
    GRAY.

8. *A clause.*

The poet who wrote " Paradise Lost " sold it for five pounds.

In each of the following sentences mention : —

1. The logical subject. 2. The grammatical subject. 3. The modifiers of the grammatical subject.

1. The willow trees are full of yellow catkins.

2. A pound of pluck is worth a ton of luck. — GARFIELD.

3. The first sharp frosts had fallen, leaving all the woodlands gay.

4. The loud winds dwindled to a whisper low.

5. The old house by the lindens
   Stood silent in the shade.

6. The brilliant cardinal flower has never seemed gay to me,

7. The angel of the flowers one day,
   Beneath a rose tree sleeping lay.

8. A certain bird in a certain wood,
   Feeling the springtime warm and good,
   Sang to it in melodious mood. — ALDRICH.

LESSON CLXII.

MODIFIERS OF THE PREDICATE.

The grammatical predicate of a sentence may be modified by : —

1. *An adverb.*

The plowman homeward plods his weary way.

2. *An infinitive.*

Full many a flower is born to blush unseen.

3. *A phrase.*

The lowing herd winds slowly o'er the lea.

4. *A clause.*

Where heaves the turf in many a moldering heap,
Each in his narrow cell forever laid,
The rude forefathers of the hamlet sleep. — GRAY.

In each of the following sentences mention : —

1. The logical predicate.   2. The grammatical predicate.
3. The modifiers of the grammatical predicate.

1. The softened sunbeams pour around
   A fairy light.
2. From peak to peak, the rattling crags among,
   ·Leaps the live thunder.
3. And the peeping sunbeam now
   Paints with gold the village spire.
4. Tall chimneys, vigorously smoking, are visible here
   and there in the distant landscape.
5. With light and mirth and melody,
   The long, fair summer days came on.
6. The setting sun stretched his celestial rods of light
   across the level landscape. — HAWTHORNE.
7. Strips of thin, fleecy cloud are driving over the
   distant hilltops.
8. I used to think, when I was small and before I
   could read, that everybody was always happy. — HOLMES.
9. The mountain ridge against the purple sky
   Stands clear and strong. — STERLING.
10. The bashfulness of the guests soon gave way before
    good cheer and affability.

11. Fairy elves, no doubt, were to have been grouped around their mistress in laughing clusters. — THACKERAY.

12. The fuchsia, that has such beautiful flowers, is a native of New Zealand.

13. In the forests of South America, the night-blooming cereus may be seen opening its white flowers to catch the first rays of the full moon.

LESSON CLXIII.

COMPLEMENTS OF THE PREDICATE.

OBJECTIVE.

If the grammatical predicate is a transitive active verb, it may be completed by : —

1. *A noun.*

How far that little candle throws his beams!
So shines a good deed in a naughty world.

SHAKESPEARE.

2. *A pronoun.*

O gentle Sleep!
Nature's soft nurse, how have I frighted thee?

SHAKESPEARE.

Melancholy marked him for her own. — GRAY.

3. *A participle.*

The riflemen have commenced shooting.

4. *An infinitive.*

We like to please our teacher.

5. *A clause.*

I know not where His islands lift
Their fronded palms in air. — WHITTIER.

Oh, fear not in a world like this,
    And thou shalt know erelong,
Know how sublime a thing it is
    To suffer and be strong. — LONGFELLOW.

Some transitive passive verbs take objective complements (see Lesson CXXXI.).

ATTRIBUTIVE.

If the grammatical predicate is an incomplete intransitive verb, it may be completed by : —

1. *An adjective.*

    The poetry of earth is never dead. — KEATS.
    A fool must now and then be right by chance.

    COWPER.

2. *A noun.*

    Imitation is the sincerest flattery. — COLTON.
    The better part of valor is discretion.

    SHAKESPEARE.

3. *A pronoun.*

    It is not we who are to blame.
    I do not think it could have been they.

4. *A participle.*

    Rest is not quitting the busy career;
    Rest is the fitting of self to its sphere.

5. *An infinitive.*

    All we want is to be let alone.

6. *A phrase.*

    Your friend is in good spirits.
    The books will be of great service to me.

7. *A clause.*

    Character is what we are: reputation is what
        others think we are.

A few transitive verbs in the passive form take attributive complements (see Lesson CLXIV.).

Point out in reference to the following sentences : —

1. The logical predicate. 2. The grammatical predicate.
3. The complement of the grammatical predicate.

1. The moonlight silvered the distant hills.

2. The light of the moon shining through gleaming clouds guided us on our way.

3. The titles of books interest me.

4. I hear the singing of the birds.

5. Each autumn sees the falling of the leaves.

6. The herdsman watched the setting of the sun.

7. The only way to have a friend is to be a friend.

8. The sleep of the laboring man is sweet.

9. His face is serious, expressive, and intellectually powerful.

10. Resolve to act honorably in all things.

11. We could never learn to be brave and patient, if there were only joy in the world.

12. Lord Beaconsfield said that progress in the nineteenth century is found to consist in a return to ancient ideas.

13. It is the end of art to inoculate men with the love of nature. — BEECHER.

14. It was the pleasant harvest time,
    When cellar bins are closely stored,
    And garrets bend beneath their load. — WHITTIER.

15. Try to know enough of a wide range of subjects to profit by the conversation of intelligent persons of different callings and various intellectual gifts and acquisitions.

LESSON CLXIV.

COMPLEMENTS OF THE PREDICATE.

DIRECT AND INDIRECT.

It has already been stated (Lesson CIX.) that a transitive verb must have a complement or an object to complete it.

Some transitive verbs having the general meaning of giving, promising, refusing, or telling, — as *give, offer, pay, promise, show, make, bring, send, forgive, ask, teach, tell,* etc., — take two objects, a direct and an indirect. The direct object is the complement of the verb; the indirect may be properly called an adverbial objective, or a dative objective (the object of the preposition *to* or *for* understood).

1. The girls sent their teacher (*indirect*) some flowers (*direct*).
2. Did you pay him (*indirect*) the money (*direct*)?
3. The lady asked the driver (*indirect*) to stop (*direct*).
4. I told the doctor (*indirect*) that the child was better (*direct*).

If a transitive verb having a direct and an indirect object is changed to the passive form, the direct object becomes the subject, while the indirect object remains an adverbial objective, or becomes the object of a preposition; thus, —

1. Charles gave her the book.
   The book was given her by Charles.
2. A messenger brought me the package.
   The package was brought me by a messenger.

Some transitive verbs used to express the general idea of cause in some peculiar way — as, *make, keep, render, proclaim, form, call,* etc. — take an object and an adjective complement; as, —

Fear kept him quiet.

Here *him* is the object of the transitive verb *kept*, and *quiet* is an adjective complement limiting the object. Changing the predicate to the passive form, the sentence would read : —

He was kept quiet by fear.

Such verbs are said to be CAUSATIVE.

Verbs signifying to make, to choose, to elect, to name, to call, etc., take an object and (in some senses) a noun complement explaining or modifying it ; thus, —

1. We chose him captain.

Here *him* is the object of the transitive verb *chose*, and *captain* is a noun complement modifying *him*.

Putting the predicate in the passive form : —

2. He was chosen captain by us.

The direct object in the first sentence becomes the subject in the second, and the noun complement becomes a predicate noun.

An object like *captain*, in the first sentence above, is sometimes called a FACTITIVE OBJECT.

In the following sentences state whether each object is direct or indirect. Point out the adjective complements and the noun complements.

Rewrite each sentence, changing the predicate to the passive form.

1. A word of praise made him happy.
2. The people of France called her extravagant.
3. I thrice presented him a kingly crown.
4. We planted some roses in our garden this morning.
5. The cruel flames have entirely devoured the house.
6. The breeze from the coast brings me the perfume of the plum trees.

LESSON CLXV.

PLAIN LANGUAGE CHANGED TO FIGURATIVE.

1. *Rewrite the following sentences, changing examples of plain language to similes or metaphors :* —

EXAMPLE. — Her cheeks are very red.
Her cheeks are like roses.
Her cheeks are roses.

1. Her teeth are very white.
2. Her hair is yellow.
3. Her eyes are bright.
4. Her disposition is happy.
5. She is free from care.
6. The dog runs rapidly.
7. He was happy.
8. Contentment is precious.
9. The cardinal flower blossomed in the meadow.
10. The cares of the day shall quickly disappear.

2. *Change the following similes to metaphors :* —

1. Thy word is like a lamp unto my feet.
2. Procrastination is like a thief of time.
3. Stars are like daisies that begem
The blue fields of the sky.
4. Her laughter is like a rippling brook.
5. Kings are like stars — they rise and set.
6. Precept is like instruction written in the sand.
7. Kindness is like the golden chain by which society
is bound together.

LESSON CLXVI.

WORDS AND THEIR MEANING.

Construct sentences illustrating the use of the following words: —

CONTEND. To contest, to struggle in opposition.
TRANSGRESS. To offend by the violation of an order.
SUBSCRIBE. To sign one's name to any document, to promise or agree by writing one's name.
ENRAGE. To excite to anger, to provoke.
DISTRACT. To draw from any point or object, to perplex, to confuse.
FALTER. To be unsteady or feeble, to hesitate in speech.
REWARD. To recompense, either good or evil.
EXHAUST. To empty by drawing out.
FORBEAR. To withhold, to control one's self.

LESSON CLXVII.

THE ELEMENTS OF A SENTENCE.

Any word, phrase, or clause performing a distinct office in a sentence is called an *element.*

The elements of a sentence may be classified with reference to 1. Form; 2. Rank; 3. Office.

1. As to form, elements are either (*a*) words, (*b*) phrases, or (*c*) clauses.

(*a*) A word that by itself is either a principal, a subordinate, or an independent element, is called a WORD ELEMENT.

18

(*b*) A prepositional, a participial, or an infinitive phrase, or a phrase adverb, used either as a principal, a subordinate, or an independent element, is called a PHRASE ELEMENT.

(*c*) A clause used in a sentence as a subject or an object, or to modify any part of it, is called a CLAUSE ELEMENT.

2. As to rank, elements are either (*a*) principal, (*b*) subordinate, or (*c*) independent.

(*a*) The grammatical subject and the grammatical predicate of a sentence are the principal elements.

(*b*) Modifiers of the subject or predicate, and complements of the predicate, are subordinate elements.

(*c*) Words, phrases, and clauses not related grammatically to the other parts of the sentence are independent elements.•

3. As to office, elements are either (*a*) substantive, (*b*) affirmative, (*c*) adjective, (*d*) adverbial, or (*e*) connective.

Each word in any sentence may be classified according to its form, its rank, or its office ; as in the sentence, —

Aha ! we have won the game.

Aha, independent word element.
We, principal word element.
Have won, principal word element.
The, subordinate word element.
Game, subordinate word element.

Classify the elements in the following sentences : —

1. With reference to rank.   2. With reference to structure.
3. With reference to office.

1. The best poetry of the best poets is touched with sadness. — WINTER.

2. It was said by Talleyrand that the object of language is to conceal thought.

3. Macbeth could scarcely understand what they said.

4. The hermit good lives in that wood
Which slopes down to the sea. — COLERIDGE.

5. Butterflies live a gay life, flitting from flower to flower, sipping the drops of honeydew, without a thought for the morrow.

LESSON CLXVIII.

PHRASES EXPANDED INTO CLAUSES.

1. Men of intelligence enjoy travel.
2. Men who are intelligent enjoy travel.

Find a clause in the second sentence equivalent to a phrase in the first.

Are the sentences equivalent in meaning?

What kind of sentence is the first? The second?

Rewrite the following sentences, expanding the Italicized phrases into equivalent clauses. State whether these clauses are substantive, adjective, or adverbial, and why.

1. *To become President* is his ambition.
2. *On receiving the letter*, I departed.
3. He is a man *of great ability*.
4. This is the house *built by Jack*.
5. I watched the workmen *building the house*.
6. *On entering the hall* of William Rufus, we recalled the trial of Warren Hastings.
7. The building *adjoining the palace* is a chapel.
8. *After seeing the procession*, the children went home.

9. Chaucer could clothe his shafts with delicate wit and poetic imagery *to an unsurpassed degree.*

10. Man's natural desire is *to know and be known.*

LESSON CLXIX.

CLAUSES CONTRACTED INTO PHRASES.

EXAMPLE. — The gates were opened that the king might enter.

The gates were opened for the king.

Rewrite the following sentences, contracting the Italicized clauses into equivalent phrases. State whether the phrases are substantive, adjective, or adverbial, and why.

1. I could read by the light *which the moon gave.*

2. *That I may convince you,* I will tell the whole story.

3. *That we should differ in opinion* is not strange.

4. *Persons who live in glass houses* should not throw stones.

5. A sentence is an assemblage of words *which make complete sense.*

6. Men *who are wise and learned* should be listened to.

7. Men *who travel on life's highway* should not be unfriendly to their fellow-travelers.

8. The prisoner *who had no friends* has been acquitted.

9. From the church tower that is in the public square, the bell tolls the hour *with a chime that is soft and musical.*

LESSON CLXX.

THE SIMPLE SENTENCE.

A simple sentence is a sentence that consists of but a single statement.

A simple sentence may be declarative, interrogative, imperative, or exclamatory.

It contains but one subject and one predicate.

Its principal and subordinate elements may be either words or phrases, but not clauses.

To break a promise is dishonorable.

Hope, the balm of life, soothes us under every misfortune.

See diagrams, pp. 346–350.

ANALYSIS.

A simple sentence is analyzed by stating : —

1. Kind of sentence, —
    (*a*) As to construction.
    (*b*) As to use.
2. The logical subject.
3. The logical predicate.
4. The grammatical subject.
5. The grammatical predicate.
6. The modifiers of the grammatical subject.
7. The modifiers and complement of the grammatical predicate.

MODELS FOR ANALYZING SIMPLE SENTENCES.

1. The old oaken bucket hangs in the well.

This is a simple declarative sentence.

The logical subject is *the old oaken bucket.*

The logical predicate is *hangs in the well.*

The grammatical subject is *bucket.*

The grammatical predicate is *hangs.*

The grammatical subject *bucket* is limited by the adjectives *old, oaken,* and *the.*

The grammatical predicate *hangs* is modified by the adverbial phrase *in the well,* in which *well* is the object of the preposition *in,* and is modified by the article *the.*

2. Hope, the balm of life, soothes us under misfortune.

This is a simple declarative sentence.

The logical subject is *hope, the balm of life.*

The logical predicate is *soothes us under misfortune.*

The grammatical subject is *hope.*

The grammatical predicate is *soothes.*

The grammatical subject *hope* is modified by the complex appositive (explanatory) phrase *balm of life,* in which *balm* is the principal term, modified by the prepositional adjective phrase *of life.*

The grammatical predicate *soothes* is completed by the objective complement *us,* and modified by the prepositional adverbial phrase *under misfortune.*

3. I prefer to ride in a carriage.

This is a simple declarative sentence.

The logical subject is *I.*

The logical predicate is *prefer to ride in a carriage.*

The grammatical subject is *I.*

The grammatical predicate is *prefer.*

The grammatical predicate *prefer* is completed by the infinitive phrase *to ride in a carriage,* used as an objective complement, in which the principal words, *to ride,* are modified by the prepositional adverbial phrase *in a carriage.*

4. The wretched prisoner, overwhelmed by his misfortunes, was on the point of putting an end to his existence.

This is a simple declarative sentence.

The logical subject is *the wretched prisoner, overwhelmed by his misfortunes.*

The logical predicate is *was on the point of putting an end to his existence.*

The grammatical subject is *prisoner.*

The grammatical predicate is *was.*

The grammatical subject *prisoner* is modified by the adjectives *the* and *wretched,* and the participial adjective phrase *overwhelmed by his misfortunes,* in which the principal word is the participle *overwhelmed,* modified by the prepositional adverbial phrase *by his misfortunes.*

The grammatical predicate *was* is modified by the complex prepositional adverbial phrase *on the point of putting an end to his existence,* in which the principal word, *point,* is modified by the adjective *the* and the complex prepositional adjective phrase *of putting an end to his existence.* The principal word of this phrase is the participle *putting,* which is completed by its object *end,* and modified by the prepositional adverbial phrase *to his existence.*

Analyze the following sentences : —

1. Memory is the storehouse of our ideas. — LOCKE.
2. A good cause makes a stout heart.
3. Employment is true enjoyment.

4. God tempers the wind to the shorn lamb. — STERNE.

5. The broad-backed billows fall faint on the shore,
In the crush of the mighty sea. — BAYARD TAYLOR.

6. And all the margin round about was set
With shady laurel trees. — SPENSER.

7. He was a short, square-built old fellow, with thick bushy hair, and a grizzled beard. — IRVING.

8. The busy lark, the messenger of day,
Saluteth in her song the morning gray. —CHAUCER.

9. There's music in the gushing of a rill.

10. According to ancient legends, the fruit of the oak served as nourishment for the early race of mankind.

11. The Puritanism of the past found its unwilling poet in Hawthorne, the rarest creative imagination of the century. — THOREAU.

12. Above all trees of the New World, the elm deserves to be considered the sovereign tree of New England.

LESSON CLXXI.

WORDS EXPANDED INTO CLAUSES.

EXAMPLE. — I shall certainly go.
It is certain that I shall go.

Expand into clauses the Italicized words in the following sentences. State whether clauses are substantive, adjective, or adverbial, and why.

1. It was *carved* ivory.
2. I shall *probably* return to-morrow.
3. A *rolling* stone gathers no moss.

4. *Intoxicating* liquors should be avoided.

5. Time has laid his hand upon my heart *gently*.

6. Abrupt and loud, a summons shook the gate.

7. *Evidently* the grass has been cut.

8. He *certainly* never deserted his post.

9. *Truly* the waves are very high.

10. *Apparently* the pool has no bottom.

11. The *blossom-bordered* path winds down to the meadow.

12. The path that runs along the sunniest side of the valley leads into a *bleak and sterile region*.

LESSON CLXXII.

CLAUSES CONTRACTED INTO WORDS.

EXAMPLE. — That we should converse is unnecessary.

Conversation is unnecessary.

Rewrite the following sentences, contracting the clauses into equivalent words. State whether these words are substantives, adjectives, or adverbs, and why.

1. Robert has a dog that is black.
2. That he is guilty will be made evident.
3. The book which was borrowed has been returned.
4. A man who sneers makes enemies.
5. Waste that is willful brings want that is woeful.
6. Persons who are industrious seldom suffer want.
7. He acknowledges that he was mistaken.
8. The man who is wise will shun evil.

9. Mary has lilies in her garden, that are white.

10. The lark that haunts the meadow sings a song that is sweet.

11. The dog that belongs to that old man looks up in his face as if he loved him.

12. The scholar who is wise does his best at all times.

13. Wellington was sure of victory, even before Blucher arrived.

14. The best sermon which was ever preached upon modern society is "Vanity Fair."

LESSON CLXXIII.

WORDS AND THEIR MEANING.

Construct sentences illustrating the use of the following words : —

RESTRICT.	To circumscribe, to restrain.
EXPLORE.	To range over for discovery, to examine.
FOREGO.	To relinquish, to renounce.
APPROVE.	To commend, to sanction.
INCLOSE.	To surround, to put in an envelope.
ENTITLED.	Denominated, qualified for, empowered.
CONSULT.	To ask advice of, to seek for information.
POSTPONE.	To defer, to adjourn.
PROVOKE.	To make angry.
RESPOND.	To answer, to act in response with.
PRESUME.	To take liberties.
COMPASSION.	Commiseration, fellow-feeling.
ANNOY.	To disturb, to harass.
FORTIFY.	To render strong, to make defensible.

LESSON CLXXIV.

THE COMPLEX SENTENCE.

A complex sentence is one that contains a principal sentence and one or more subordinate clauses.

A pupil who gives attention learns easily.
Have you found the book which you lost?

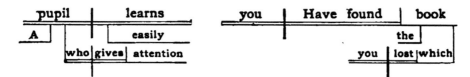

When we shall leave this place is uncertain.

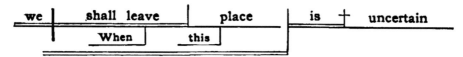

1. The subordinate clause may be an adjective element, and as such may modify any word that can be modified by an adjective.

(*a*) *It may modify the subject.*

The man whom you would select should possess all of these qualities.

The book that was lost has been found.

(*b*) *It may modify the object complement.*

I saw the man who gave you that book.

(*c*) *It may modify any noun in the subject or predicate.*

We went in the steamer which sailed yesterday.

The progress of a pupil who studies diligently will be rapid.

2. It may be an adverbial element, and as such it may be used in any way in which a simple adverb can be used. It is generally a modifier of the predicate. The following are examples of the more common forms of adverbial clauses : —

> He lived where his father lived.
> We were there when the train arrived.
> No message has come since you went away.
> Whither I go ye cannot come.
> My teacher is wiser than I.
> I am so weary that I can go no further.
> If you persevere, you will succeed.

3. A subordinate clause may be a substantive element, performing the office of a noun : —

(*a*) *As subject of a verb.*

> That the cause is lost, cannot be denied.

(*b*) *As objective complement.*

> We have learned that the earth is round.

(*c*) *As attributive complement.*

> His advice was that I should go.

(*d*) *As object of a preposition.*

> It depends on how soon the moon rises.

The connectives which join the subordinate clause to the principal sentence are subordinate conjunctions, relative pronouns, and a few conjunctive adverbs.

ANALYSIS OF COMPLEX SENTENCES.

A complex sentence is analyzed by stating : —

1. The kind of sentence.

2. The logical subject and the logical predicate of the entire sentence.

3. The principal sentence.

4. The subordinate clause or clauses.

5. The connective which introduces the subordinate clause, or joins it to the principal sentence.

6. The analysis of the principal sentence and subordinate clauses separately, as simple sentences.

MODELS FOR ANALYZING COMPLEX SENTENCES.

1. The reason why you cannot succeed is evident.

This is a complex declarative sentence.
The logical subject is *the reason why you cannot succeed.*
The logical predicate is *is evident.*
The principal sentence is *the reason is evident.*
The subordinate clause is *why you cannot succeed.*
The connective is the conjunctive adverb *why.*
The logical subject of the principal sentence is *the reason.*
The logical predicate is *is evident.*
The grammatical subject is *reason.*
The grammatical predicate is *is.*

The grammatical subject *reason* is modified by the adjective *the*, and the adjective clause *why you cannot succeed.*

The grammatical predicate *is* is completed by the attributive complement *evident.*

The subject, logical and grammatical, of the subordinate clause, is *you.*

The logical predicate is *cannot succeed why.*

The grammatical predicate *can succeed* is modified by the adverbs *not* and *why.*

2. I will give you the book when I see you.

This is a complex declarative sentence.
The logical subject is *I.*

The logical predicate is *will give you the book when I see you.*

The principal sentence is *I will give you the book.*

The subordinate clause is *when I see you.*

The connective is the conjunctive adverb *when.*

The subject, logical and grammatical, of the principal sentence, is *I.*

The logical predicate is *will give you the book.*

The grammatical predicate *will give* is completed by the objective complement *book* and the dative complement *you,* and is modified by the adverbial clause *when I see you.*

The objective complement *book* is modified by the adjective *the.*

The subject, logical and grammatical, of the subordinate clause, is *I.*

The logical predicate is *see you when.*

The grammatical predicate *see* is completed by the objective complement *you,* and modified by the adverb *when.*

3.　That he was the author of the book is generally believed.

This is a complex declarative sentence.

The logical subject is the substantive clause *that he was the author of the book.*

The logical predicate is *is generally believed.*

The principal sentence is the entire sentence, because the subordinate clause is substantive.

The subordinate clause is *that he was the author of the book.*

The subordinate clause is introduced by the conjunction *that.*

The grammatical subject of the sentence is the substantive clause *that he was the author of the book.*

The grammatical predicate *is believed* is modified by the adverb *generally.*

The subject, logical and grammatical, of the subordinate clause, is *he*.

The logical predicate is *was the author of the book.*

The grammatical predicate *was* is completed by the attributive complement *author*, which is modified by the adjective *the*, and the prepositional adjective phrase *of the book.*

4. I will give you no more money till I see how you use what you have.

This is a complex declarative sentence.

The logical subject is *I.*

The logical predicate is *will give you no more money till I see how you use what you have.*

The principal sentence is *I will give you no more money.*

The subordinate clause is *till I see how you use what you have.*

The connective is the conjunctive adverb *till.*

The subject, logical and grammatical, of the principal sentence, is *I.*

The logical predicate is *will give you no more money.*

The grammatical predicate *will give* is completed by the objective complement *money*, and the dative complement *you*, and is modified by the complex adverbial clause *till I see how you use what you have.*

The objective complement *money* is modified by the adjective *more*, which is modified by the adverb *no.*

The subordinate clause is itself complex.

The logical subject is *I.*

The logical predicate is *till I see how you use what you have.*

The grammatical subject is *I.*

The grammatical predicate *see* is modified by the adverb *till*, and completed by the complex substantive clause *how you use what you have*, which is used as an objective complement.

Of this complex substantive clause, the subject, logical and grammatical, is *you.*

The logical predicate is *use what you have how.*

The grammatical predicate *use* is modified by the adverb *how*, and completed by the substantive clause *what you have,* used as an objective complement.

In the clause *what you have*, the subject, logical and grammatical, is *you.* The logical predicate is *have what.*

The grammatical predicate is *have*, which is completed by the objective complement *what.*

Analyze the following sentences :—

1. He liveth long who liveth well.
2. I loved to walk where none had walked before.

    CRABBE.

3. As we approached the woods, we heard the music of the leaves.
4. Small service is true service while it lasts.

    WORDSWORTH.

5. Even a fool, when he holdeth his peace, is counted wise.
6. He who sets a great example is great.
7. Those deeds of charity which we have done
    Shall stay forever with us.
8. Persistent people begin their success where others end in failure.
9. He has not learned the lesson of life who does not every day surmount a fear. —EMERSON.
10. On waking, he found himself on the green knoll whence he had first seen the old man of the glen.

    IRVING.

11. Recollection is the only Paradise from which we cannot be turned out. — RICHTER.

12. The true grandeur of nations is in those qualities which constitute the true greatness of the individual.

SUMNER.

13. The road ambition travels is too narrow for friendship, too crooked for love, too rugged for honesty, and too dark for conscience. — ACROPOLITA.

14. It ever is weak falsehood's destiny
That her thick mask turns crystal to let through
The unsuspicious eyes of honesty. — LOWELL.

15. In the latter part of his life, when impressed with the sublime events brought about through his agency, Columbus looked back upon his career with a sublime and superstitious feeling. — IRVING.

16. The goodliest cedars which grow on the high mountains of Libanus thrust their roots between the clefts of hard rocks, the better to bear themselves against the strong storms that blow there. — RALEIGH.

17. My walk under the pines would lose half its summer charm were I to miss that shy anchorite, the Wilson's thrush, nor hear in haying time the metallic ring of his song, that justifies his rustic name of scythe-whet.

LOWELL.

18. Nature and Time seem to have conspired to make the development of the Mississippi basin and the Pacific slope the swiftest, easiest, completest achievement in the whole record of the civilizing progress of mankind since the founder of the Egyptian monarchy gathered the tribes of the Nile under one government. — BRYCE.

LESSON CLXXV.

RECASTING THE SENTENCE.

Iron is the most useful of metals.

1. Iron is more useful than any other metal.
2. No other metal is so useful as iron.
3. Every other metal is less useful than iron.
4. Iron surpasses all other metals in usefulness.
5. The usefulness of iron is not equaled by that of any other metal.
6. The king of all metals is iron.
7. No other metal equals iron in usefulness to mankind.
8. In usefulness, iron surpasses even gold and silver.
9. More than any other metal, iron advances civilization.
10. Strongest and best of our servants is iron.

Do these sentences all express the same idea?
Which sentence do you like best?

Express the following thoughts in as many ways as possible : —

1. Industry is the cause of prosperity.
2. Many who conquer their anger cannot conquer their pride.
3. Henry IV. said that James I. was the wisest fool in Christendom.
4. Let another man praise thee, and not thine own mouth; a stranger, and not thine own lips. — BIBLE.
5. Beware of desperate steps.   The darkest day,
   Live till to-morrow will have passed away. — COWPER.

6. The noblest mind the best contentment has.

SPENSER.

7. There is a pleasure in the pathless woods,
   There is a rapture on the lonely shore. — BYRON.

8. But words are things; and a small drop of ink,
   Falling like dew upon the thought, produces
   That which makes thousands, perhaps millions, think.

BYRON.

9. I find the great thing in this world is not so much where we stand, as in what direction we are moving. — HOLMES.

10. They are never alone who are accompanied with noble thoughts. — SIDNEY.

LESSON CLXXVI.

THE COMPOUND SENTENCE.

A compound sentence consists of two or more coördinate sentences so united as to express closely related propositions, but having no grammatical dependence upon each other.

The vine still clings to the moldering wall,
And at every gust the dead leaves fall.

He that observeth the winds shall not sow; and he that regardeth the clouds shall not reap.

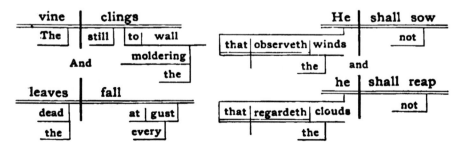

The coördinate sentences which are united to form a compound sentence are called MEMBERS.

The members of a compound sentence may be : —

1. *Simple.*

> The vine still clings to the moldering wall,
> And at every gust the dead leaves fall.

2. *Simple and complex.*

> He that is soon angry dealeth foolishly; and a man of wicked device is hated.

3. *Complex.*

> If thine enemy be hungry, give him bread to eat;
> if he be thirsty, give him water to drink.

Compound sentences may be divided into two general classes, coördinate and illative.

COÖRDINATE SENTENCES.

In coördinate sentences the members have no grammatical dependence, but are connected to show natural sequence of thought, comparison, contrast, etc. They may be classed as, —

1. Copulative ; 2. Disjunctive ; 3. Antithetic or adversative.

The copulative sentence consists of two or more members having no logical dependence, but expressing a natural sequence, one independent statement added to another ; as, —

Appoint a time for everything, and do everything in its time.

The connective is frequently omitted, and such omission often makes the style more vigorous ; as, —

Appoint a time for everything ; do everything in its time.
Just men alone are free ; the rest are slaves.
You may remain ; I will go myself.

The connectives in copulative sentences are *and, also, likewise, moreover, further, both, as well as,* etc.

The disjunctive sentence consists of two or more members united, but having their meaning distributed; as, —

He must return soon, or his affairs will go wrong.

You must assist me, otherwise I cannot succeed.

He will neither go himself, nor permit any one else to go.

The connectives in disjunctive sentences are *such as, either, or, neither, nor, otherwise, else, but,* etc.

When two members of a compound sentence express contrast or opposition, the sentence is called ANTITHETIC or ADVERSATIVE; as, —

Abel was a keeper of sheep; but Cain was a tiller of the ground.

Wise men lay up knowledge; but the mouth of the foolish is near destruction.

The following are the principal connectives of antithetic sentences: *but, however, only, on the one hand, on the other hand, yet, still.*

ILLATIVE SENTENCES.

Illative sentences are those in which a second member stands in some logical relation to the first, to express cause, conclusion, or effect.

Learn of me, for I am meek and lowly in heart.

His friends trusted him because he was honorable.

I believed, therefore I have spoken.

As Cæsar loved me, I weep for him; as he was valiant, I honor him; but as he was ambitious, I slew him.

The connectives in illative sentences are *such as, therefore, wherefore, because, hence, thereupon,* etc.

ANALYSIS OF COMPOUND SENTENCES.

A compound sentence is analyzed by stating: —

1. That it is compound.
2. Its class, — whether copulative, disjunctive, antithetic, or illative.
3. Its coördinate members.
4. The conjunction (or other word) by which they are connected.
5. The analysis of each member as a simple or a complex sentence.

MODELS FOR ANALYZING COMPOUND SENTENCES.

1. Righteousness exalteth a nation; but sin is a reproach to any people.

This is a compound declarative sentence, antithetic, composed of the two coördinate simple sentences, *righteousness exalteth a nation*, and *sin is a reproach to any people*, connected by the disjunctive conjunction *but*.

The subject, logical and grammatical, of the first member, is *righteousness*.

The logical predicate is *exalteth a nation*.

The grammatical predicate *exalteth* is completed by the objective complement *nation*, which is modified by the adjective *a*.

The subject, logical and grammatical, of the second member, is *sin*.

The logical predicate is *is a reproach to any people*.

The grammatical predicate *is* is completed by the attributive complement *reproach*, which is modified by the adjective *a* and the prepositional adjective phrase *to any people*.

2. If thine enemy be hungry, give him bread to eat; and if he be thirsty, give him water to drink.

This is a compound declarative sentence, copulative, composed of the two coördinate complex sentences, *if thine enemy be hungry, give him bread to eat,* and *if he be thirsty, give him water to drink,* the connective being *and.*

The logical subject of the first complex member is *thou* understood.

The logical predicate is *give him bread to eat, if thine enemy be hungry.*

The principal clause is *give him bread to eat.*

The subordinate clause is *if thine enemy be hungry.*

The connective is the subordinate conjunction *if.*

The subject, logical and grammatical, of the principal clause, is *thou* understood.

The logical predicate is *give him bread to eat.*

The grammatical predicate *give* is completed by the objective complement *bread* and the dative complement *him.*

The objective complement *bread* is modified by the infinitive *to eat,* used as an adjective.

The logical subject of the subordinate clause is *thine enemy.*

The logical predicate is *be hungry.*

The grammatical subject *enemy* is modified by the possessive pronoun *thine.*

The grammatical predicate *be* is completed by the attributive complement *hungry.*

The logical subject of the second complex member is *thou* understood.

The logical predicate is *if he be thirsty, give him water to drink.*

The principal clause is *give him water to drink.*

The subordinate clause is *if he be thirsty.*

The connective is the subordinate conjunction *if.*

The subject, logical and grammatical, of the principal clause, is *thou* understood.

The logical predicate is *give him water to drink.*

The grammatical predicate *give* is completed by the objective complement *water* and the dative complement *him*.

The objective complement *water* is modified by the infinitive *to drink*, used as an adjective.

The subject, logical and grammatical, of the subordinate clause, is *he*.

The logical predicate is *be thirsty*.

The grammatical predicate *be* is completed by the attributive complement *thirsty*.

3. A moral, sensible, and well-bred man
    Will not affront me, and no other can. — COWPER.

This is a compound declarative sentence, copulative, composed of the two coördinate simple sentences, *a moral, sensible, and well-bred man will not affront me*, and *no other can*, connected by the conjunction *and*.

The logical subject of the first member is *a moral, sensible, and well-bred man*.

The logical predicate is *will not affront me*.

The grammatical subject *man* is modified by the adjectives *a, moral, sensible,* and *well-bred*, the last two connected by the conjunction *and*.

The grammatical predicate *will affront* is modified by the adverb *not*, and completed by the objective complement *me*.

The logical subject of the second member is *no other*.

The logical predicate is *can affront me*.

The grammatical subject *other* is modified by the adjective *no*.

The grammatical predicate *can affront* is completed by the objective complement *me*.

Analyze the following sentences : —

1. Wisdom is better than rubies, and all things that may be desired are not to be compared to it. — BIBLE.

2. Mankind is always happier for having been happy; if you make them happy now, you make them happy twenty years hence by the memory of it. — SMITH.

3. To have a respect for ourselves guides our morals; and to have a deference for others governs our manners. — STERNE.

4.   Beside a sandal tree a woodman stood,
   And swung an ax; and as the strokes were laid
   Upon the fragrant trunk, the generous wood
With its own sweets perfumed the cruel blade.

BRYANT.

5. Heaven is above all; there sits a Judge
   That no King can corrupt. — SHAKESPEARE.

6. Every day is a little life;
   And life is but a day repeated. — BISHOP HALL.

7. The robins are not good solo singers; but their chorus, as, like primitive fire worshipers, they hail the return of light and warmth to the world, is unrivaled. — LOWELL.

8. The hearts of men are their books; events are their tutors; great actions are their eloquence. — MACAULAY.

9. Blessed is he who has found his work : let him ask no other blessedness. — CARLYLE.

10. I do not count the hours I spend
    In wandering by the sea;
    The forest is my loyal friend,
    A Delphic shrine to me. — EMERSON.

11. Reading furnishes the mind only with materials of knowledge : it is thinking that makes what we read ours.

LOCKE.

12. The woods are gay with the clustered flowers of the laurel; the air is perfumed with the sweetbrier and the wild rose; the meadows are enameled with clover blossoms. — IRVING.

13. Thence look the thoughtful stars, and there
The meek moon walks the silent air. — BRYANT.

14. Cowards die many times before their deaths;
The valiant never taste of death but once.

SHAKESPEARE.

15. Keep your head and heart full of good thoughts, and the bad ones will find no room.

LESSON CLXXVII.

PUNCTUATION. — THE SEMICOLON.

Place a semicolon (;) between the two members of a compound sentence, if one is complete in itself and the other added for the sake of contrast or explanation; thus,—

The miser grows rich by seeming poor; but an extravagant man grows poor by seeming rich.

Do not think yourself perfect; for imperfection is natural to humanity.

When the members of a compound sentence are but slightly connected in thought or construction, they are separated by semicolons; thus,—

Everything grows old; everything passes away; everything disappears.

There is good for the good; there is virtue for the faithful; there is victory for the valiant.

The members of a compound sentence are separated by a semicolon, if either member contains elements separated by commas; thus,—

Without dividing, he destroyed party; without corrupting, he made a venal age unanimous.

His best impulses become a snare to him; and he is led astray because he is social, sympathetic, and warm-hearted.

Tell why the semicolon is used in the following sentences. Write the sentences from dictation.

1. On this side were tyranny, ignorance, superstition; on that, culture, progress, freedom.

2. A man's country is not a certain area of land, but it is a principle; and patriotism is loyalty to that principle.

CURTIS.

3. The noise of running brooks and the dripping of the fertilizing rain are music to his ears; the whispering of the great trees of the forest is sweet to him; his eye is trained to note the changeful phases of the sky, and his mind quick to interpret them. — HOFFMAN.

4. France arrests the attention; Napoleon rose and seated himself on the throne of the Bourbons; he pointed the thunder of his artillery at Italy, and she fell before him; he leveled his lightning at Spain, and she trembled; he sounded the knell of vengeance on the plains of Austerlitz, and all Europe was at his feet; he was greater than Cæsar; he was greater than Alexander.

5. A bullet kills a tyrant; but an idea kills tyranny.

CURTIS.

6. A halo of martial glory surrounds them, then fades

away; their marble thrones crumble; their iron limbs are broken; their proud navies are sunk. — OSTRANDER.

7. France wavered; Germany stood back; England was lukewarm; Italy sided with Spain.

8. The miser grows rich by seeming poor; an extravagant man grows poor by seeming rich. — PROVERB.

9. The shadow of the earth in every position is round; consequently the earth is a globe.

10. Some must watch, while some must sleep:
So runs the world away. — SHAKESPEARE.

11. There is good for the good; there is virtue for the faithful; there is victory for the valiant; there is spirituality for the spiritual.

12. To be content with what is sufficient is the greatest wisdom; he who increases his riches increases his cares.

13. The man of the world does not make a speech; he takes a low business tone, avoids all brag, dresses plainly, promises not at all, performs much.

14. When a writer reasons, we look only for perspicuity; when he describes, we expect embellishment; when he decides or relates, we desire plainness and simplicity.

15. A slender acquaintance with the world must convince every man that actions, not words, are the true criterion of the attachment of friends; and that the most liberal professions of good will are very far from being the surest marks of it. — WASHINGTON.

16. Words learned by rote a parrot may rehearse,
But talking is not always to converse;
Not more distinct from harmony divine
The constant creaking of a country sign.

COWPER.

LESSON CLXXVIII.

COMPOSITION.

A LETTER.

BAY ST. LOUIS, MISS.,
Feb. 15, 1889.

To the Editor of the "Critic."

Dear Sir,—When I was a boy, an edition of the writings of Edgar A. Poe came to my hand, and I read it amid the hills of Cherokee, Ga. Attached to the work was a little essay by Mr. Lowell. That was in 1859, some ten years after Poe's death. From then till now (and I can feel the influence projecting itself into the future), what Mr. Lowell has written has been a part of my education. From my point of view, no living American, in assuming to speak for American culture, has so thoroughly justified himself as has Mr. Lowell. While our novelists have been showing us how ill bred and plebeian we are, and while our critics in general have been taking the pitch of their strain from London masters, there have been in his writings a vigor, a manliness, and a patriotic independence, always pure, racy, and refreshing, which have made us aware of our own value as the creators of a new civilization of which the old is not competent to judge. Wherever the most healthful and most fertilizing influence of American republicanism has gone, wherever the best essence of American aspiration has insinuated itself to liberalize human thought, or to give vigor to reforms, there have been felt the sincere force and the subtle earnestness of Mr. Lowell's words set in the phrasing of a master of style. His seventieth birthday marks the threescore and ten of a life very precious to America and to all the enlightened world.   To me it is a privilege of the highest kind to have this opportunity to join the "Critic's" distinguished guests in paying this small but sincere tribute of respect to America's most distinguished critic, and to wish him every good.   Yours very truly,

MAURICE THOMPSON.

After studying the above letter of appreciation, write a similar one, telling what author has given you pleasure or inspiration.

LESSON CLXXIX.

THE USE OF WORDS.

Illustrate by an original sentence the precise use of each of the following words : —

ACKNOWLEDGE. CONFESS.	I acknowledge the kindness I have received, and confess my fault.
APPLAUD. PRAISE.	One applauds in public, and praises at all times and under all circumstances.
DEFEND. PROTECT.	We defend what is attacked, and protect what is weak.
RECEIVE. ACCEPT.	To receive can be used either in a voluntary or involuntary sense; but to accept implies, at least, readiness.
AFFECT.	We affect with the view not only of impressing, but of misleading others.
EFFECT.	The carrying of pollen to distant plants is effected by the wind.

LESSON CLXXX.

PUNCTUATION. — THE SEMICOLON.

Two or more clauses having a common grammatical relation are usually separated by semicolons; thus, —

The affections which spread beyond ourselves, and stretch far into futurity; the workings of mighty passions; the innocent and irrepressible joy of infancy; the bloom and buoyancy and dazzling hopes of youth; the tones and looks which only a mother's heart can inspire, — these are all poetical.

Place a semicolon before *as* and *namely* when they precede an example or specification of particulars; thus, —

He traded in country produce; as, grain, vegetables, and fruit.

There are four seasons; namely, spring, summer, autumn, winter.

Tell why the semicolon is used in the following sentences. Write the sentences from dictation.

1. To Greece we are indebted for the three principal orders of architecture; namely, the Doric, the Ionic, and the Corinthian.

2. To be really wise, we must labor after knowledge; to be learned, we must study; to be great in anything, we must have patience.

3. According to a late writer, London surpasses all other great cities in four particulars; namely, size, commerce, fogs, and pickpockets.

4. Some men distinguish the period of the world into four ages; namely, the golden age, the silver age, the brazen age, and the iron age.

5. If we neglected no opportunity of doing good; if we fed the hungry and ministered to the sick; if we gave up our own luxuries to secure necessary comforts for the destitute, — though no man might be aware of our generosity, yet in the applause of our own conscience we should have an ample reward.

6. A sensible man has one mode of articulation, and one only; namely, always to pronounce his words in such a manner as to be readily understood, but never in such a manner as to excite remark. — LEGOUVÉ.

7. Philosophers assert that Nature is unlimited in her operations; that she has inexhaustible treasures in reserve; that knowledge will always be progressive; and that all future generations will continue to make discoveries of which we have not the slightest idea.

8. As for jest, there be certain things which ought to be privileged from it; namely, religion, matters of state, great persons, any man's present business of importance, any case that deserveth pity. — BACON.

LESSON CLXXXI.

SENTENCES WITH COMPOUND ELEMENTS.

A sentence may have two or more elements having a common relation to other words.

Grammar and arithmetic are important studies.
The teacher worked and explained the example.

Webster was a statesman and an orator.

John and James study and recite history and geography.

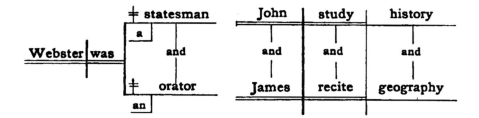

A sentence may have : —

1. *A compound subject.*

   (*a*) The boy and his sister are obedient.

   (*b*) John and James resemble each other.

   (*c*) Mercy and truth are met together.

2. *A compound predicate.*

   (*a*) The man read and appreciated the letter.

   (*b*) I feel your kindness, and wish for an opportunity to requite it.

3. *A compound complement.*

   (*a*) Objective.

   God created the heavens and the earth.

   (*b*) Predicate adjective.

   The sky is bright and clear.

   Be ye therefore wise as serpents, and harmless as doves.

   (*c*) Predicate noun.

   He was a prince and a conqueror.

4. *A compound adjective element.*

   He is an honest and industrious man.

5. *A compound adverbial element.*

> He spoke eloquently and forcibly.
> He was trusted by his neighbors and by all who knew him.

6. *All its elements compound.*

> John and his sister study and recite grammar and arithmetic.

A sentence with a compound element is usually equivalent to a compound sentence ; thus, —

The above sentences are respectively equivalent to : —

1. (*a*) The boy is obedient, and his sister is obedient.

2. (*a*) The teacher read the lesson, and the teacher explained the lesson.

3. (*a*) God created the heavens, and God created the earth.

    (*b*) The sky is bright, and the sky is clear.

    (*c*) He was a prince, and he was a conqueror.

4. He is an honest man, and he is an industrious man.

5. He spoke eloquently, and he spoke forcibly.

6. John studies grammar, and his sister studies grammar ; John recites grammar, and his sister recites grammar ; John studies arithmetic, and his sister studies arithmetic ; John recites arithmetic, and his sister recites arithmetic.

Sentences having compound elements that may be thus expanded into a compound sentence are properly called *contracted compound sentences.*

Some sentences, however, having compound elements, cannot be thus expanded into compound sentences ; thus, —

The clematis and ivy cover the wall is a sentence with a compound subject; but it is not equivalent to the compound sentence, *the clematis covers the wall, and the ivy covers the wall,* for the wall is not covered by either alone, but by both together.

Sentences similar to this are properly called *simple sentences with compound elements.*

ANALYSIS OF SENTENCES WITH COMPOUND ELEMENTS.

A sentence with a compound element is analyzed by stating: —

1. The element that is compound.
2. The regular analysis.

MODELS FOR ANALYZING SENTENCES WITH COMPOUND ELEMENTS.

1. The clematis and ivy cover the wall.
2. On land and sea he is equally at home.
3. He most lives who thinks most, feels the noblest acts the best.

1. The clematis and ivy cover the wall.

This is a simple declarative sentence with a compound subject.

The logical subject of the sentence is the compound subject *the clematis and ivy.*

The logical predicate is *cover the wall.*

The grammatical subject is compound, comprising the two simple subjects *clematis* and *ivy; clematis* being limited by the adjective *the,* and *clematis* and *ivy* being connected by the conjunction *and.*

The grammatical predicate is *cover.* This is completed by the objective complement *wall,* which is modified by the adjective *the.*

2. On land and sea he is equally at home.

This is a simple declarative sentence.

The subject, logical and grammatical, is *he.*

The logical predicate is *is equally at home on land and sea.*

The grammatical predicate is *is,* which is modified by the adverbial phrase *at home,* which is in turn modified by the adverb *equally,* and the compound adverbial phrase *on land and sea;* the two parts of this phrase being connected by the conjunction *and.*

3. He most lives who thinks most, feels the noblest, acts the best.

This is a complex declarative sentence, the subordinate clause having a compound predicate.

The logical subject is *he who thinks most, feels the noblest, acts the best.*

The logical predicate is *lives most.*

The principal sentence is *he most lives.*

The subordinate clause is *who thinks most, feels the noblest, acts the best.*

The connective is the relative pronoun *who.*

The subject, logical and grammatical, of the principal sentence, is *he.*

The logical predicate is *lives most.*

The grammatical predicate *lives* is modified by the adverb *most.*

The subject, logical and grammatical, of the subordinate clause, is *who.*

The logical predicate is the compound predicate *thinks most, feels the noblest, acts the best.*

The grammatical predicate is compound, comprising the simple predicates *thinks, feels,* and *acts. Thinks* is modified by the adverb *most; feels,* by the adverb *noblest,* which is modified by the adverb *the;* and *acts*, by the adverb *best*, which is modified by the adverb *the*.

Analyze the following sentences : —

1. The calm gray sky of early morn
    Was flecked and barred with golden clouds.

   HOOD.

2. The professor will examine, decipher, and classify them.

3. Princes and lords are but the breath of kings.

   BURNS.

4. The heroic soul does not sell its justice and its nobleness. — EMERSON.

5. Our intellectual and active powers increase with our affection. — EMERSON.

6. Carlyle's reverence and affection for his kindred were among his most beautiful traits. — BURROUGHS.

7. Those ivy-covered walls and ruins, those finished fields, those rounded hedgerows, those embowered cottages, and that gray massive architecture, all contribute to the harmony and to the repose of the landscape.

8. It is faith in something, and enthusiasm for something, that makes a life worth looking at. — HOLMES.

9. Politeness is to do and say
    The kindest thing in the kindest way.

10. The greatest pleasure I know is to do a good action by stealth, and to have it found out by accident. — LAMB.

11. The south wind searches for the flowers
     Whose fragrance late he bore,
     And sighs to find them in the wood
     And by the stream no more. — BRYANT.

12. But the good deed, through the ages,
   Living in historic pages,
   Brighter grows, and gleams immortal,
   Unconsumed by moth or rust. — LONGFELLOW.

13. A faint sound of organ music floating from the cathedral, and seeming to deepen the hush of the summer wind, delighted me with its sweetness.

14. The chime of bells remote, the murmuring sea,
   The song of birds in whispering copse and wood,
   The distant voice of children's thoughtless glee,
   And maiden's song, are all one voice of good.
                                        STERLING

15. Out of the bosom of the air,
   Out of the cloud folds of her garment shaken
Over the woodlands brown and bare,
   Over the harvest fields forsaken,
Silent and soft and low,
   Descends the snow. — LONGFELLOW.

LESSON CLXXXII.

STUDY OF POEM.

THE CHAMBERED NAUTILUS.

This is the ship of pearl, which, poets feign,
   Sails the unshadowed main, —
   The venturous bark that flings
On the sweet summer wind its purpled wings
In gulfs enchanted, where the Siren sings,
   And coral reefs lie bare,
Where the cold sea-maids rise to sun their streaming hair.

Its webs of living gauze no more unfurl;
    Wrecked is the ship of pearl!
    And every chambered cell,
Where its dim dreaming life was wont to dwell,
As the frail tenant shaped his growing shell,
    Before thee lies revealed, —
Its irised ceiling rent, its sunless crypt unsealed!

Year after year beheld the silent toil
    That spread his lustrous coil;
    Still, as the spiral grew,
He left the past year's dwelling for the new,
Stole with soft step its shining archway through,
    Built up its idle door,
Stretched in his last-found home, and knew the old no more.

Thanks for the heavenly message brought by thee,
    Child of the wandering sea,
    Cast from her lap, forlorn!
From thy dead lips a clearer note is born
Than ever Triton blew from wreathèd horn!
    While on mine ear it rings,
Through the deep caves of thought I hear a voice that
    sings : —

Build thee more stately mansions, O my soul,
    As the swift seasons roll!
    Leave thy low-vaulted past!
Let each new temple, nobler than the last,
Shut thee from heaven with a dome more vast,
    Till thou at length art free,
Leaving thine outgrown shell by life's unresting sea!

OLIVER WENDELL HOLMES.

Copy the poem carefully, and commit it to memory.

Have you ever seen the beautiful pearly shell of the chambered nautilus? Have you seen a picture of the living nautilus? Why is it called "chambered"? How many chambers in the shell? How do they compare in size? In which chamber does the nautilus live? Are the other chambers empty?

What do you understand by "sunless crypt"? What do you think is meant by "irised ceiling"? Note the beauty of the line, "Stole with soft step its shining archway through." Point out other figurative expressions.

In which stanza is the thought suggested by what the poet saw? In which does he express what he heard?

What are the "stately mansions of the soul"? How are they built? State in your own words the meaning of the last stanza.

Many persons think the third stanza the richest. Which do you like best?

Write from memory the entire poem.

LESSON CLXXXIII.

PUNCTUATION.— THE COLON.

If the first member of a compound sentence is followed by some remark or illustration that is not introduced by a conjunction, the clauses are separated by a colon (:); thus, —

Study to acquire the habit of thinking : no study is more important.

The two principal members of a compound sentence are separated by a colon, if either of them contains members or clauses separated by a semicolon; thus, —

Education does not commence with the alphabet : it begins with a mother's look ; with a father's nod of approbation, or a sign of reproof ; with a sister's gentle pressure of the hand, or a brother's noble act of forbearance.

Place a colon after the formal introduction of a quotation, speech, or series of particulars ; thus, —

We all admire this sublime passage : " God said, ' Let there be light ; ' and there was light."

A colon should be placed after *yes* or *no*, when followed by a statement in continuation or repetition of the answer ; thus, —

Yes : I am a foreigner.   But who was Lafayette, who was Pulaski, and who was Arnold ?

Tell why the colon is used in the following sentences. Write the sentences from dictation.

1. Nature never hurries : atom by atom, little by little, she achieves her work.

2. His genius embodied the three essential characteristics of a great general : forethought, abstraction, will.

3. Never flatter people : leave that to such as mean to betray them.

4. Homer was the greater genius ; Virgil, the better artist : in the one, we most admire the man ; in the other, the work. — POPE.

5. The quality of mercy is not strained ;
   It droppeth as the gentle rain from heaven
   Upon the place beneath : it is twice blessed ;
   It blesseth him that gives, and him that takes.

   SHAKESPEARE.

LESSON CLXXXIV.

FIGURES OF RHETORIC.

A figure of rhetoric is an intentional deviation from the ordinary application of words with a view to making the meaning more effective.

The figures of speech most frequently used are those which imply closeness of relation, likeness, or unlikeness. The simile and the metaphor have been already considered.

Other figures of speech in common use are : metonymy, synecdoche, personification, allusion, climax, hyperbole, and pleonasm.

1. *Metonymy* means a change of name. It is a figure in which the name of one thing is put for another which it suggests.

Common forms of metonymy : —

Cause for effect.

　　He writes a plain hand

Effect for cause.

　　Gray hairs should be respected.

Container for thing contained.

　　The kettle boils.

Sign for thing signified.

　　The pen is mightier than the sword.

Name of an author for his works.

　　We study Shakespeare.

2. *Synecdoche* is the putting of a part for the whole, the whole for a part, or a definite number for an indefinite ; as, —

I welcome you to my fireside.

France was devastated by **war**.

Ten thousand fleets sweep over thee in vain.

3. *Personification* is the assigning of personality and intelligence to inanimate or irrational objects : —

By the use of epithet.

Smiling fields.

By ascribing action to inanimate things.

The waves beckon to us.

By addressing inanimate things.

Break, break, break,

At the foot of thy crags, O Sea !

4. *Allusion* is a reference to some historical or literary incident, fact, or saying, supposed to be so well understood that it may be denoted by some word or phrase, without being fully described ; as, —

Quebec is the Gibraltar of America.

5. *Climax* consists of an arrangement of ideas by which the sentence rises, as it were, step by step, in importance, force, or dignity ; as, —

I came, I saw, I conquered.

6. *Hyperbole* is an exaggerated form of statement. It should be used sparingly.

And fired the shot heard round the world.

7. *Pleonasm* is the using of more words than are necessary to the construction ; as, —

The boy — oh ! where was he ?

The prophets — do they live forever ?

Point out and explain the figures of rhetoric in the following : —

1. The cattle upon a thousand hills.

2. His steel gleamed on high.

3. He beheld a sea of faces.

4. White as a sea fog landward bound,
    The spectral camp was seen. — LONGFELLOW.

5. But look! the morn, in russet mantle clad,
    Walks o'er the dew of yon high eastern hill.

    SHAKESPEARE.

6. Night's candles are burnt out, and jocund day
    Stands tiptoe on the misty mountain tops.

    SHAKESPEARE.

7.   For Pleasure and Revenge
    Have ears more deaf than adders, to the voice
    Of any true decision. — SHAKESPEARE.

8. Now dark in the shadow, she scatters the spray,
    As the chaff in the stroke of the flail;
    Now white as the sea gull, she flies on her way,
    The sun gleaming bright on her sail.

9. The world to him, as to all of us, was like a medal,
    on the obverse of which is stamped the image of Joy, and
    on the reverse that of Care. — LOWELL.

10. Dreams are bright creatures of poem and legend,
    sporting on earth in the night season, and melting away
    in the first beams of the sun, which lights grim Care and
    stern Reality in their pilgrimage through the world.

    DICKENS.

LESSON CLXXXV.

REVIEW. — SENTENCES.

1. Define a sentence.

2. Distinguish between simple and modified subject; simple and modified predicate.

3. What is meant by an element? Classify the elements of a sentence with respect to rank, office, and structure.

4. In how many ways may the grammatical subject of a sentence be modified?

5. Name the possible modifiers of the grammatical predicate.

6. Distinguish between the direct and the indirect object.

7. Write three simple sentences, three complex sentences, three compound sentences.

8. Write two sentences in each of which the subject is a phrase used as a noun.

9. Write two sentences in each of which the subject is a clause used as a noun.

10. Write three sentences in each of which the verb has two or more subjects connected by *and*.

11. Write three sentences in each of which the verb has two or more singular subjects connected by *or* or *nor*.

12. Write sentences, using as the predicate, —

    (*a*) A transitive verb with an infinitive as direct object.

    (*b*) An intransitive verb completed by an adjective.

    (*c*) A transitive verb with an object clause.

    (*d*) A verb in the passive voice with an adverbial clause.

LESSON CLXXXVI.

REVIEW.

Give the reasons for the punctuation of the following sentences : —

1. Economy is no disgrace; for it is better to live on a little than to outlive a great deal.

2. He was heard to say, " I have done with the world."

3. Three properties belong to wisdom : nature, learning, and experience.

4. Study to acquire a habit of thinking : no study is more important.

5. A great man will be great in misfortune, great in prison, great in chains.

6. This must be owned, that to love one's relatives is not always an easy task ; to live with one's neighbor is not amusing. — THACKERAY.

7. Self-reverence, self-knowledge, self-control,
    These three alone lead life to sovereign power.
    Yet not for power (power of herself would come
        uncalled for), but to live by law,
    Acting the law we live by without fear ;
    And because right is right, to follow right,
    Were wisdom in the scorn of consequence.
                                        TENNYSON.

8. How sweet the moonlight sleeps upon this bank !
    Here will we sit, and let the sounds of music
    Creep in our ears. — SHAKESPEARE.

9. Consider the lilies of the field ; they toil not, neither do they spin.

APPENDIX.

RULES OF SYNTAX.

1. **A noun or a pronoun used as the subject of a verb must be in the nominative case.**

A substantive clause used as the subject of a sentence is frequently placed after the verb; the pronoun *it* introducing the sentence, and standing as the representative subject, with which the subject clause is said to be in apposition ; as, —

> It is not true that I said so =
> It, that I said so, is not true.   (What is not true?)

The word *there*, used simply for euphony, often introduces a sentence, the subject following the verb; as, —

> There is no terror, Cassius, in your threats.
> There came to the beach a poor exile of Erin.

2. **A noun or a pronoun used as the complement of an intransitive or a passive verb must be in the nominative case; as, —**

> It is I.   He became a scholar.
> This is he.   He shall be called John.

A noun or pronoun following the infinitive of the verb *be*, or of any other incomplete verb, must be in the same case as the word whose act, being, or state of being, the infinitive expresses (that is, in the same case as the subject); as, —

> I did not suppose it to be him (objective).
> He desires to become a scholar (nominative).

3. **A noun or a pronoun used simply in address is in the nominative independent; as,** —

> O thou that rollest above! whence are thy beams?
> There is no terror, Cassius, in thy threats.

(1) A noun in the nominative independent may be the antecedent of a relative pronoun; as, —

> Ye stars, that are the poetry of heaven.

(2) A noun used in mere exclamation, in the manner of an interjection, is in the nominative independent; as, —

> My gold! my iron chest! they will break in, and rob my iron chest!

(3) A noun or a pronoun used by *pleonasm* is in the nominative independent; as, —

> The prophets, do they live forever?

4. **A noun or a pronoun limited by a participle, and not in grammatical relation with any other word in a sentence, is in the nominative absolute; as,** —

> The sun having risen, we pursued our journey.

Sometimes the participle, or some governing word, is understood; as, —

> Hat in hand, he stood and gazed.

5. A noun or a pronoun used as the object of a transitive verb or a preposition, must be in the objective case.

6. A noun or a pronoun used to limit another noun by denoting possession, origin, or fitness, must be in the possessive case.

(1) A noun or a pronoun in the possessive case may relate to a participle used as a noun, even when the participle retains its verb character of governing an objective case ; as, —

His having done his duty was a sufficient reward.

(2) When two or more possessives are used jointly to limit the same noun, only the last takes the sign of the possessive ; as, —

Mason and Dixon's line.

(3) When separate possession is indicated, each possessive should have the sign ; as, —

Webster's and Worcester's dictionaries.
John's and William's books are new.

(4) When two or more possessives are in apposition, and precede the noun which they limit, only the last takes the sign of the possessive ; as, —

Webster the statesman's speeches.
My friend the poet's latest work.

(5) But when the possessive in apposition forms the abridged complement of an intransitive or a passive verb, the first may take the sign ; as, —

This speech is Webster's, the defender of the Constitution.

7. A noun or a pronoun in apposition must agree in case with the noun or pronoun which it explains.

Substantives in the same member of a sentence, and standing for the same person or thing, are said to be in apposition ; as, —

Hope, the balm of life, soothes us under misfortune (nominative).

Jack the giant-killer's wonderful exploits (possessive).

We saw Forrest, the great trágedian, in " Hamlet " (objective).

8. A pronoun must agree with its antecedent in gender, person, and number.

The case of a pronoun is determined by its construction.

(1) When a pronoun has two or more antecedents connected by *and*, it must be in the plural number ; as, —

He sought wealth and fame ; but they alike eluded him.

John and I do our duty.

(2) When a pronoun has two or more singular antecedents connected by *or* or *nor*, it must agree with each in the singular number ; as, —

Neither the man nor the boy was in his place.

If you have a pencil or a pen, bring it to me.

(3) But when one of the antecedents is plural the pronoun also must be in the plural ; as, —

Either the girl or her brothers have come, and they will assist us.

(4) A collective noun denoting unity must have a pronoun in the singular ; as, —

> The class was in its room when I arrived.

(5) A noun of multitude requires a pronoun in the plural ; as, —

> The people ran to their houses.
> The clergy began to withdraw themselves.

(6) The words *one, each, every, either, neither*, take a pronoun in the singular ; as, —

> Every one of the men had his own business to attend to.

(7) Antecedents of different persons, numbers, or genders, connected by *or* or *nor*, should not, as a rule, be represented by a common pronoun, as there is no pronoun equally applicable to each of them. The plural is, however, used by reputable authors in such instances as the following : —

> Neither my brother nor I can say our lessons to-day.
> Either you or I will be in our place in due time.

If in doubt, make distinct statements ; as, —

> Either I shall be in my place, or you will be in yours.

The antecedents, though of different numbers or persons, may be in such relation that the pronoun denotes common possession ; as, —

> Either my brother or I must take our father's place.

When the gender is common or indeterminate, the masculine pronoun in the third person is generally used ; as, —

> No one can tell how long he may live.

(8) When singular nouns, taken separately, are of different genders, for the want of a singular pronoun of common
gender, we are reduced to the alternative of repeating the
pronoun for each gender, or of violating the rule by using
a pronoun in the plural ; as, —

If any man or woman shall violate his or her pledge, he or she
shall pay a fine, *or*
If any man or woman shall violate their pledge, they shall pay
a fine.

Generally the latter is preferable to the clumsy circum-
locution of the former.

It is better, however, so to construct the sentence, that
by means of separate clauses, or by inversion, the necessity
for the pronoun shall be avoided ; as, —

Any man violating his pledge, or any woman violating hers, shall
pay a fine.
A fine shall be paid by any man or woman who shall violate this
pledge.

9. **An adjective modifies a noun or pronoun.**

(1) The comparative is used when only two things, or
two classes of things, are compared ; the superlative, when
more than two are compared ; as, —

Homer was the greater genius ; Virgil, the better artist.
John is the best scholar in his class (of several).

(2) When the comparative is used, the latter term of
comparison must exclude the former ; thus, —

Rhode Island is smaller than any other State in the Union.

(3) When the superlative is used, the latter term of comparison must include the former; as, —

Rhode Island is the smallest State in the Union.

(4) *Either* and *neither* are used to designate one of two objects only. When more than two objects are referred to, we should use *any, any one, none, no one;* as, —

Here are two books : take either of them.
Neither of these (two) houses is for sale.
You may have any one of those (three).

(5) *Either* should not be used to refer to two objects collectively or distributively in the sense of *both* or *each.* Thus we should not say, —

Trees grow on either side of the road (both sides, or each side).

(6) To express reciprocal relation, the terms *each other* and *one another* are often used.

Each other refers to two persons only ; as, —

The boy and his brother help each other.

One another refers to more than two ; as, —

Those three houses resemble one another.

10. An adverb modifies a verb, an adjective, or another adverb.

(1) Adverbs modify also participles and infinitives. An adverb may modify an adverbial phrase ; as, —

The path of glory leads but to the grave.
He sailed nearly round the globe.

(2) A few adverbs modify nouns or pronouns.

> The men only, not the women, were present.
> I, even I, do bring a flood.
> And chiefly thou, O Spirit! instruct me.
> His being there was merely an accident.

The adverbs used in this way are such as *chiefly, particularly, especially, entirely, altogether, only, merely, partly, also, likewise, too.*

(3) Adverbs modifying nouns usually restrict some idea of number or quantity (adjective or adverbial idea) contained in the noun; as, —

> I alone am left to tell thee.
> He lives nearly a mile from the village.

11. A verb must agree with its subject in person and number.

(1) Ellipsis of the principal verb is not admissible when the auxiliaries require it to be of a different form; as, —

> This opinion never has and never can prevail, *for*
> This opinion never has prevailed, and never can prevail.

When a pronoun is the subject of a verb, the number and person are determined by the antecedent.

(2) A collective noun standing for many considered as one whole must have a verb in the singular; as, —

> The army was defeated.
> The regiment consists of one thousand men.

(3) When the verb affirms something of many as individuals (noun of multitude), it must be in the plural; as, —

> People are of different opinions.

(4) The word *number*, followed by *of* with a plural noun, meaning many or several, must have a verb in the plural; but *number* preceded by *the* takes a singular verb; as, —

A number of persons were injured.

A very great number of our words are derived from the Latin.

The number of pupils present was six.

(5) When a verb has two or more subjects connected by *and*, it must agree with them in the plural; as, —

Temperance and exercise preserve health.

When two subjects are connected, one of which is taken affirmatively and the other negatively, the verb must agree with the affirmative subject, and be understood with the other in its own person and number; as, —

My poverty, but not my will, consents.

Ambition, and not the safety of the state, was concerned.

(6) Several singular subjects, though connected by *and*, if preceded by *each, every*, or *no*, must have a verb in the singular; as, —

Each paper and each book was in its place.

Every leaf and every twig teems with life.

No oppressor and no tyrant triumphs here.

(7) When two nominatives are connected by *as well as*, the verb agrees with the first, and may be understood with the second in the person and number required; as, —

You, as well as your brother, are to be blamed.

They, as well as I, are invited.

(8) When several terms are used to describe only one person or thing, the verb must be in the singular; as, —

The saint, the father, and the husband prays.

This philosopher and poet was banished from his country.

(9) When a verb has two or more singular subjects connected by *or* or *nor*, it must be in the singular number; as, —

>   Either Mary or her sister was in the house.
>   Neither silk nor cotton is produced in Great Britain.

Reputable authors use a plural verb after *neither — nor*, because by implication what is denied of each of the subjects is denied of all; as, —

> Neither you nor I are in fault; *that is*, we are not in fault.

(10) If one of the subjects is plural, it should be placed next to the verb, and the verb must be in the plural; as, —

>   Either the captain or the sailors were to blame.

(11) If two or more subjects connected by *or* or *nor* differ in person, the verb should generally agree with the one next to it; as, —

>   Either you or I am expected at the meeting.
>   Thou or he may have the book.

It is better, however, to avoid doubtful usage by repeating the verb whenever practicable, or by changing the structure of the sentence; as, —

> Either the captain was to blame, or the sailors were (to blame).
> You are expected at the meeting, or I am (expected).
> It is expected that either you or I shall attend the meeting.
> Thou mayst have the book, or he may have it.

12. A preposition introduces a phrase, and shows the relation of its object to the word which the phrase modifies.

13. A conjunction connects words, phrases, clauses, or sentences.

14. **An interjection has no grammatical relation to the other words in the sentence.**

15. **A participle is used as a noun or as an adjective.**

16. **An infinitive is used as a noun, an adjective, or an adverb.**

LIST OF IRREGULAR VERBS.

The following list comprises nearly all the irregular verbs in the language. Those conjugated regularly, as well as irregularly, are marked with an R. Those in *Italics* are obsolete, or but little used at the present time. The present participle is omitted in this table, as it is always formed regularly from the simple root by annexing *ing*.

PRESENT.	PAST.	PAST PART.	PRESENT.	PAST.	PAST PART.
abide	abode	abode	blow	blew	blown
am	was	been	break	broke / *brake*	broken / *broke*
arise	arose	arisen	breed	bred	bred
awake	awoke, R	awaked	bring	brought	brought
bake	baked	baked, *baken*	build, *re-*	built, R	built, R
bear	bore, *bare*	born	burn	burnt, R	burnt, R
(*to bring forth*)			burst	burst	burst
bear, *for-*	bore, *bare*	borne	buy	bought	bought
(*to carry*)			cast	cast	cast
beat	beat	beaten, beat	catch	caught, R	caught, R
begin	began	begun	chide	chid	chidden / chid
bend	bent, R	bent, R	choose	chose	chosen
bereave	bereft, R	bereft, R	cleave	clove / cleft	cloven / cleft
beseech	besought	besought	(*to split*)		
bet	bet, R	bet, R	cling	clung	clung
bless	blest, R	blest, R	clothe	clad, R	clad, R
bid	bid, bade	bidden, bid	come, *be-*	came	come
bind, *un-*	bound	bound	cost	cost	cost
bite	bit	bitten, bit			
bleed	bled	bled			

PRESENT.	PAST.	PAST PART.	PRESENT.	PAST.	PAST PART.
creep	crept	crept	hide	hid	hidden, hid
crow	crew, R	crowed	hit	hit	hit
cut	cut	cut	hold, *be-*	held	held, *holden*
dare	durst, R	dared	hurt	hurt	hurt
(*to venture*)			keep	kept	kept
deal	dealt	dealt, R	kneel	knelt, R	knelt, R
dig	dug, R	dug, R	knit	knit, R	knit, R
dive	dove, R	dived	know	knew	known
do, *mis-un-*	did	done	lade	laded	laden, R
draw	drew	drawn	lay	laid	laid
dream	dreamt, R	dreamt, R	lead, *mis-*	led	led
dress	drest, R	drest, R	leave	left	left
drink	drank	{ drank { drunk	lean	leant, R	leant, R
			leap	leapt, R	leapt, R
drive	drove	driven	lend	lent	lent
dwell	dwelt, R	dwelt, R	let	let	let
eat	ate, *ăt*	eaten	lie (*recline*)	lay	lay
fall, *be-*	fell	fallen	light	lit, R	lit, R
feed	fed	fed	lose	lost	lost
feel	felt	felt	make	made	made
fight	fought	fought	mean	meant	meant
find	found	found	meet	met	met
flee	fled	fled	mow	mowed	mown, R
fling	flung	flung	pass	past, R	past, R
fly	flew	flown	pay, *re-*	paid	paid
forsake	forsook	forsaken	pen	pent, R	pent, R
freeze	froze	frozen	(*to inclose*)		
freight	freighted	freighted	put	put	put
get, *be- for-*	got, *gat*	got, gotten	quit	quit, R	quit, R
gild	gilt, R	gilt, R	rap	rapt, R	rapt, R
gird, *be- en-*	girt, R	girt, R	read	rĕad	rĕad
give, *for-*	gave	given	rend	rent	rent
go, *under-*	went	gone	rid	rid	rid
grave	graved	graven	ride	rode, *rid*	ridden, *rid*
grind	ground	ground	ring	rang, rung	rung
grow	grew	grown	rise	rose	risen
hang	hung	hung	rive	rived	riven, R
have	had	had	run	ran, *run*	run
hear	heard	heard	saw	sawed	sawn, R
heave	hove, R	hoven, R	say	said	said
hew	hewed	hewn, R	see	saw	seen

PRESENT.	PAST.	PAST PART.	PRESENT.	PAST.	PAST PART.
seek	sought	sought	steal	stole	stolen
seethe	sod, R	sodden, R	stick	stuck	stuck
sell	sold	sold	sting	stung	stung
send	sent	sent	stride, *be-*	{ strode / *strid* }	stridden / *strid*
set, *be-*	set	set			
shake	shook	shaken	strike	struck	{ struck / *stricken* }
shape, *mis-*	shaped	shapen, R			
shave	shaved	shaven, R	string	strung	strung
shear	sheared	shorn, R	strive	strove	striven
shed	shed	shed	*strow, be-*	*strowed*	*strown,* R
shine	shone, R	shone, R	swear	{ swore / *sware* }	sworn
shoe	shod	shod			
shoot	shot	shot	sweat	sweat	sweat, R
show	showed	shown, R	sweep	swept	swept
shrink	{ shrunk / *shrank* }	shrunk	swell	swelled	swollen, R
			swim	{ swam / *swum* }	swum
shred	shred	shred			
shut	shut	shut	swing	swung	swung
sing	sang, sung	sung	take	took	taken
sink	sunk, *sank*	sunk	(*be- mis- re-*)		
sit	sat	sat	teach	taught	taught
slay	slew	slain	tear	tore, *tare*	torn
sleep	slept	slept	tell	told	told
slide	slid	{ slidden / slid }	think, *be-*	thought	thought
			thrive	{ thrived / *throve* }	thriven, R
sling	slung, *slang*	slung			
slink	slunk	slunk	throw	threw	thrown
slit	slit	slit	thrust	thrust	thrust
smite	smote	smitten	tread	{ trod / *trode* }	trodden / trod
sow	sowed	sown, R			
speak, *be-*	{ spoke / *spake* }	spoken	wax	waxed	waxen, R
			wear	wore	worn
speed	sped	sped	weave	wove	woven
spend, *mis-*	spent	spent	weep	wept	wept
spin	spun, *span*	spun	wet	wet, R	wet, R
spit.	spit, *spat*	spit	whet	whet, R	whet, R
split	split	split	win	won	won
spread, *be-*	spread	spread	wind	wound, R	wound
spring	{ sprang / sprung }	sprung	work	wrought, R	wrought, R
			wring	wrung	wrung
stand, *with-*	stood	stood	write	wrote	written

A BRIEF SKETCH OF THE ENGLISH LANGUAGE.

If we listen to persons of different nations speaking their own tongues, or if we look over books or papers printed in different languages, there appear at first to be no resemblances between them ; but if we study several languages, we find that the words used to mean the same thing (particularly common things) are often similar. We shall find that certain grammatical forms appear in some languages, and are not found in others. By comparing these resemblances and differences, scholars have been able to find evidences of the common origin of certain languages, and to arrange the languages of the world in groups or families.

Our English speech has been traced back to the language of a people called "Aryans," who lived thousands of years ago in Iran, the country in the neighborhood of the Hindu Kush Mountains. The great family of languages that has descended from this old Aryan speech is called the "Aryan or Indo-Germanic family."

As these Aryans became numerous, large numbers of them moved southward and westward from Iran. Later other bands followed, and the pioneers were pushed farther westward or southward. Wherever the Aryans settled, the demands of a new country, new conditions of life, and strange objects, made changes in their speech. These changes were the easier because they had no means of communication — railroads, mails, telegraph lines, or newspapers — to connect them with the friends they had left behind.

In the course of centuries, the original Aryan language became greatly changed in different localities, and numbers of new languages were the result.

Indo-Germanic Family. — The Aryans that moved southward into India gave rise to the Asiatic division of the Indo-Germanic family, of which the branches are : —

1. The *Indian*, including Sanskrit, the ancient sacred language of India, the modern languages of India (such as Hindustani), and the Gypsy language.

2. The *Iranian* or *Persian* branch, the ancient and modern languages of Persia.

The Aryans that moved westward gave rise to the European division, of which the chief branches are : —

1. The *Greek* branch, including Ancient Greek, Modern Greek, Romaic, and other dialects.

2. The *Italic* branch, including Latin and the several Romance languages derived from the Latin; namely, Italian, French, Spanish, Portuguese, and a few others.

3. The *Celtic* branch, including various ancient dialects, and Welsh, Cornish, Irish, Manx, and Highland Scotch.

4. The *Slavonic* branch, including Russian, Polish, Old Prussian, Bulgarian, and Bohemian.

5. The *Teutonic* or *Germanic* branch, including Gothic, Old German, Modern High German, Scandinavian languages (Icelandic, Danish, Swedish, Norwegian), Low German, Dutch, Flemish, Anglo-Saxon English.

Some of the other families of language are the Semitic, Hamitic, Monosyllabic, Turanian, Dravidian, Malay-Polynesian, Oceanic, Bantee, Central African, and American ; and each of these, like the Aryan, is subdivided into branches.

The **earliest knowledge** that we have of England is from the invasion of Britain by the Romans in 55 B.C. It was not then called England, and there was then no English language.

The people spoke a Celtic dialect, something like the Welsh or Cornish of the present day. A few of these old Celtic words have come down to us in our modern English, such as the names of many rivers, — *Avon, Esk, Thames, Cam, Ouse*, etc., — besides a few common words, — *crock, cradle, cart, down, pillow, glen, havoc, kiln, pool*, etc.

The Romans conquered the southern part of the island, and held it nearly five centuries; but they made so little change in the language of the people that it is said that fewer than a dozen Latin words (and their derivatives) can be traced to this period. Some of these are *castra* (a camp), in Man*chester*, Lan*caster*, Lei*cester*; *strata-via* (a paved way), in *street*, *Strat*ford; *portus* (a harbor), in *Port*smouth, Bridge*port*; *colonia* (a settlement), in Lin*coln*; *vallum* (a rampart), in *wall*; *mille passu*um (a thousand *paces*), in *mile*.

In the middle of the fifth century began the Saxon conquest of Britain. The Romans, busy in other parts of their crumbling empire, were unable to help the Britons to resist the Pagan invaders. These were the Jutes from the shores of the Cattegat, the Saxons from the vicinity of the Weser, the Angles from what is now Sleswick. They all spoke dialects of the same Teutonic language; and these dialects remained distinct for several centuries after the people settled in Britain. Because the Saxons came first, the Britons called all the Teutonic invaders "Saxons." When the invaders became united, three or four centuries later, they called themselves "Angles," or "English," because the Angles were most numerous.

The language of these united Teutonic conquerors is known as " Anglo-Saxon," or " Old English."

It is in this Anglo-Saxon that we find our parent language, and not in the Celtic of the early Britons, nor in the Latin of their Roman conquerors.

The Angles and Saxons drove the Britons before them into the remote parts of the island, just as the English in America drove the Indians farther and farther westward.

As the language of the conquering English became the language of America, so the language of the Angles and Saxons became the language of England. And as the Indians have left but slight impression on our language, so did the Britons leave but few of their words in the speech of the Teutons.

The Anglo-Saxon is a very different language from our modern English ; but nearly half of all the words in use in English to-day, and more than half of the most useful words, come to us from the Anglo-Saxon.

Anglo-Saxon Words. — Among the English words of Anglo-Saxon origin are the pronouns, the numerals, nearly all the irregular or strong verbs (and the auxiliaries), nearly all the prepositions and conjunctions, nouns forming their plurals by change of vowel, and adjectives that are irregularly compared.

General terms are usually Latin, particular terms are Saxon : thus, *color* is Latin ; *red, yellow, green, brown*, etc., are Saxon : *number* is Latin ; *one, two, three, four*, etc., are Saxon : *move* is Latin ; *run, leap, ride, spring, fly, crawl*, etc., are Saxon.

The Anglo-Saxon words in English are generally short words of one or two syllables.

The following classes of words are among those obtained from the Anglo-Saxon : —

1. Short names of trees, plants, and flowers ; as, *apple, ash, bean, berry, blade, bough, corn, daisy, elm, ivy, leaf, limb, maple, oak, oats, root, rye, sap, walnut, wheat*, etc.

2. The short names of common animals ; as, *ant, bear, bird, bull, calf, cat, colt, cow, dog, duck, fly, fowl, frog, goat, hen, horse, lamb, mouse, owl, pig, sheep, snake, toad, wasp, worm*, etc.

3. The more commonly used names of parts of the body ; as, *ankle, arm, beard, blood, breast, brain, cheek, chin, ear, eye, fat, foot, hair, hand, hip, leg, lip, mouth, nail, neck, nose, rib, skin, thigh, throat, thumb, wrist*, etc.

4. Many of the names of the parts of houses, and things in and around them ; as, *ax, barn, bed, bush, beam, bolster, bowl, broom,*

floor, glass, grass, house, hovel, hammer, harrow, knife, ladder, latch, lath, oven, roof, rake, room, shed, sheet, spoon, stool, saw, scythe, shovel, spade, shelf, shop, stair, tongs, wedge, yoke, etc.

5. Many of the most useful adjectives; as, *bare, black, broad, brown, busy, chilly, clean, cold, cool, damp, dark, deep, dim, dingy, dreary, dry, early, empty, fair, fresh, full, glad, good, great, green, hard, high, lame, lazy, loud, low, mad, mean, near, new, poor, proud, quick, raw, red, rich, right, ripe, rough, sick, silly, slow, sly, sorry, sour, stark, stiff, strong, thin, tough, true, warm, wet, white, wide, wise, wrong, young.*

6. Some of the earliest and dearest words we learn; as, *home, friend, father, mother, son, daughter, brother, sister, wife, husband, child, heart, song, love, fireside, hearth.*

Latin Words. — Next in importance to the Anglo-Saxon words in English, but outnumbering them, come the Latin words. We have noticed how a few Latin words came into the language. Let us glance at the chief causes that have brought in the others.

During the seventh century, the Pagan Anglo-Saxons were converted by the Roman Church to Christianity. Latin was then, as now, the language of the Church, and from it were introduced many words; as, *bishop, chalice, clerk, deacon, presbyter, priest,* and others.

In the tenth century, another branch of the Teutonic race, the Northmen, settled in France. They learned from their neighbors to speak a Latin dialect called " Norman French." In 1066 the Normans, under their duke, William, invaded England, defeated Harold, the last Saxon king, and conquered the country.

The conquerors introduced their language into the camps, the courts, the churches, and the schools, and thus came in thousands of Latin words. The Anglo-Saxons held fast to their language. It long remained the language of the field, the market, and the home.

The Norman conquerors gave names in their language to the

castle, cellar, chapel, college, edifice, fort, hotel, partition, spire, tower, etc. The Saxon name held good for the *barn, house, hovel, roof, shed, shop, shelf,* etc.

The Normans brought in more luxury, new ideas, refinement; and they gave names to the new things, such as *carpet, curtain, cushion, fork, mirror, napkin, scissors, table,* etc.; but the Anglo-Saxon names for the plainer, common things, held fast; as, *bed, bowl, knife, looking-glass, shears, spoon, tongs,* etc. The Norman names for some of the common animals came to designate the flesh of these animals in the market or on the table; as, *beef, mutton, pork, veal;* but the Anglo-Saxon names for the animals alive still held good; as, *ox, sheep, pig,* and *calf.*

These two peoples, then, lived side by side; the Anglo-Saxons speaking their Teutonic language, the Normans their Latin speech. Very gradually they came to know each other, to unite their interests and their languages; and from this union came our English. Bear in mind continually that there was no English language until long after the Norman Conquest, and that it was neither Anglo-Saxon nor Norman French, but a union of the two.

The Crusades, the establishment of universities, the invention of printing, the revival of the commercial spirit, all contributed to a revival of learning, one feature of which was a great interest in Latin and Latin literature in England in the sixteenth century. This interest in learning and in Latin added many words to our language.

It has been estimated that ninety per cent of the words in English are derived, as outlined above, from the Anglo-Saxon and the Latin. The remaining ten per cent have been taken from many sources.

The instinct for conquest that drove the Angles, the Saxons, and the Normans to England, has sent the Englishman to the most remote parts of the earth. Where he has not gone to conquer by war, he has gone to conquer by trade. He has taken back with him to his island home gold, jewels, and other valuable things. He has gained from nearly every language on the globe some word or words.

From the Arabic he has taken *algebra, almanac, zero, coffee, sirup, alcohol, magazine, cotton, sugar, lemon, assassin,* and others.

From the Persian, *azure, caravan, chess, scarlet, lilac, shawl, orange, paradise, dervish, bazaar,* and *horde.*

From the Italian, *gazette, opera, piano, soprano, piazza, malaria, studio, umbrella, carnival,* and *regatta.*

From the Spanish, *alligator, cork, cigar, negro, mosquito, tornado,* and *vanilla.*

From the Dutch, *boor, brandy, measles, jeer, ballast, sloop, schooner, yacht, yawl, reef, skates, smack,* and *smuggle.*

From the Chinese, *china, tea, serge, junk, nankeen, silk,* and *typhoon.*

From Africa, *gorilla, kraal, zebra, guinea, oasis.*

From South America, *hammock, potato, guano, mahogany, tolu, caoutchouc, pampas, tapioca.*

Other Languages. — *Damask,* from Damascus; *tariff,* from Tarifa; *cambric,* from Cambray; *muslin,* from Mosul, etc.

The demands of science for new terms, and of invention and discovery for new names, have introduced hundreds of words into the English language within a few decades. These words are mostly (but not all) from the Greek; as, *telegraph, phonograph, photograph,* etc.

ANALYSIS OF WORDS.

just　　　　un*just*　　　　*just*ify

The word *just* means right, fair. If we place the syllable **un** before it, we make a new word, *un*just, meaning *not* right or *not* fair.

If we place the syllables *ify* after the word *just,* we make another word, just*ify,* meaning *to make* right or fair.

A word like *just,* that is not formed from any other word in the language, is called a PRIMITIVE or PRIME WORD.

A word like *unjust* or *justify,* made up of two or more parts, each expressing an idea, is called a COMPOSITE or DERIVATIVE WORD.

The component parts of a composite or derivative word are called *elements*.

de*pend*   *pend*ent

To *depend* is to *hang* from : *pend*ent means *hang*ing. Here we find that the syllable *pend* means to *hang*.

An element of a word that may be used in composition with syllables placed before or after it to form new words is called a STEM.

A stem may be used *only* as an element of a *derivative* word. A *prime* word may be used *alone*, or as an *element* of a composite word.

An element of a word placed *before* a primitive or a stem (like *un*just or *de*pend), to modify its meaning in combination, is called a PREFIX.

An element of a word placed *after* a primitive or a stem (like just*ify* or pend*ent*), to modify its meaning in combination, is called a *suffix*.

When *both* elements of a word are *prime* words, the *derivative* is called COMPOUND, as *blacksmith, wheelwright.*

PREFIXES.

1. Study carefully the following prefixes, then analyze each illustrative word, determining the prefix, the stem, and the suffix.

2. Look in the following lists for the meanings of the elements of the words.

3. Compare your knowledge of the word with the definition given in the dictionary.

4. Construct a sentence to illustrate the use of the word.

MODEL. — Diameter. Prefix, *dia*, through ; stem, *meter*, measure. A measure through. The length of a straight line through the center of an object.

The *diameter* of the earth is nearly eight thousand miles.

A, AB, ABS, from ; *a*vert, *ab*jure, *abs*cess.

AD (AC, AG, AL, AM, AN, AP, AR, AS, AT), to, toward ; *ad*apt, *ac*cede, *al*lude, *ap*pend, *as*sume.

AMB (AMBI), around ; *amb*iguous (ig = act).

AMPHI, on both sides ; *amphi*bious (bi = life).

AN, without, not ; *an*archy (arch = rule).

ANA, back, again ; *ana*lysis (lysis = loosen).

ANT (ANTI), against ; *anti*pathy (path = feeling).

ANTE, before ; *ante*cedent.

APO, from, off ; *apo*state (sto = stand).

BE, cause, etc. ; *be*calm, *be*foul, *be*dim.

BENE, well ; *bene*factor, *bene*diction.

BI, double, two ; *bi*ped.

BIS, twice ; *bis*cuit (cuit = cooked).

CATA, down ; *cata*logue.

CIRCUM, around ; *circum*spect.

CON (CO, COL, COM, COR), with, together ; *con*struct, *co*equal, *com*pel, *com*pose.

CONTRA (CONTRO, COUNTER), against ; *contra*dict, *counter*mand.

DE, down, from ; *de*cline, *de*pend, *de*pose.

DIA, through ; *dia*meter, *dia*logue.

DIS (DI), apart ; *dis*pel, *di*vert.

DU (DUO), two ; *du*plicate.

E (EX), out ; *e*duce, *e*ject, *ex*port, *ex*act.

EPI, upon ; *epi*gram (graph).

EU, well ; *eu*logy, *eu*phony.

EXTRA, beyond ; *extra*ordinary.

HEMI, half ; *hemi*sphere.

IN (IL, IM, IR), in, into ; *in*cline, *im*pel.

IN (IG, IL, IM, IR), not ; *in*animate, *il*liberal.

INTER, between ; *inter*pose.

OB (OF), against ; *ob*loquy, *of*fer.

PEN, almost ; *pen*insula (insula = island).

PER, through ; *per*spire, *per*ceive.

POLY, many ; *poly*gon (gon = angle).

POST, after ; *post*pone.

PRE, before ; *pre*cede, *pre*lude.

PRO, before ; *pro*mote, *pro*pel.

RE (RED), back ; *re*cline.

SEMI, half ; *semi*circle.

SUB (SUC, SUF, SUG, SUP, SUR, SUS), under, after ; *sub*marine, *suc*cor, *suf*fer, *sup*pose.

SUPER, over ; *super*visor.

SUR, over ; *sur*vive.

TRANS, across ; *trans*late, *trans*pose.

SUFFIXES.

1. Study carefully the following suffixes, then analyze each illustrative word, determining the prefix, the stem, and the suffix.

2. Find in the accompanying lists the meanings of the elements of the word.

3. Compare your knowledge of the word with the definition given in the dictionary.

4. Construct a sentence to illustrate the use of the word.

MODEL. — Excursion. Prefix, *ex*, out; stem, *curs*, run; suffix, *ion*, the act of. A running out, or a trip for pleasure.

On Saturday there will be an *excursion* to Niagara Falls.

ABLE (IBLE, BLE), may be, can be, worthy of; inhabit*able*, discern*ible*.

ACEOUS (ACIOUS), of, consisting of, like, resembling; cap*acious*.

ACITY (ICITY, OCITY), state or quality of; cap*acity*, dupl*icity*.

AGE, collection of, state of, allowance for; bagg*age*, bond*age*, post*age*.

AL, of, pertaining to, befitting or becoming; manu*al*, ment*al*, person*al*.

AN (ANE), pertaining to, one who; Europe*an*, histori*an*.

ANCE (ANCY), being, state of being; perform*ance*, abund*ance*.

ANT, one who, the person that, ing; merch*ant*, adjut*ant*, pli*ant*.

ARY, one who, the place where, the thing that; advers*ary*, diction*ary*, liter*ary*, bound*ary*.

ATE, having, being, one who, to make, to put, to take; inanim*ate*, gradu*ate*, facilit*ate*, anim*ate*.

DOM, the place where, state of being; king*dom*, free*dom*, wis*dom*.

ED, past tense and past participle ending; wish*ed*, jump*ed*, hunt*ed*.

EN, made of, to make, little; wood*en*, deep*en*, maid*en*.

ENT, one who, the person that, ing, being; ag*ent*, anteced*ent*, concurr*ent*, equival*ent*.

ER, one who, the person that; build*er*, buy*er*.

ERLY (ERN), direction; east*erly*, west*ern*.

ERY (RY), place where, collection, art of; scen*ery*, pan*try*.

EST, most (superlative degree); high*est*, sharp*est*, soft*est*.

FUL, full of; doubt*ful*, hope*ful*, sin*ful*.

FY, to make; magni*fy*, clari*fy*.

IC (ICAL), of, belonging, relating or pertaining to; her*oic*, ocean*ic*, poet*ical*.

ILE, belonging to, may or can be, easily; duct*ile*, frag*ile*, project*ile*.

INE, of or belonging to; infant*ine*, mar*ine*.

ING, present participle ending; wear*ing*, see*ing*, hear*ing*.

ION, the act of, state of being, ing; ex-puls*ion*, animat*ion*, elect*ion*.

ISE (IZE), to make, to give; fertil*ize*.

ISH, to make, somewhat, belonging to, like; fin*ish*, green*ish*, Span*ish*, child*ish*.

ISM, state of being, an idiom, doctrine of; hero*ism*, Gallic*ism* (Gallia = France), Tory*ism*.

IST, one who, the person that; jur*ist*, ocul*ist*.

ITY (TY), being, state of being; brev*ity*, equ*ity*.

LESS, without; child*less*, fruit*less*, power*less*.

LET, little (diminutive); brook*let*, rivu*let*.

LING, little, young; duck*ling*, gos*ling*, lord*ling*.

LY, like or resembling; beast*ly*, father*ly*, prince*ly*.

MENT, being, state of being, act of, the thing that; abase*ment*, manage*ment*, frag*ment*.

MONY, the state of being, the thing that; matri*mony*, patri*mony*.

NESS, being, state of being; cool*ness*, fond*ness*, idle*ness*.

OR, one who, the person that; collect*or*, inspect*or*, jur*or*.

ORY, the place where, thing that; deposit*ory*, fact*ory*.

PLE, fold; multi*ple*, quadru*ple*, sim*ple*, tri*ple*.

RY, being, act of, place where; brave*ry*, cook*ery*, nurse*ry*.

SHIP, office of, state of; clerk*ship*, friend*ship*, professor*ship*.

SOME, somewhat, full of; glad*some*, burden*some*.

TUDE (UDE), being, state of being; alti*tude*, apti*tude*, grati*tude*.

Y, being, state of being, ing, full of, consisting of ; honest*y*, colloqu*y*, dirt*y*, sand*y*.

STEMS.

1. Study carefully the following stems, then analyze each illustrative word, determining the stem, the prefix, and the suffix.

2. Combine into a definition the meanings of the elements of the word as you find them in the accompanying lists.

3. Compare your knowledge of the word with the definition given in the dictionary.

4. Construct a sentence to illustrate the use of the word.

MODEL. — Emigrant.   Stem, *migr*, wander ; prefix, *e*, out ; suffix, *ant*, one who.   One who wanders.

Many *emigrants* from Sweden have settled in America.

ELEMENTARY LIST.

AG, ACT, drive, urge, act; *ag*ent, ex*act*, trans*act*.

ALT, high; *alt*ar, ex*alt*.

ANIM, mind, soul, spirit; *anim*us, equ*anim*ity.

ANN, ENN, year; *ann*als, per*enn*ial, cent*enn*ial.

APT, fit, join; ad*apt*, *apt*ly, *apt*ness.

BAS, low; a*bas*e, *bas*e, *bas*ement, *bas*s, de*bas*e.

BREV, short; *brev*ity, *brev*e, ab*brev*iate.

CAD, CAS, CID, fall; de*cad*ence, oc*cas*ion, ac*cid*ent.

CAP, CAPT, take, hold; *cap*able, *cap*acious, *capt*or.

CARN, flesh; *carn*al, *carn*age, in*carn*ate.

CED, CESS, go, yield; *ced*e, con*ced*e, ac*cess*.

CENT, hundred; *cent*ipede, *cent*, *cent*enary.

CING, CINCT, bind; pre*cinct*, suc*cinct*.

CLIN, lean, bend; de*clin*e, in*clin*ation, re*clin*e.

COR, CORD, heart; *cord*ial, con*cord*, dis*cord*.

CUR, care; *cur*ious, pro*cur*e, ac*cur*acy.

CURR, CURS, CUR, run; *curr*ent, ex-*curs*ion, re*cur*.

DICT, speak, say; *dict*ion, e*dict*, pre-*dict*.

DIGN, worthy; *dign*ify, in*dign*ant.

DUC, DUCT, lead, bring; ab*duct*, con-*duct*, e*duc*ate.

EQU, equal; *equ*ation, *equ*ivocal, *equ*ality.

FA, speak; *fa*ble, inef*fa*ble, pre*fa*ce, in*fa*nt.

FAC, FACT, FECT, FIC, make, form, do; *fac*tor, ef*fect*, de*fic*ient.

FERR, FER, carry, bear, bring; pre*fer*, suf*fer*, re*fer*ence.

FID, FY, faith; con*fid*e, dif*fid*ent, in*fid*el, de*fy*.

FIN, end, limit; *fin*ish, af*fin*ity, de*fin*i-tion.

FRANG, FRACT, break; *frag*ment, *fract*ion, re*fract*.

FUND, FUS, pour, melt; re*fund*, trans*fus*e, re*fus*e.

GEN, GENER, kind, race; *gen*eral, *gen*-uine, *gen*der.

GRAD, GRESS, step, go; de*grad*e, e*gress*.

GRAPH, write; *graph*ic, bio*graph*y, photo*graph*.

GRAT, pleasing; *grat*ify, in*grat*e.

HOSPIT, HOST, guest; *hospit*ality, *host*, *host*ess.

JECT, cast, hurl; e*ject*, ab*ject*, re*ject*, sub*ject*.

JUNCT, join; *junct*ion, ad*junct*.

JUR, swear; ab*jur*e, con*jur*e, *jur*y.

JUR, law, right; in*jur*e, *jur*isdiction.

LAT, carry, lift, bring; col*lat*e, re*lat*e, trans*lat*e.

LEG, send; de*leg*ate, re*leg*ate, *leg*ation.

LEG, LECT, gather, choose; col*lect*, e*lect*, *leg*ion.

LIBER, free; *liber*al, *liber*ate.

LIN, flax; *lin*en, *lin*ing, *lin*seed, *lin*e.

LITER, letter; *liter*al, ob*liter*ate.

LOC, place; *loc*omotion, dis*loc*ate, *loc*-ate.

LOG, speech, word, reason; epi*log*ue, eu*log*y.

LOQU, LOCUT, speak, talk; *loqu*acious, e*locut*ion.

LUD, LUS, sport, play; e*lud*e, pre*lud*e, col*lus*ion.

MAGN, great; *magn*ificent, *magn*ani-mous.

MAN, hand; *man*age, *man*uscript, e*man*cipate.

MAR, the sea; *mar*iner.

MATER, mother; *mater*nal.

MEDI, middle, between; im*medi*ate, *medi*ate.

MENT, mind; de*ment*ed, *ment*ion, *ment*al.

MERC, merchandise, trade; com*merc*e, *merc*enary.

MERG, MERS, dip, sink, mingle; e*merg*e, im*mers*e.

METER, measure; dia*meter*.

MIGR, wander; *migr*ation, e*migr*ant, im*migr*ate.

MIR, wonder, look; ad*mir*ation.

MITT, MIT, MISS, send, throw; com*mit*, o*mit*, *miss*ion.

MON, MONIT, advise, remind; sum*mon*, pre*monit*ion.

MORT, death; *mort*al, *mort*ify, *mort*uary.

MOT, move; *mot*ion, re*mot*e, pro*mot*e.

MULT, many; *mult*iply, *mult*itude.

MUN, MUNIT, fortify; am*munit*ion.

NAT, born; in*nat*e, *nat*al.

NAV, ship; *nav*igate, *nav*al.

NOT, known; *not*ify, *not*ion.

NUMER, number; e*numer*ate.

NUNCI, NOUNCE, tell; pro*nounce*, e*nunci*ate.

OCUL, eye; bin*ocul*ar, in*ocul*ate.

PAR, get ready; pre*par*e, re*pair*.

PARL, speak; *parl*iament, *parl*or.

PART, PARTIT, divide; im*part*, *partit*ion, *party*.

PAST, feed; *past*or, re*past*.

PAT, PASS, suffer, feel, endure; *pat*ient, com*pat*ible, com*pass*ion.

PATER, father; *pater*nal.

PED, foot; *ped*al, im*ped*e, ex*ped*ite.

PELL, PULS, drive, urge; re*pel*, im*puls*e, ex*pel*.

PEND, PENS, hang, weigh; *pend*ant, *pens*ion, ex*pend*.

PET, PETIT, attack, seek, ask; *petit*ion, com*pet*ent.

PHIL, PHILO, fond, loving; *phil*ology.

PLE, PLET, fill; de*plet*ion, im*ple*ment, sup*ple*ment.

PLIC, fold, bend; sup*plic*ate, ex*plic*it, com*plic*ate, sim*plic*ity.

PON, place, put; de*pon*ent, op*pon*ent, post*pon*e.

PORT, carry, bring; *port*able, im*port*, trans*port*.

PORT, gate, door; *port*, op*port*une.

POS, place, put; dis*pos*e, ex*pos*e, op*pos*e.

PRIM, first; *prim*ary, *prim*er, *prim*e.

SACR, holy; *sacr*ament, conse*cr*ate, exe*cr*ate.

SCI, know; *sci*ence, con*sci*ence, pre*sci*ence.

SCRIB, SCRIPT, write; in*scrib*e, pre*scrib*e, post*script*.

SENT, SENS, feel, think; con*sent*, *sens*ible.

SEQU, SECUT, follow; *sequ*ence, sub*sequ*ent, prose*cut*e.

SOL, alone; *sol*e, *sol*itude, *sol*iloquy.

SPEC, SPECT, SPIC, look, appear; de*spic*able, circum*spect*.

SPIR, breathe; a*spir*e, ex*pir*e, per*spir*e.

STRU, STRUCT, build; in*struct*, ob*struc*tion.

SUM, SUMPT, take; pre*sum*e, re*sumpt*ion.

TACT, touch; *tact*, *tact*ile, in*tact*.

UN, one; *un*animous, *un*ion, *un*ity.

UT, use; *ut*ilize, *ut*ility.

VERT, VERS, turn; *vers*ion, con*vers*e, re*vert*.

VID, VIS, see, appear; pro*vid*e, *vis*ion, *vis*or.

VIV, live; *viv*acity, *viv*ify, *viv*isection.

VOC, call; ad*voc*ate, con*vok*e, re*vok*e.

ADVANCED LIST.

APER, APERT, open; *aper*ient, *apert*ure.

ARCH, rule, govern; an*arch*y, patri*arch*.

ART, skill; *art*ist, *art*isan.

AUD, hear, listen; *aud*ible, *aud*ience.

AUR, gold; *aur*iferous.

BAT, beat; *bat*ter, com*bat*, de*bat*e, re*bat*e.

BIT, bite; *bit*ter, *bait*.

CANT, sing; *cant*icle, *cant*o, in*cant*ation.

CAPIT, head; *capit*al, de*capit*ate.

CELER, swift; ac*celer*ate.

COMMOD, fit, suitable; ac*commod*ate, in*commod*e.

COMMUN, common; *commun*icate.

CORON, crown; *coron*et, *coron*er.

CORPUS, CORPOR, body; in*corpor*ate.

CRED, believe; *cred*ence, *cred*it.

CYCL, circle; bi*cycl*e.

DAT, give; *dat*e, tra*dit*ion.

DENT, tooth; in*dent*.

DI, day; *di*al.

DOMIN, lord, master; *domin*ion.

DORM, sleep; *dorm*itory.

FAC, face; sur*fac*e, de*fac*e.

FELIC, happy; *felic*ity.

FESS, acknowledge; con*fess*, pro*fess*.

FORM, shape; con*form*, de*form*, re*form*.

FORT, strong; com*fort*.

GEST, carry, bring; sug*gest*, regi*ster*.

GRAN, grain; *gran*ary.

GROSS, fat, thick; *gross*, *groc*er.

HOR, hour; *hor*oscope.

INTEGR, entire, whole; *integer*, *integr*ity.

JUDIC, judge; *judic*ial, pre*judice.*

LINGU, tongue; *lingu*al, *langu*age.

MAJOR, greater; *major, major*ity.

MAN, MANS, stay, dwell; *mans*e, per*man*ent, re*main.*

MEDIC, physician; *medic*ine, *medic*al.

MENS, measure; di*mens*ion.

PAN, bread; com*pan*y, *pan*try.

PAR, equal; dis*par*age, *peer.*

PASS, step; *pass*age, *pace.*

PEN, pain, punishment; *pen*alty, im*pun*ity.

PETR, stone, rock; *petr*ify.

PHON, sound; *phon*ograph, eu*phon*y.

PHYSI, nature; *physi*ology, *physi*c.

PICT, paint; de*pict.*

PLAC, please; com*plac*ent.

PLEN, full; *plen*ary.

PLUM, feather; *plum*e, *plum*age.

PLUMB, lead; *plumb, plumb*er.

POT, drink; *pot*ion, *pot*able.

POTENT, powerful; *potent*ial, pleni*potent*iary.

PREHEND, PREHENS, take, grasp; com*prehend*, ap*prehend.*

PUNCT, prick, point; *punct*ual, *punct*uate.

QUADR, square, fourfold; *quadr*uped.

QUANT, how much; *quant*ity.

QUER, QUISIT, seek, ask; in*quir*y, dis*quisit*ion.

QUIET, quiet; re*quit*e, ac*quit.*

RADI, ray; *radi*ate, *radi*ant.

RAP, RAPT, seize, grasp; *rap*acious.

RAT, think, calculate; *rat*ional, *rat*ify.

REG, RECT, rule, straight, right; *reg*ent, *rect*ify.

RID, RIS, laugh; *rid*iculous, *ris*ible.

RIV, stream; *riv*er, de*riv*e.

ROG, ROGAT, ask; inter*rog*ate.

RUPT, break; e*rupt*ion, ir*rupt*ion.

SAL, salt; *sal*t, *sal*ary.

SAL, leap; *sal*ient, *sal*ly.

SANCT, holy; *sanct*uary, *sanct*ify.

SAT, SATIS, enough, sufficient; *sat*iate, *satis*fy.

SCOP, watch, view; epi*scop*al.

SEC, SECT, cut; *sec*ant, dis*sect*, in*sect.*

SEN, old; *sen*ate, *sen*ile.

SERV, serve, keep; ob*serv*e, re*serv*e.

SIST, place, stand; per*sist*, sub*sist.*

SON, sound; dis*son*ant, re*son*ant.

SORT, lot, kind; con*sort, sor*cery.

SPECI, kind; *speci*al, *speci*fy.

STANT, standing; di*stant*, circum*stance.*

STELL, star; con*stell*ation.

STRING, STRICT, draw tight, bind; *string*ent, re*strict.*

SU, follow; *su*e, pur*su*e.

SUAD, SUAS, persuade; dis*suad*e, per*suas*ion.

SURG, SURRECT, rise; in*surg*ent, insur*rect*ion.

TAILL, cut; de*tail*, re*tail.*

TANG, touch; *tang*ible, con*tag*ious.

TEG, TECT, cover; *teg*ument, pro*tect.*

TEMPOR, time; *tempor*al, con*tempor*ary.

TEND, TENT, stretch, reach; at*tend*, dis*tend*, pre*tend.*

TEST, witness; pro*test, test*ify, con*test.*

TORT, twist, wring; ex*tort, tor*ment.

TRACT, draw; con*tract*, re*tract*, dis*tract.*

TRIT, rub; at*trit*ion, de*trit*ment.

TRUD, TRUS, thrust; pro*trud*e, in*trus*ion.

UND, wave; red*und*ant, in*und*ate.

VAD, VAS, go; per*vad*e, in*vas*ion.

VAL, be strong; *val*iant, pre*vail.*

VEN, VENT, come; inter*ven*e, pre*vent*, con*vent*ion.

VERS, VERT, turn; in*vert, vers*e, re*vers*e, anni*vers*ary.

VI, VIA, way, road; ob*vi*ous, de*via*te.

VIC, a change, turn; *vic*ar.

VOLV, VOLU (VOLUT), roll; e*volv*e, *volu*ble, re*volut*ion.

VOT, vow; *vot*ary, de*vot*e.

DIAGRAMS.

The chief value of a diagram is to indicate the analysis of a sentence in a manner that will make it possible for the teacher to see at a glance whether or not the pupil has a correct idea of its structure.

It is believed that the system here presented will be found both simple and comprehensive.

The grammatical subject and grammatical predicate are written over a double line, and separated from each other by a heavy vertical line, as in No. 1. A complement of the predicate is written after the verb, over a single line, and, if an object, is separated from it by a light vertical line, as in No. 2; if an adjective, a horizontal bar cuts this line, as in No. 3; if an attributive noun, a double bar, as in No. 4.

Limiting words, phrases, or clauses are attached by a vertical line underneath to the word limited; and the single line upon which the limiter is written opens to the left or to the right according as the limiter comes in construction before or after the element which it limits (see Nos. 5, 6, 7, 8). Subordinate elements are shown to be limited in the same way (see Nos. 9, 10, 24). The relation intended to be shown will be evident, for the most part, without further explanation.

I. SIMPLE SENTENCES.

1. Stars shine.   2. Children gather flowers.

1.

Stars | shine

2.

Children | gather | flowers

3. Sugar is sweet.   4. Men become friends.

5. Every man started back.

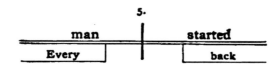

6. A large flock of idle crows sported about the tree.

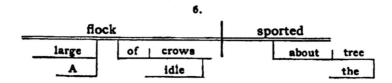

7. Our northern seasons have a narrow streak of spring.

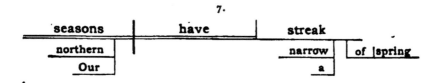

8. The church was a large, handsome brick structure.

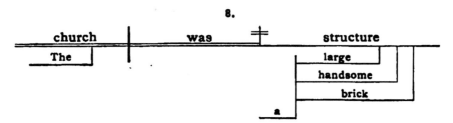

9. The merry song of the birds mingled with the sound of
the rustling leaves.

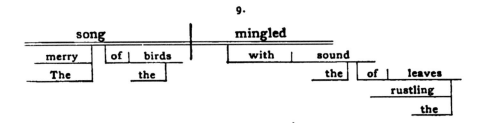

10. Kate's book is in my desk.

11. Now he patted his horse's side.

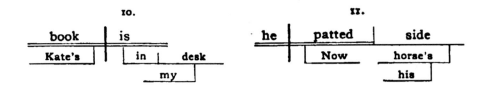

12. The calla, a common plant, is a native of Africa.

13. There is always somewhere a weakest spot.

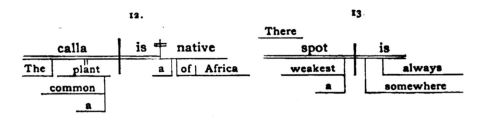

14. The peasant gave the traveler a night's lodging.

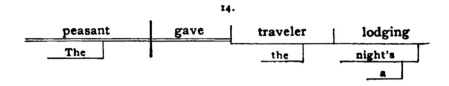

15. A night's lodging was given the traveler by the peasant.

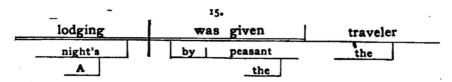

16. The boy made the stick straight.
17. The stick was made straight by the boy.

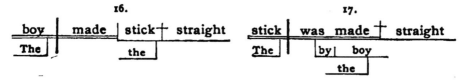

18. His friends called him a spendthrift.
19. He was called a spendthrift by his friends.

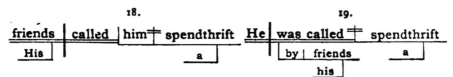

20. The horseman saw the gilded weathercock swim in the moonlight.

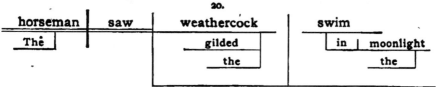

21. The gilded weathercock was seen by the horseman to swim in the moonlight.

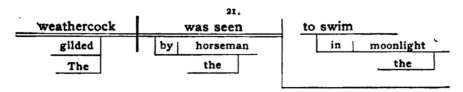

22. Helen's believing this story was remarkable.

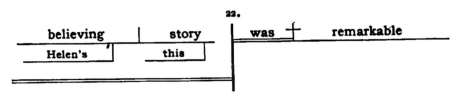

23. Education is learning the rules of the game of life.

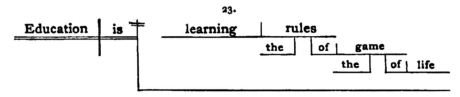

24. The farmers gave them ball for ball, chasing the red-coats down the lane.

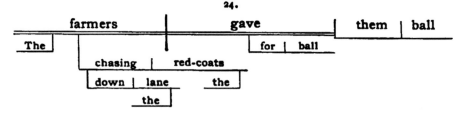

25. Manners are the happy ways of doing things.

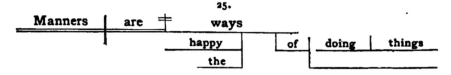

26. There is work to do.

27. I will be ready to spread the alarm.

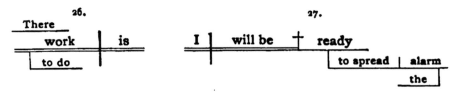

II. COMPLEX SENTENCES.

In the complex sentence, the elements of the principal sentence and of each clause are arranged as if each were a simple sentence. If the subordinate clauses are modifiers, they are annexed in the same way as adjective and adverbial phrases (see 28–33).

If a clause is used as a subject or as an object, it occupies the usual place of subject or object in the diagram of the principal sentence (see 34–38).

The elements of a participial or an infinitive phrase, however, whether the phrase is used as a subject, an attribute (see 23), or a modifier (see 24), are written over a single line.

28. The ornament of a house is the friends who frequent it.

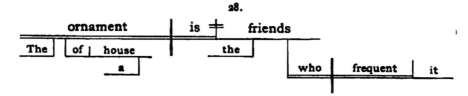

29. The left hand is the hand which we leave.

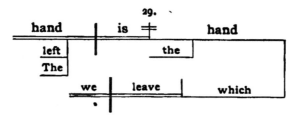

30. Everything around me wore that happy look which makes the heart glad.

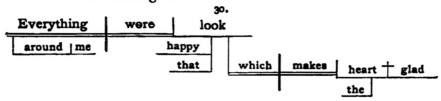

31. Some children, whose names we did not know, brought the wild flowers yesterday.

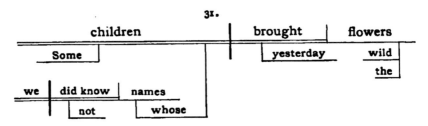

32. Where the drift was deepest, we made a tunnel.

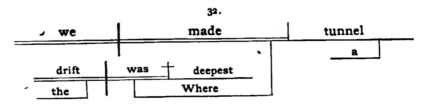

33. We never make a new word till we have made a new thought.

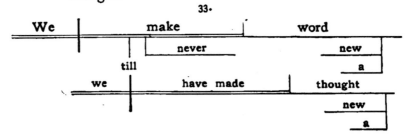

34. How the robin builds her nest is easily discovered.

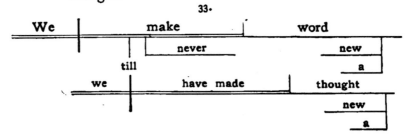

35. Tom saw that the boat was gaining steadily

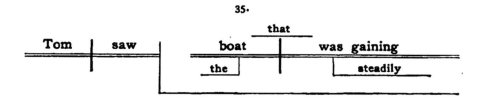

36. The fisherman did not know where he left his pole.

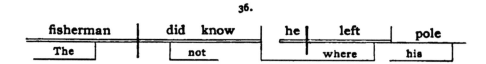

37. The dog understood what his master said.

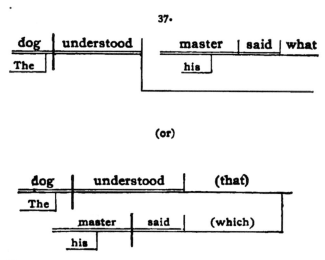

(or)

38. What these men did will long be remembered.

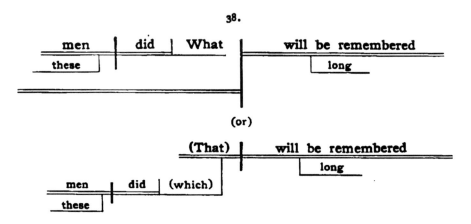

39. He bought the deserted farm of which he had read.
40. Hardy, to whom this was addressed, seized the boathook.

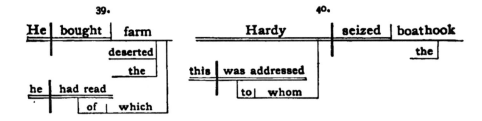

41. The poorest cobbler whose labor pays for his existence, is more useful to the state than a rich idler.

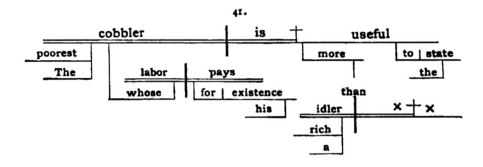

42. One who talks without thinking resembles a hunter who shoots without aiming.

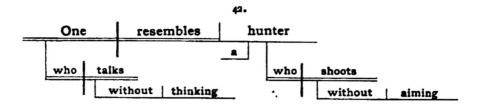

43. The man who says to one Go, and to another Come, has often more sense of restraint than the man who obeys him.

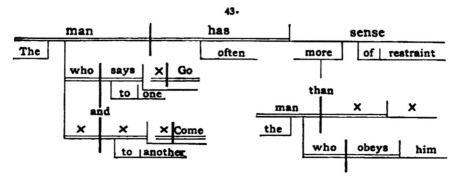

44. The beautiful estate which I have thus described to you, was ornamented by no suitable dwelling house at the time when it was purchased by Mr. Wilson.

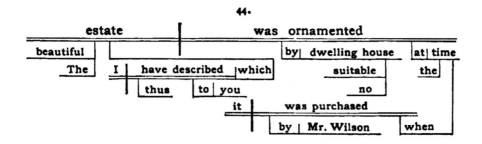

III. COMPOUND SENTENCES.

The diagram of the compound sentence shows the elements of the separate members of which it is composed : the conjunction is written as in 45, 46, or 50.

45. Labor makes thought healthy, and thought makes labor happy.

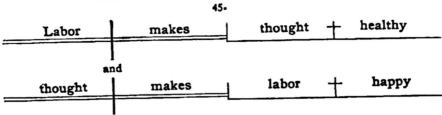

46. Temperance promotes health : intemperance destroys it.

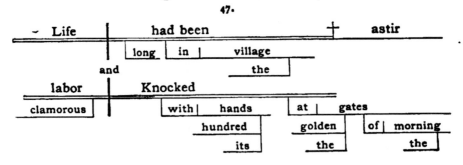

47. Life had long been astir in the village, and clamorous labor Knocked with its hundred hands at the golden gates of the morning.

47.

| Life | had been | | astir |

48. Then came the laborers home from the field, and serenely
the sun sank
Down to his rest.

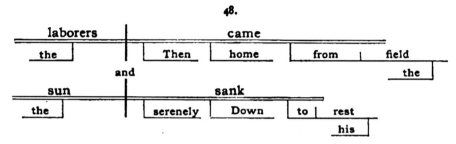

49. The eye always sees what it wants to see, and the ear
always hears what it wants to hear.

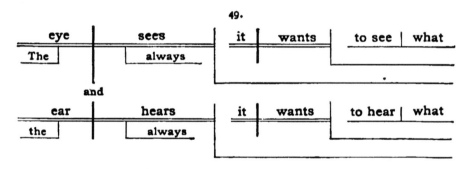

50. If thine enemy be hungry, give him bread to eat; if he be
thirsty, give him water to drink.

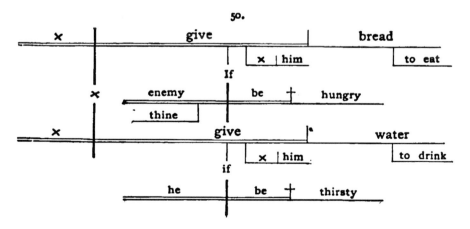

IV. SENTENCES WITH COMPOUND ELEMENTS.

51. Dandelions and buttercups gild the lawn.
52. The squirrel found and ate the corn.

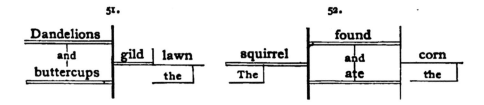

53. Few and short were the prayers we said.
54. Men and women heard and praised the music and the speeches.

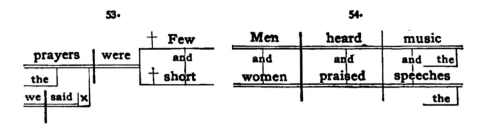

55. I neither saw nor heard you.
56. The squirrel leaps among the boughs,
  And chatters in his leafy house.

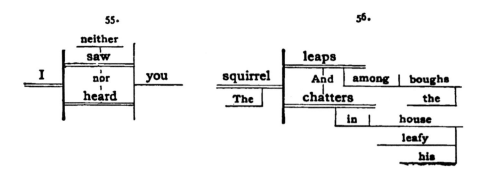

57. Between the dark and the daylight,
   When the night is beginning to lower,
   Comes a pause in the day's occupations,
   That is known as the Children's Hour.

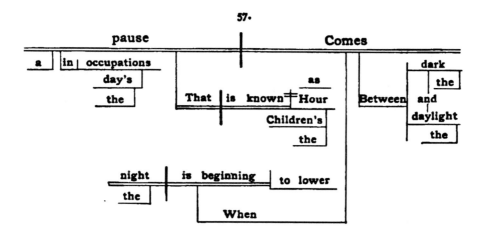

58. There are great truths that pitch their shining tents
   Outside our walls ; and though they are but dimly seen
   In the gray dawn, they will be manifest
   When the light widens into perfect day.

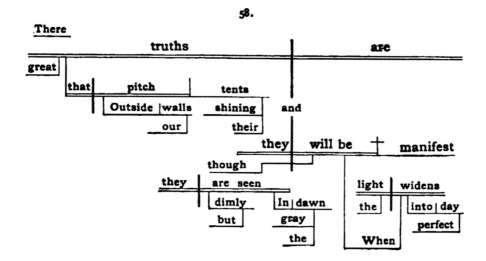

59. And pleasantly under the silver moon, and under the silent, solemn stars, ring the steel shoes of the skaters on the frozen sea, and voices, and the sound of bells.

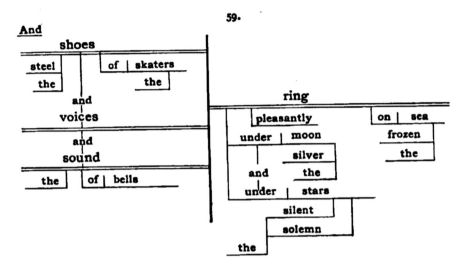

60. Thoughts that great hearts once broke for, we
Breathe cheaply in the common air;
The dust we trample heedlessly
Throbbed once in saints and heroes rare,
Who perished, opening for their race
New pathways to the commonplace.

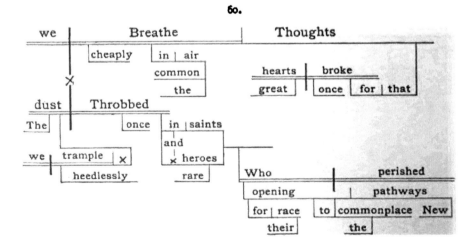

VERSIFICATION.

Verse is a species of composition in which the words are arranged in lines containing a definite number and succession of accented and unaccented syllables ; as, —

And still | they gazed, | and still | the won | der grew
That one | small head | could car | ry all | he knew. — GOLDSMITH.

Rhythm is the recurrence of accent at regular intervals of duration. The unit of rhythm is commonly called a FOOT.

A foot, or measure, is a portion of a verse or line, consisting of two or three syllables combined according to accent.

The kinds of poetic feet most used in English are four ; namely, the iambus, the trochee, the anapest, the dactyl.

An iambus is a foot of two syllables, having the first unaccented, the second accented ; as, *reflect'*.

A trochee is a foot of two syllables, the first accented, the second unaccented ; as, *on'ward*.

An anapest is a foot of three syllables, having the third syllable accented, the first and second unaccented ; as, *intervene'*.

A dactyl is a foot of three syllables, having the first accented, the second and third unaccented ; as, *ten'derly*.

Meter is the arrangement into lines of definite measures of sounds definitely accented.

The number of feet in a line determines the name of the meter.

The following are the most common English meters : —

    Monometer, a line containing a single foot.
    Dimeter, a line containing two feet.
    Trimeter, a line containing three feet.
    Tetrameter, a line containing four feet.

Pentameter, a line containing five feet.

Hexameter, a line containing six feet.

Heptameter, a line containing seven feet.

Octameter, a line containing eight feet.

Verse is classified according to two characteristics ; namely, —

    1. The *kind* of foot prevailing in a line.

    2. The *number* of feet in a line.

If the feet composing a verse or line are all *of one kind,* the verse is said to be PURE.

If the feet composing the verse or line are *of different kinds,* the verse is said to be MIXED.

The division of a verse or line into feet is called SCANNING.

Iambic measures, the most frequent in English verse, have the accent placed upon the *second* syllable, the *fourth,* etc. Iambic measures are peculiarly fitted for long poems.

One iambus, iambic monometer : —

> How bright
> The light!

Two iambuses, iambic dimeter : —

> Here, here, | I live
> And some | what give. — HERRICK.

Three iambuses, iambic trimeter : —

> O let | the sol | id ground
> Not fail | beneath | my feet! — TENNYSON.

Four iambuses, iambic tetrameter : —

> Ring out | the old, | ring in | the new,
>   Ring hap | py bells | across | the snow;
>   The year | is go | ing, let | him go,
> Ring out | the old, | ring in | the new. — TENNYSON.

Four iambuses with added syllable : —

> Ah me, | how quick | the days | are flit | ting!

Five iambuses, iambic pentameter : —

> The cur | few tolls | the knell | of part | ing day. — GRAY.

Five iambuses with added syllable : —

> I come | to bur | y Cæ | sar, not | to praise | him.
>
> SHAKESPEARE.

Six iambuses, iambic hexameter : —

> The hills | and val | leys ring, | and e'en | the ech | oing air
> Seems all | composed | of sounds | about | them ev | erywhere.
>
> DRAYTON.

Seven iambuses, iambic heptameter : —

> The mel | anchol | y days | are come, | the sad | dest of | the year,
> Of wail | ing winds | and na | ked woods | and mead | ows brown |
> and sear. — BRYANT.

Trochaic measures have the accent placed upon the *first* syllable, the *third*, etc. Trochaic lines have a light, tripping movement, and are well fitted for lively subjects.

One trochee, trochaic monometer : —

> Splashing,
> Dashing. — SOUTHEY.

Two trochees, trochaic dimeter : —

> Hope is | banished,
> Joys are | vanished.

Three trochees, trochaic trimeter : —

> Singing | through the | forest.

Four trochees, trochaic tetrameter : —

> Willows | whiten, | aspens | quiver,
> Little | breezes | dusk and | shiver.

Five trochees, trochaic pentameter : —

> Spake full | well, in | language | quaint and | olden. — LONGFELLOW.

Five trochees with added syllable : —

> Think when | e'er you | see us | what our | beauty | saith.
> LEIGH HUNT.

Six trochees, trochaic hexameter : —

> Dark the | shrine, and | dumb the | fount of | song thence | welling.

Seven trochees, trochaic heptameter : —

> Gently | at the | evening | hour when | fading | was the | glory.

Eight trochees, trochaic octameter : —

> Dear my | friend and | fellow | student, | I would | lean my | spirit | o'er
> you. — MRS. BROWNING.

Anapestic measures have the accent placed on the *third* syllable, the *sixth*, etc.

One anapest, anapestic monometer : —

> Far away
> O'er the bay.

Two anapests, anapestic dimeter : —

> In my rage | shall be seen.

Two anapests with added syllable : —

> He is gone | on the moun | tain,
> He is lost | to the for | est. — SCOTT.

Three anapests, anapestic trimeter : —

> Not a pine | in my grove | is there seen.

Four anapests, anapestic tetrameter : —

> Look aloft, | and be firm | and be fear | less of heart.

Five anapests, anapestic pentameter : —

> And they sleep | in the dried | river chan | nel where bul | rushes tell
> That the wa | ter was wont | to go war | bling so soft | ly and well.
> BROWNING.

Dactylic measures have the accent placed upon the *first* sylla-, ble, the *fourth*, etc.

One dactyl, dactylic monometer : —

> Memory !
> Tell to me. — GEORGE ELIOT.

Two dactyls, dactylic dimeter : —

> Emblem of | happiness.

Three dactyls, dactylic trimeter : —

> Brighter than | summer's green | carpeting.

Four dactyls, dactylic tetrameter : —

> Cold is thy | heart, and as | frozen as | charity.

Five dactyls with added trochee : —

> This is the | forest pri | meval; but | where are the | hearts that be | neath it,
> Leaped like the | roe, when he | hears in the | woodland the | voice of the |
> huntsman? — LONGFELLOW.

Six dactyls, dactylic hexameter : —

> Land of the | beautiful, | land of the | generous, | hail to thee | heartily !

Rhyme. — Metrical language in which the concluding syllables of the lines have a similarity of sound is called RHYME : —

> The vine still clings to the moldering *wall*,
> But at every gust the dead leaves *fall*. — LONGFELLOW.

Rhymes may occur also in the middle of lines : —

> The splendor *falls* on castle *walls*
> And snowy summits old in *story*:
> The long light *shakes* across the *lakes*,
> And the wild cataract leaps in *glory*. — TENNYSON.

Verse without rhyme is called BLANK VERSE : —

> All things in earth and air
> Bound were by magic spell
> Never to do him harm,
> Even the plants and stones,
> All save the mistletoe,
> The sacred mistletoe. — LONGFELLOW.

Stanzas. — The variety of arrangement in English verse is almost indefinite.

The shortest and simplest English stanza is a two-line rhyming couplet : —

> As it fell upon a day
> In the merry month of May. — BARNFIELD.

The three-line rhyming stanza, or triplet, is occasionally found in English poetry : —

> O thou child of many prayers,
> Life hath quicksands, life hath snares,
> Care and age come unawares. — LONGFELLOW.

The four-line rhyming stanza, or quatrain, is the commonest of all forms of English poetry : —

> I held it truth, with him who sings
> To one clear harp in divers tones,
> That men may rise on stepping-stones
> Of their dead selves to higher things. — TENNYSON.

> With many a curve my banks I fret
> By many a field and fallow,
> And many a fairy foreland set
> With willow-weed and mallow. — TENNYSON.

> Rocked in the cradle of the deep,
> I lay me down in peace to sleep;
> Secure I rest upon the wave
> For thou, O Lord! hast power to save. — WILLARD.

The five-line stanza is rarely used : —

> Hail to thee, blithe spirit!
> Bird thou never wert,
> That from heaven, or near it,
> Pourest thy full heart
> In profuse strains of unpremeditated art. — SHELLEY.

The six-line stanza has several forms, and is much used in English poetry : —

> Ethereal minstrel! pilgrim of the sky!
>   Dost thou despise the earth where cares abound?
> Or, while the wings aspire, are heart and eye
>   Both with thy nest upon the dewy ground?
> Thy nest, which thou canst drop into at will,
> Those quivering wings composed, that music still!
>   WORDSWORTH.

The seven-line stanza is but little used : —

> Under my window, under my window,
>   All in the midsummer weather,
> Three little girls with fluttering curls
>   Flit to and fro together.
> There's Belle with her bonnet of satin sheen,
> And Maud with her mantle of silver-green,
>   And Kate with her scarlet feather. — WESTWOOD.

The eight-line stanza has many forms of great beauty : —

> 'Tis sweet to hear the watchdog's honest bark
>   Bay deep-mouthed welcome as we draw near home;
> 'Tis sweet to know there is an eye will mark
>   Our coming, and look brighter when we come;
> 'Tis sweet to be awakened by the lark,
>   Or lulled by falling waters; sweet the hum
> Of bees, the voice of girls, the song of birds,
> The lisp of children and their earliest words. — BYRON.

The nine-line combination is known as the Spenserian stanza : —

> Ah! then and there was hurrying to and fro,
> And gathering tears, and tremblings of distress,
> And cheeks all pale, which but an hour ago
> Blushed at the praise of their own loveliness;
> And there were sudden partings, such as press
> The life from out young hearts, and choking sighs
> Which ne'er might be repeated; who could guess
> If ever more should meet those mutual eyes,
> Since upon night so sweet such awful morn could rise! — BYRON.

The sonnet stanza is the most complex of all. The lines are more numerous, the rhyming more frequent, and any error in versification more marked and injurious. It is made up of fourteen lines : —

> When I consider how my light is spent,
> Ere half my days, in this dark world and wide,
> And that one talent which is death to hide,
> Lodged with me useless, though my soul more bent
> To serve therewith my Maker, and present
> My true account, lest he returning chide;
> "Doth God exact day-labor, light denied?"
> I fondly ask: but Patience, to prevent
> That murmur, soon replies, "God doth not need
> Either man's work or his own gifts; who best
> Bear his mild yoke, they serve him best: his state
> Is kingly; thousands at his bidding speed,
> And post o'er land and ocean without rest;
> They also serve who only stand and wait." — MILTON.

INDEX.

———◦•◦———

24

CPSIA information can be obtained at www.ICGtesting.com
Printed in the USA
LVOW051509150212

268849LV00007B/18/P